2ND EDITION

Jim George

Making Vocational Choices

A theory of vocational personalities and work environments

JOHN L. HOLLAND

Professor Emeritus
Johns Hopkins University

PRENTICE-HALL, INC.   Englewood Cliffs, New Jersey 07632

Library of Congress Cataloging in Publication Data

HOLLAND, JOHN L.
    Making vocational choices.

    Bibliography: p.
    Includes index.
    1. Vocational guidance. I. Title.
HF5381. H5668 1985   331.7'02   84-6796
ISBN 0-13-547597-x

Editorial/production supervision: Linda Benson
Cover design: Debbie Holland of DK Holland Unlimited, Inc.
Manufacturing buyer: Ron Chapman/Barbara Kelly Kittle

To Elsie and all my other collaborators here and abroad

Printed in the United States of America

10   9   8   7   6   5   4   3

ISBN 0-13-547597-X   01

Prentice-Hall International, Inc., *London*
Prentice-Hall of Australia Pty. Limited, *Sydney*
Editora Prentice-Hall do Brasil, Ltda., *Rio de Janeiro*
Prentice-Hall Canada Inc., *Toronto*
Prentice-Hall of India Private Limited, *New Delhi*
Prentice-Hall of Japan, Inc., *Tokyo*
Prentice-Hall of Southeast Asia Pte. Ltd., *Singapore*
Whitehall Books Limited, *Wellington, New Zealand*

CONTENTS

TABLES

FIGURES

PREFACE

This book is the story of my life. More accurately, I have spent most of my working hours preoccupied with my own career and the careers of others. Employers, family, friends, golf, music, teaching, and woodworking have sometimes been pushed aside by this task—producing and revising a theory of careers and personality.

The purpose of this book is to justify my obsession—it is all right to have a narrow range of interests and to neglect some obligations to others, if you produce something of value. I hope practitioners, researchers, students, and workers will continue to find the theory helpful in research, in career counseling, and in understanding their own careers. And although I have written primarily for behavioral scientists and their students, I have tried to write so that an intelligent person can find the principal ideas clear and helpful.

To accomplish these goals, I have presented the theory as directly as I could without the customary asides, doubts, and cautions. These traditional worries are summarized in Chapter 5, "Some Evidence" and in Chapter 6, "The Classification System." These comprehensive summaries are intended to persuade social scientists and educators that the theory has a full complement of technical investigations with prestigious terms and techniques. The evaluations at the end of these chapters provide the reader with an assessment of the theory's strengths and weaknesses without the pain of a tedious technical review.

This book is the fifth account of the theory. The first was a journal article based largely upon my experience as a vocational counselor and as a reader of the vocational literature (Holland, 1959). This first formulation led to some encouraging research, so that a second and more systematic formulation became possible—a brief book (Holland, 1966b). The little book was written to provide more explicit definitions of the main concepts, to provide more comprehensive formulations, and to attract the help of other researchers. Much to my surprise, other researchers appeared, and more than a hundred studies of the theory's usefulness were performed. The third statement (Holland, 1973) offered a theory that better complied with scientific standards of logic and evidence and suggested more practical applications. It was more properly a theory of careers, for it dealt more completely and successfully with vocational problems throughout a person's life: vocational choice, work history, job changes, and occupational achievement. Most importantly, the theory was restructured so that it had both a clearer structure and a simpler statement. The 1973 statement was amended later by Gary Gottfredson and myself in a journal article (1976) in which we attempted to clarify the theory and show more completely how it could be applied to people of all ages.

I hope this fifth statement is my last revision. I am 65 and entitled to a different career or at least some rest. This book continues the tidying-up process, but the theory still closely resembles the 1973 statement and its clarification by Gottfredson and myself (1976).

At the same time, the present statement differs from the earlier statements in several ways: (1) The theory and its application are more comprehensive and explicit; (2) The construct of identity is added as another secondary construct to prop up the formulations for both types and environments. "Consistency" has been demoted for weak performance; (3) The limits (boundary conditions) of the theory are made clearer. The role of age, sex, SES, intelligence and other influences are now given more explicit consideration; (4) I have used Staats' (1975) work on learning, vocational interests, and psychometrics to relate the assessment of personality types to the formulations for the types and their development, and I have used Barker's (1968) concept of behavior setting to alleviate some deficiencies in the environmental models; and, finally (5) The evidence (number of research investigations) reviewed here is now more than four times that in 1973.

The intellectual roots of the theory lie mainly in the traditions of differential psychology—especially the interest measurement literature—and of typologies of personality. The interest literature provided the stimulus for assuming that people with different interests and in different jobs were in fact different people with different life histories.

I saw a typology of persons and occupations as a useful way to organize the massive information we have accumulated about people and jobs. The typology differs from nearly all earlier typologies in many ways: (1) The typology has been revised three times in response to data; (2) It is a typology of persons and environments. It always has been an interactive model; (3) Degrees and patterns of resemblance to models have been substituted for all-or-none distinctions among types so that the theory can cope more successfully with the complexity of personalities and environments; (4) The processes of development, stability, and change are now outlined in more typological terms; (5) All major concepts have been given empirical definition; and (6) A single spatial model (a hexagon) has been used to coordinate the major concepts in the theory.

Last, my thinking has been shaped by my work in counseling centers, in hospitals, and in my curbstone counseling of adolescents and adults. I have become addicted to seeing careers from an individual's perspective—how can a person's difficulties be resolved within the present personal and environmental resources? I have neglected the restructuring of educational institutions, businesses, and public policy, although I have indicated some of the implications of the theory for these institutions. My concern for individuals has led to a related goal—to construct a formulation that can be understood and used by practitioners. Consequently, I have stuck to simple measures of all theoretical constructs. Fortunately, these simple measures usually work as well as more complex ones.

I wrote the first draft of this book, but I am indebted to many friends who have provided valuable criticisms and ideas for renovating the theory itself. They include: Paul T. Costa, Jr., Gary D. Gottfredson, Linda S. Gottfredson, Geoffrey I. Kelso, Aaron M. Pallas, Paul G. Power, Jack R. Rayman, Arnold R. Spokane, Keith F. Taylor, and W. Bruce Walsh.

I remain obligated to many other colleagues who helped me at earlier stages of this venture. They include: William A. Alston, Alexander W. Astin, Leonard L. Baird, Fred H. Borgen, John D. Black, Charles F. Elton, Paul M. Muchinsky, John D. Krumboltz, Thomas M. Magoon, Samuel H. Osipow, Donald P. Hoyt, Robert C. Nichols, James M. Richards, John M. Stalnaker, Donald L. Thistlethwaite, Nancy S. Cole, Mary Cowan Viernstein, Harold F. Giedt, William F. Fairweather, Douglas R. Whitney, and Thelma Baldwin Zener.

Finally I am indebted to Shirley Sult who survived my directions and misdirections in typing the manuscript.

These and other colleagues have provided so much help for such a long time that I can no longer discriminate their ideas from my own or always remember their special contribution. I am in their debt for much of what is useful in this book.

John L. Holland

CHAPTER 1
INTRODUCTION
TO THE THEORY

The purpose of this book is to present a revised theory of careers and its applications to vocational life. I show more completely than before (Holland, 1973) how a theory of careers can be used to explain common career phenomena, to report some new insights and supportive research, and to spell out the implications of these ideas for career counseling and other forms of vocational assistance.

The theory provides explanations for three common and fundamental questions.

1. What personal and environmental characteristics lead to satisfying career decisions, involvement, and achievement, and what characteristics lead to indecision, dissatisfying decisions, or lack of accomplishment?
2. What personal and environmental characteristics lead to stability or change in the kind of level and work a person performs over a lifetime?
3. What are the most effective methods for providing assistance to people with career problems?

The primary concern of the theory is to explain vocational behavior and suggest some practical ideas to help young, middle-aged, and older people select jobs, change jobs, and attain vocational satisfaction. To a lesser degree, the theory also concerns personal competence, educational

behavior, social behavior, and personality. The inclusion of these areas is
the natural outcome of the development of the theory as it has acquired
greater clarity of statement and more evidence for a wider range of usefulness. The following section summarizes the main ideas. The remainder
of the book elaborates these ideas, summarizes the scientific evidence for
their validity, and shows how to apply them to selected vocational, personal, educational, and industrial problems.

A SUMMARY OF THE THEORY

The theory consists of several simple ideas and their more complex elaborations. First, we can characterize people by their resemblance to each of
six personality types: Realistic, Investigative, Artistic, Social, Enterprising,
and Conventional. The more closely a person resembles a particular type,
the more likely he or she is to exhibit the personal traits and behaviors
associated with that type. Second, the environments in which people live
can be characterized by their resemblance to six model environments: Realistic, Investigative, Artistic, Social, Enterprising, and Conventional. Finally,
the pairing of persons and environments leads to outcomes that we can
predict and understand from our knowledge of the personality types and
the environmental models. These outcomes include vocational choice, vocational stability and achievement, educational choice and achievement,
personal competence, social behavior, and susceptibility to influence.

Four working assumptions constitute the heart of the theory. They
indicate the nature of the personality types and environmental models,
how the types and models are determined, and how they interact to create
the phenomena—vocational, educational, and social—that the theory is
meant to explain.

  *1. In our culture, most persons can be categorized as one of six types:
realistic, investigative, artistic, social, enterprising, or conventional.* The description of each type (see Chapter 2) is both a summary of what we know
about people in a given occupational group and a special way of comprehending this information: It is a theoretical or ideal type. A *type* is a model
against which we can measure the real person.

Each type is the product of a characteristic interaction among a
variety of cultural and personal forces including peers, biological heredity, parents, social class, culture, and the physical environment. Out of this
experience, a person learns first to prefer some activities as opposed to
others. Later, these activities become strong interests; such interests lead
to a special group of competencies. Finally, a person's interests and competencies create a particular personal disposition that leads him or her to
think, perceive, and act in special ways. For example, people who resemble the Social type are more likely to seek out social occupations such

as teaching, social work, or the ministry. They would be expected to see themselves as friendly and social and to have more social competencies (such as helping others with personal problems) than realistic competencies (such as using tools or understanding machines). They would value socially oriented problems or tasks: helping others, serving a community, upholding religion.

In short, each type has a characteristic repertoire of attitudes and skills for coping with environmental problems and tasks. Different types select and process information in different ways, but all types seek fulfillment by exercising characteristic activities, skills, and talents and by striving to achieve special goals. Consequently, types are often active rather than passive recipients of environmental influence, for they both seek and avoid environments, problems, and tasks.

By comparing a person's attitudes with those of each model type, we can determine which type he or she most resembles. That model becomes a person's personality type. Then we can also determine what other types a person resembles. For example, a person might resemble a social type most, then an enterprising type, then the other types in descending order. The total resemblance to each of the six types forms a pattern of similarity and dissimilarity—the individual's personality pattern. Thus we obtain a profile of resemblances that allows for the complexity of personality and avoids some of the problems inherent in categorizing a person as a single type. A six-category scheme built on the assumption that there are only six kinds of people in the world is unacceptable on the strength of common sense alone. But a six-category scheme that allows a simple ordering of a person's resemblance to each of the six models provides the possibility of 720 different personality patterns or repertoires for coping with the environment.

To estimate a person's profile or personality pattern, we can use one of several methods: a person's scores on selected scales from interest and personality inventories, choice of vocation or field of training, work history or history of preemployment aspirations, or combinations of these data. For example, certain scales of the Vocational Preference Inventory, the Self-Directed Search, and the Strong-Campbell Interest Inventory have been designated as estimates of the types. The procedure is to have a person take an inventory, score it, and profile the appropriate scales. The profiles can then be interpreted by applying the descriptions of the types.

2. There are six model environments: realistic, investigative, artistic, social, enterprising, and conventional.   Each environment is dominated by a given type of personality, and each environment is typified by physical settings posing special problems and opportunities. For example, Realistic environments are "dominated" by Realistic types of people—that is, the largest percentage of the population in the Realistic environment resembles the Realistic type. A Conventional environment is dominated by Conventional types.

Because different types have different interests, competencies, and dispositions, they tend to surround themselves with special people and materials and to seek out problems that are congruent with their interests, competencies, and outlook on the world. Thus, where people congregate, they create an environment that reflects the types they are, and it becomes possible to assess the environment in the same terms as we assess people individually. One method of accomplishing this task is to count the number of different types in an environment. The distribution of types is then converted to percentages of the total number of people in the environment. The environment is represented by six percentages and is interpreted by the environmental formulations given in Chapter 3.

3. People search for environments that will let them exercise their skills and abilities, express their attitudes and values, and take on agreeable problems and roles.   Realistic types seek realistic environments, Social types seek Social environments, and so forth. To a lesser extent, environments also search for people through friendships and recruiting practices. The person's search for environments is carried on in many ways, at different levels of consciousness, and over a long period of time. The personality types epitomize some common ways in which people develop in our culture. They also illustrate how personal development channels goals, vocational choices, and mobility.

4. Behavior is determined by an interaction between personality and environment.   If we know a person's personality pattern and the pattern of his or her environment, we can, in principle, use our knowledge of personality types and environmental models to forecast some of the outcomes of such a pairing. Such outcomes include choice of vocation, job changes, vocational achievement, personal competence, and educational and social behavior.

These four key assumptions are supplemented by several secondary assumptions that can be applied to both persons and environments. The purpose of the secondary concepts is to moderate or qualify predictions or explanations that are derived from the main concepts. For example, a well-differentiated, consistent, Realistic type with a clear sense of identity, as opposed to a Realistic type without these attributes, would be expected to exhibit more realistic attitudes, behaviors, and choices.

Consistency.   Within a person or an environment, some pairs of types are more closely related than others. For example, Realistic and Investigative types have more in common than Conventional and Artistic types. Consistency is the degree of relatedness between personality types or between environmental models. Degrees of consistency or relatedness are assumed to affect vocational preference. For instance, a person who resembles the Realistic type most and next most resembles the Investigative type (a Realistic-Investigative person) should be more predictable than a Realistic-Social person.

Differentiation. Some persons or environments are more clearly defined than others. For instance, a person may closely resemble a single type and show little resemblance to other types, or an environment may be dominated largely by a single type. In constrast, a person who resembles many types or an environment that is characterized by about equal numbers of the six types is undifferentiated or poorly defined. The degree to which a person or an environment is well defined is its degree of differentiation.

Identity. This concept provides an estimate of the clarity and stability of a person's identity or the identity of an environment. Personal identity is defined as the possession of a clear and stable picture of one's goals, interests, and talents. Environmental identity is present when an environment or organization has clear, integrated goals, tasks, and rewards that are stable over long time intervals.

Identity, consistency, and differentiation are all concerned with the clarity, definition, or focus of the main concepts—types and environmental models. They probably represent three techniques for assessing the same concept.

Congruence. Different types require different environments. For instance, Realistic types flourish in Realistic environments because such an environment provides the opportunities and rewards a Realistic type needs. Incongruence occurs when a type lives in an environment that provides opportunities and rewards foreign to the person's preferences and abilities—for instance, a Realistic type in a Social environment.

Calculus. The relationships within and between types or environments can be ordered according to a hexagonal model in which the distances between the types or environments are inversely proportional to the theoretical relationships between them. This spatial arrangement provides explicit definitions of both consistency of a person or an environment (three levels) and congruence of person and environment (four levels). In this way, the internal relationships of the theory are defined and organized by a single geometrical model (see Figure 3, p. 29).

BACKGROUND CONCEPTS AND ORIGINS

The theory comes from and rests upon the work of many others. This section provides a brief account of the main origins of the theory and some additional background principles that I have proposed or borrowed from others. These ideas are important to the theory but usually less so than the main ideas summarized earlier.

Origins

The formulations for the types grew out of my experience as a vocational counselor in educational, military, and clinical settings. That experience, the vocational literature, and the construction of the Vocational Preference Inventory (Holland, 1958) gradually led me to the notion that it might be helpful to categorize people in terms of interest or personality types.

The idea for a typology resulted from the frequent observation that several broad classes account for most human interests, traits, and behaviors. In a now obscure article, Darley (1938) suggested the potential value of organizing our knowledge according to occupational stereotypes. As a beginning I used six scales of the Vocational Preference Inventory that correspond to the present personality types: Realistic, Investigative, Artistic, Social, Enterprising, and Conventional. Somewhat later, I was impressed and reassured by Guilford's (1954) comprehensive factor analysis of human interest, in which he obtained six major factors to account for the diversity of interests and personality traits: mechanical, scientific, social welfare, clerical, business, and esthetic.

The present types are analogous in some ways to the types proposed earlier by Adler (1939), Fromm (1947), Jung (1933), Sheldon (1954), Spranger (1928), and more recently by Gordon (1975) and Welsh (1975). They differ from the earlier typologies in their origin (which is largely the vocational literature) and in their empirical definitions (see Chapter 2). In addition, I have tried to formulate a clear, testable structure for each type and to conform with as many scientific principles of logic and evidence as possible.

The notion of assessing environments by characterizing the people in a particular environment came from Linton (1945), who suggested that a major portion of the force of the environment is transmitted through other people. The typology thus became a method for engineering Linton's idea—that is, by calculating the distribution of types in an environment, you will know the environment. This hypothesis led to the development of the Environmental Assessment Technique (Astin and Holland, 1961), which has been used to describe college environments.

The assumption that human behavior depends upon *both* personality and the specific environment in which a person lives has a long history. However, Murray's (1938) formulations of personal "needs" and environmental "pressures" were the immediate stimulus for the use of personality types and environmental models here.

Throughout the development and study of the theory, I have been impressed with the need for pragmatism. Any research study requires much time and resources, so I have tried to limit the use of the theory to simple, inexpensive, practical definitions and measures. Further, I have hoped that the elaboration of these simple approaches would be sufficient to cope with much of the complexity of human behavior and human environments, and much of the research now supports the value of these strategies.

I have also been concerned with developing an elegant and symmetrical theory. The development of parallel sets of types and environments and the discovery of the hexagonal model (Figure 3, p. 29) came partly from an irrational belief and feeling about symmetry. I agree with Mohr (1982) that longer lists of variables and more elaborate theories are unlikely to succeed and will be less likely to be tested or used.

Background Principles

In developing the typology and the environmental models, a number of principles seemed plausible, or at least hard to imagine as false. These are enumerated below, along with some arguments for their acceptance.

The choice of a vocation is an expression of personality.   For many years it was popular to interpret people's scores on vocational interest inventories and their choices of vocation as a function of their "vocational interests," as if these interests were different from or independent of personality. Some early work of Strong (1943) and Super and Crites (1962) epitomizes the view that vocational interests measure only interests, vocational choices, and vocational preferences. A long history of adherence to this concept produced an independent literature known as "interest measurement."

More recent knowledge about the personal and environmental factors associated with vocational choice, job changes, and vocational achievement has revealed the need for a broader conception. We have learned that vocational preferences are sometimes moderately correlated with personality and originality scales (Holland, 1963), self-ratings of ability and personalty traits and life goals (Baird, 1970), parental attitudes (Medvene, 1969), objective perceptual tests (Crutchfield, Woodworth, and Albrecht, 1958), and many other psychological and sociological variables. For many years, writers have suggested the need for a more comprehensive view of vocational preferences and interests: "Interest inventory scores are measures of self-concept" (Bordin, 1943); "vocational interest measurement is a special case in personality theory" (Darley and Hagenah, 1955); "vocational choice is a developmental process" and is, in large part, "the implementation of a person's self-concept" (Super, 1972). These orientations consistently imply that people's vocational interests flow from their life history and personality.

If vocational interests are construed as an expression of personality, then they represent the expression of personality in work, school subjects, hobbies, recreational activities, and preferences. In short, what we have called "vocational interests" are an important aspect of personality. Just as we have developed theories of personality from our knowledge of sex and parental relationships, so we can construct theories of personality from our knowledge of vocational life. We can then reinterpret vocational interests as an expression of personality. The theory is mainly an elaborate engineering of this key idea.

Interest inventories are personality inventories. If vocational interests are an expression of personality, then it follows that interest inventories are personality inventories. Forer (1948) was probably the first to develop an inventory to assess personality from interests and activities and to illustrate how a person's responses to apparently neutral content (vocational interests and activities) could be interpreted as expressions of various dimensions of personality. Although Forer did not put his ideas to a direct scientific test, he did show that we can distinguish a great variety of medical and psychiatric groups (asthmatics to schizophrenics) by their scores on various scales of one interest inventory, the Kuder Preference Record (Forer, 1951). Forer's theorizing led to the construction of my Vocational Preference Inventory (1958, 1977), a personality inventory composed entirely of occupational titles. In general, the scales were developed by hypothesizing that preferences for occupations are expressions of personality. The rationale for the development of the inventory contains a more complete statement of this hypothesis:

> The choice of an occupation is an expressive act which reflects the person's motivation, knowledge, personality, and ability. Occupations represent a way of life, an environment rather than a set of isolated work functions or skills. To work as a carpenter means not only to use tools but also to have a certain status, community role, and a special pattern of living. In this sense, the choice of an occupational title represents several kinds of information: the S's motivation, his knowledge of the occupation in question, his insight and understanding of himself, and his abilities. In short, item responses may be thought of as limited but useful expressive or projective protocols. (Holland, 1977, p. 5)

The development and validation of the Vocational Preference Inventory (Holland, 1977) make it clear that vocational preferences are indeed signs of personality traits. Work by Baird (1970), Campbell (1971), and others also shows that interest scales are related to a person's values, academic achievement, liberalism, adventurousness, and other personal characteristics. And Staats et al. (1973) have applied Staats' attitude-reinforcer-discriminative theory to selected items of the Strong Vocational Interest Blank and demonstrated in three experiments that interest items have emotional-eliciting properties, that items can serve as rewards or punishments, and that measured interests can indicate the stimuli that have discriminative control over the individual's approach and avoidance behavior. Staats et al. supply persuasive and explicit data for assuming that a person's interests are useful for understanding personality and that earlier assumptions such as "an interest inventory is a record of a person's reinforcement history" have merit. Or, in Staats' words, "an interest inventory . . . samples the events that have learned emotional value."

To summarize, it seems useful to interpret vocational interest inventories as personality inventories. Moreover, the content of vocational interest inventories provides scales whose reliabilities and validities approximate those obtained for other methods for assessing personality.

Vocational stereotypes have reliable and important psychological and sociological meanings. Just as we judge people by their friends, dress, and actions, so we judge them by their vocations. Our everyday experience has generated a sometimes inaccurate but apparently useful knowledge of what people in various occupations are like. Thus we believe that carpenters are handy, lawyers aggressive, actors self-centered, salespeople persuasive, accountants precise, scientists unsociable, and the like. In earlier years, social scientists were skeptical of the accuracy of this amorphous folklore of vocational stereotypes (some still are), but recent work makes it clear that many have some validity.

O'Dowd and Beardslee (1960, 1967) have demonstrated that occupations are perceived in much the same way by high school students, college students, college faculty, and men versus women. They also found that demographic differences (that is, one's social status) make only small differences in the perception of occupations, and that occupational stereotypes change only slightly during four years of college. And Marks and Webb (1969) demonstrated that students entering the field of industrial management or electrical engineering possess "a fairly accurate image— assuming the professionals know what they are talking about—of the typical incumbent of the intended occupation." Their elaborate study of two occupational titles by three levels of experience—freshmen, seniors, and professionals before, during, and after training—practically closes the door on the argument that inexperienced and experienced people do not see an occupation in similar ways. In addition, L. Gottfredson (1981) has provided a more recent summary that supports and extends these early studies. In short, people of different ages and backgrounds have characteristic perceptions of an occupation: its appropriateness for men and women, its level of prestige, and the personal traits of the typical incumbent.

These findings have considerable and pervasive importance for vocational behavior. Most interest inventories rest heavily on the assumptions that people perceive occupations and their associated activities accurately and that these perceptions remain the same over long periods of time. In the same way, a person's vocational preferences and choices rest on the same assumptions. If perceptions of occupations had no validity, interest inventories would have little or no validity, and the average person would have great difficulty in selecting suitable jobs.

The members of a vocation have similar personalities and similar histories of personal development. If a person enters a given vocation because of a particular personality and history, it follows that each vocation attracts and retains people with similar personalities. Laurent's (1951) study of engineers, physicians, and lawyers documents the similarities in life histories for the members of a vocation. Other studies—for example, Roe (1956), Kulberg and Owens (1960), Chaney and Owens (1964), Nachmann (1960), and Eberhardt and Muchinsky (1982)—support this assumption. And, if we should form classes made up of vocations demanding similar personalities, we would get groups of people who are alike. For example, groups of scientists such as physicists, chemists, and mathematicians should be grossly similar, because the evidence indicates that physical scientists have something in common.

Because people in a vocational group have similar personalities, they will respond to many situations and problems in similar ways, and they will create characteristic interpersonal environments. Although we cannot test this assumption directly, we do have some indirect evidence. For example, Astin and Holland (1961) were able to predict what college students would say about their college and about fellow students. The method entails a simple census of the number of students in each of six curricular groups: Realistic, Investigative, Social, Conventional, Enterprising, and Artistic. The percentage of students in each curricular group at a given college becomes the profile of that college. In the first study, Astin and Holland found, for example, that the percentage of students in the realistic group was correlated with a student's description of the college and its students as pragmatic rather than humanistic. It is possible then to describe a college by a simple census of its members if one has a way to interpret the meaning of membership in various curricula. Other studies (Astin, 1968; Richards, Seligman, and Jones, 1970) have validated these ideas in large-scale analyses of educational environments.

Vocational satisfaction, stability, and achievement depend on the congruence between one's personality and the environment in which one works. Just as we are more comfortable among friends whose tastes, talents, and values are similar to our own, so we are more likely to perform well at a vocation in which we "fit" psychologically. Vocational interest inventories are based in part on this assumption. Moreover, the vocational literature is filled with evidence that supports the assumption, although that evidence is not usually interpreted as relating to the interaction between a particular personality and a particular environment. In the present theory, the congruence of person and environment is defined in terms of the *structure* of personality types and environmental models. For example, a congruent or fitting environment is one in which a person's preferred activities and special competencies are required, and his or her personal disposition and its associated characteristics—a special outlook on the world, role preferences, values, and personal traits—are reinforced.

LOOSE ENDS

The theory, like most theories, has some ambiguities, limitations, and omissions and is prone to some misunderstandings. This brief section is to place the theory in the context of related career and personality theory, to emphasize how stability and change in career pathways occur, and to indicate the role of influential variables such as intelligence, gender, and social class.

Theoretical Context

The theory is a structural-interactive or a typological-interactive theory. It is "structural" or "typological" because it attempts to organize the vast sea of information about people and jobs. And it is "interactive" because it assumes that many career and social behaviors are the outcome of people and environments acting on one another. It is not a one-way street; jobs change people, and people change jobs.

Compared with other theories of personality, the theory is a fulfillment model, for it assumes that all people look for enjoyment and seek to reach goals that actualize talents, skills, and interests. It is further assumed that some goal-oriented activities are conscious and some are not. In addition, it is assumed that all people are active and that "all psychological agents give direction to behavior. Stimuli, prior learning, genes, physiological conditions, developmental processes, almost any psychological or sociological influence exerts its influence by making some response classes more probable than others" (Robert Bolles, 1978, p. 11).

Here it is assumed that interest inventories provide a potent assessment of both psychological and sociological agents, or the behavioral repertoires that such influences create. And the Environmental Assessment Technique (EAT) or job analyses provide information about the environmental characteristics or demands that press for the expression of different activities, goals, coping behaviors, and values.

A particular disposition develops because different people have different biological capacities and life histories. The developmental outcomes of these interactions are characterized as personality types and tend to become well defined between 18 and 30.

Stability and Change

The average career is both focused and stabilized by relatively constant dispositions, special talents, expectations, irreversible choices, credentials, and other baggage that workers acquire, and by the benign and biased environments everyone encounters at every age. At the same time, some workers do change (or become different types), although career changes or changes in personality are difficult to accomplish and sustain. People trying to change themselves or their careers receive little environmental support and must overcome the cumulative learning associated with a particular job or self-concept such as "I am a teacher, not an executive," or "I am an inferior person, not a confident one."

In short, stability is the norm, because workers soon become active seekers of a limited range of congruent jobs, and because employers discourage change through common hiring practices and biases of age, appearance, sex, training, and work history. Family, friends, co-workers, and relatives also press for stability, because they usually have a stake in a worker's income, friendship, and power. These generalizations are elaborated as theoretical explanations in Chapter 4.

Although the guts of the theory is the interaction of a particular person (personality pattern) in a particular work environment (environmental pattern) in a "closed" system of six personal and six environmental concepts, the theory is at the same time an "open" system within a particular culture. For instance, as the American culture shifts toward greater equality for women, that influence will be reflected in the interest profiles of women. This appears to be happening already. And, as the interests of incumbents and the demands of a particular occupational environment shift, these changes will alter the data used to characterize that occupational environment. Some informal data and older work by David Campbell (1971) imply that some small cultural changes in vocational interests and therefore personality have occurred between the 1930s and the 1960s and may be occurring now.

"Other Things Being Equal . . ."

The theory cannot be applied successfully without the observance of a few boundary conditions. These are comparable to the instructions supplied with a new sewing machine or table saw. You can ignore them, but don't complain to the manufacturer when things go wrong.

In this instance I want to emphasize that "other things being equal . . ." applies to the entire theory and consists of the following characteristics of the person and environment: age, gender, ethnicity, geography, social class, physical assets or liabilities, educational level attained, intelligence, and influence. Most of these variables are incorporated indirectly in the theory, but direct assessments of these variables are also required to secure more positive applications.

For example, the distribution of influence and status within a person's social environment makes a difference, so researchers must control their experiments for influence and status, and practitioners must make some estimate of the role of influence and status in evaluating environments for their clients. People also acquire perceptions of job-self compatibility—especially sex type, prestige, and required effort associated with a job—that focus and limit a person's job search in adolescence (L. Gottfredson, 1981) and probably in adulthood. These influences appear most powerful at the extremes of age, sex-role socialization, social class, intelligence, and physical disability. For example, visually impaired college students frequently want to become teachers, tutors, or therapists, because these occupations represent the world they know best.

In short, these variables—age, gender, social class, effort required—circumscribe (L. Gottfredson, 1981) or reduce the range of careers a person will consider. At the same time, the number of options remaining after the effects of these variables are considered is still large. It is at this point that interest inventories become especially useful for comprehending and sorting out the remaining pool of possibilities. I hope readers will at least include measures of age, gender, social class, and intelligence as well as gross characteristics of the work environment so that the contributions of these and the theoretical constructs can be applied or studied in a more integrated way.

Kind and Level of Work

All three versions of the theory (Holland, 1959, 1966, 1973) have focused more on the *kind* of work a person performs (for example, sales, clerical, scientific, mechanical, artistic, educational) than on the *level* of work a person performs (its prestige, income, level of talent required, and so on). The earlier versions included a few testable hypotheses about the level of vocational choice and achievement, but these ideas attracted little research attention and apparently got lost among the numerous hypotheses about kind of work. The earlier theoretical statements proposed that the level of vocational choice or career attainment followed the following formulas: occupational level, attained or expected, equals (a) intelligence plus status (Holland, 1959), (b) consistency of personality pattern . . . social and enterprising types . . . and other things being equal ("intelligence and social background") (Holland, 1966, p. 47), and (c) "other things being equal, vocational achievement will be associated with the model types in the following order: E, S, A, I, C, and R . . . consistency and differentiation of the personality pattern . . . congruency of person and environment" (Holland, 1973, pp. 25 and 39–40).

This time around I have spelled out the meaning of "other things being equal" more explicitly and in several places. I have indicated that vocational achievement follows the 1973 hypotheses with the addition of identity (see Chapter 2), and I have suggested how the individual hypotheses might interact. I hope someone tests these ideas.

SUMMARY

A typology of six personality types, six corresponding occupational environments, and their interactions is offered as a tool for understanding work histories, vocational satisfaction, achievement, and vocational interventions and for organizing and interpreting personal and occupational data. Some secondary concepts—congruence, consistency, differentiation, and identity—are included to increase the explanatory value of the main concepts—types and environmental models. The origins, theoretical context, and some ambiguities and misunderstandings of the theory are reviewed. The following chapters offer a more complete exposition. Chapter 2, "The Personality Types," provides detailed descriptions of the theoretical types and their expected performance. Chapter 3 specifies "The Environmental Models." Chapter 4, "People in Environments," shows what happens when different personalities live in different environments, and Chapter 5 summarizes the evidence for the usefulness of the theory. Chapter 6 describes the classification system and summarizes the evidence of its validity. And Chapter 7 outlines the practical applications of the theory to personal, educational, and industrial problems.

CHAPTER 2
THE PERSONALITY TYPES

This chapter provides the theoretical formulations for each of the six personality types. Separate sections summarize how types develop, what each type is like, how types are assessed, how types resemble one another, and how types behave.

DEVELOPMENT OF TYPES

The purpose of this section is to outline how personality types develop and to do so in the context of the formulations for these types. These speculative statements are intended to make the theory more complete and to facilitate its study and application.

To some degree, types produce types. Although parental attitudes play a minor and complex role in the development of a child's interests (Roe, 1956; Roe and Siegelman, 1964), the assumption here is that each parental type provides a large cluster of environmental opportunities, as well as some deficits which extend well beyond parental attitudes. For example, Realistic parents (their child-rearing attitudes aside) engage in characteristic Realistic activities in and out of the home; surround themselves with particular equipment, possessions, materials, and tools; and select Realistic friends and neighborhoods. At the same time, Realistic parents tend to ignore, avoid, or reject some activities and types more than others. For instance, Realistic parents will be expected to reject social activities, people, and situations. In short, parents create characteristic environments that include attitudes as well as a great range of obvious environmental experiences.

Parents also transmit a particular biological endowment of physical and psychological potentials, and although the absolute impact of these biological potentials is not clear, we are not created with equal potentials. For instance, a large-scale investigation (Grotevant et al., 1977) of families with biological and adopted children implies, as did the earlier studies of identical and fraternal twins (Roberts and Johansson, 1974), that vocational interests have a small inherited component. These data even suggest that the *shape* of the interest profile is inherited. I do not mean to imply that inheritance equals immutability, but it does imply a little push in one direction as opposed to another.

Further, children create their own environment to a limited degree by their demands upon parents and by the manner in which parents react to and are influenced by children (Bell, 1968; Bell and Harper, 1977; Thomas, Chess, and Birch, 1970). Children's demands are assumed to be a function of both biological endowment and social learning—not one or the other. Presumably, the more a child resembles a particular parent, the more reward he or she will receive—so parent-child relationships, like other personal relationships, may demonstrate that types are attracted to types. When parental and child data are organized in the typology, positive associations among types should occur because large clusters of characteristic activities, competencies, vocational preferences, and so on are being assessed, not just subtle attitudes that can be easily distorted by the assessment process and that constitute only a small portion of the multiple and varied influences parents exert.

A child's special biology and experience first lead to preferences for some kinds of activities and aversions to others. Later, these preferences become well-defined interests from which the person gains satisfaction as well as reward from others. Still later, the pursuit of these interests leads to the development of more specialized competencies as well as to the neglect of other potential competencies. At the same time, a person's differentiation of interests with age is accompanied by a crystallization of correlated values. These events—an increasing differentiation of preferred activities, interests, competencies, and values—create a characteristic disposition or personality type that is predisposed to exhibit characteristic behavior and to develop characteristic personality traits, attitudes, and behaviors that in turn form repertoires or collections of skills and coping mechanisms. These include:

1. Self-concepts
2. Perception of the environment
3. Values
4. Achievement and performance
5. Differential reaction to environmental rewards, stress, and so on
6. Preference for occupation and occupational role
7. Coping style
8. Personal traits
9. Repertoires of "skills" formed by 1 to 8.

This simplified account of personality development avoids any consideration of the complex and involuted ways in which personality is usually assumed to develop. The simplification is achieved by limiting the account to a general discussion of easily observed developments. These events *do* happen and, for the purposes of this theory, that is sufficient. Thus we can substitute a straightforward account of activities, competencies, values, and interests for a more complex model of sex, siblings, and parental relationships. The simple model provides a useful form for explaining some human behavior without the usual complexities.

Figure 1 illustrates how types may develop. To summarize, some of a child's initial activities lead to long-term interests and competencies. That experience creates a person who is predisposed to exhibit a characteristic self-concept and outlook and to acquire a characteristic disposition. This general formula is used to structure the formulations in the next section.

The loops (half circles in Figure 1) suggest how types may become more differentiated or how a person may become more like one type than another over the life course. For instance, persons of a particular type may become more like that type with age as they experience more and more activities and acquire more and more associated competencies and rewards. In contrast, a person of a particular type may get an opportunity, or be forced, to perform the activities and acquire the competencies of a different type, and discover that this experience (prevented earlier because of traditional sex role socialization, racial discrimination, poverty, or the special ghettos that everyone grows up in) is congenial so that a shift in disposition may occur. Such shifts are usually expected to be minor rather than major because of the cumulative learning and environmental barriers that must be overcome. Finally, it is assumed that the probability of change via the loops becomes smaller with age, because the impact of cumulative learning and of environmental resistance to change grows stronger.

This brief account of how types develop is most consistent with Staats' (1981) theory of social behaviorism and Krumboltz's (1979) social learning theory of career decision making, but it is most closely related to the Staats theory. According to Staats:

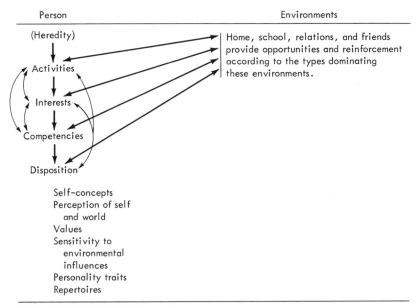

Note: The order of development usually is from activities to dispositions. Preferred activities develop out of the initial global and diffuse activities that characterize infants. The loops with arrows on both ends indicate the many other ways in which types may develop. We also assume that differences in heredity affect the choice of activity and the likelihood of reinforcement. For example, sheer size, sex, coordination, etc., influence the choice of sport, role in that sport, etc.

FIGURE 1   How Types May Develop

The individual begins from birth to learn *systems* of "skills," according to the principles of conditioning, in three areas: language-cognitive processes, emotional-motivational processes, and sensori-motor acts. These systems are called . . . personality repertoires and are considered to be the basic constituents of personality in several ways. First, the way an individual *responds* to a situation is not only a function of the behaviorally significant acts of the situation but a function (in part) of the individual's personality repertoires. Second, this is true for what the person *experiences* in a situation as well as for what he or she *learns*. Each behavioral occurrence depends in part on the situation and in part on the individual's own personality repertoires . . . The person who has a rich repertoire of aggressive sensori-motor skills that are elicited by situations involving physical hostility is different in personality from the person who has never acquired such skills or who has acquired other skills in their place, that is, various forms of escape and avoidance behaviors. Sensori-motor skills are involved in work, sex, recreation. (1981, p. 244)

In the context of the Staats theory, the six types are models of six common clusters of personality or behavioral repertoires that occur in our society. The six parallel environments are the major, but not the exclusive, stimuli for the creation of special repertoires.

FORMULATIONS OF THE TYPES

The types are assumed to represent common outcomes of growing up in our culture. Each type is described in terms of a theoretical model created with several goals in mind: (1) To outline only the bare bones of the experiences that lead to a particular kind of person; (2) to show how a person's experience leads to a special disposition and how that disposition leads to a wide range of human behavior; and (3) to provide theoretical models that will fit both the old and the new evidence about the types.

The Realistic Type

The special heredity and experiences of the Realistic person lead to a preference for activities that entail the explicit, ordered, or systematic manipulation of objects, tools, machines, and animals and to an aversion to educational or therapeutic activities. These behavioral tendencies lead in turn to the acquisition of manual, mechanical, agricultural, electrical, and technical competencies and to a deficit in social and educational competencies.

This development of a Realistic pattern of activities, competencies, and interests creates a person who is predisposed to exhibit the following behavior:

1. Prefers realistic occupations or situations (for example, electrician) in which one can engage in preferred activities and avoid the activities demanded by social occupations or situations.
2. Uses realistic competencies to solve problems at work and in other settings.
3. Perceives self as having mechanical and athletic ability and lacking ability in human relations.
4. Values concrete things or tangible personal characteristics—money, power, and status.

Because the Realistic person possesses these preferences, competencies, self-perceptions, and values, the Realistic person is apt to be:

Asocial	Materialistic	Self-effacing
Conforming	Natural	Inflexible
Frank	Normal	Thrifty
Genuine	Persistent	Uninsightful
Hard-headed	Practical	Uninvolved

The Investigative Type

The special heredity and experiences of the Investigative person lead to a preference for activities that entail the observational, symbolic, systematic, and creative investigation of physical, biological, and cultural phenomena in order to understand and control such phenomena; and to an aversion to persuasive, social, and repetitive activities. These behavioral tendencies lead in turn to an acquisition of scientific and mathematical competencies and to a deficit in persuasive competencies.

This development of an Investigative pattern of activities, competencies, and interests creates a person who is predisposed to exhibit the following behavior:

1. Prefers investigative occupations or situations in which one can engage in preferred activities and competencies and avoid the activities demanded by enterprising occupations or situations.
2. Uses investigative competencies to solve problems at work and in other settings.
3. Perceives self as scholarly, intellectual, having mathematical and scientific ability, and lacking in leadership ability.
4. Values science.

Because the Investigative person possesses these preferences, competencies, self-perceptions, and values, the Investigative person is apt to be:

Analytical	Independent	Rational
Cautious	Intellectual	Reserved
Critical	Introspective	Retiring
Complex	Pessimistic	Unasssuming
Curious	Precise	Unpopular

The Artistic Type

The special heredity and experiences of the Artistic person lead to a preference for ambiguous, free, unsystematized activities that entail the manipulation of physical, verbal, or human materials to create art forms or products, and to an aversion to explicit, systematic, and ordered activities. These behavioral tendencies lead, in turn, to an acquisition of artistic competencies—language, art, music, drama, writing—and to a deficit in clerical or business system competencies.

This development of an Artistic pattern of activities, competencies, and interests creates a person who is predisposed to exhibit the following behavior:

1. Prefers artistic occupations or situations in which one can engage in preferred activities and competencies and avoid the activities demanded by conventional occupations or situations.
2. Uses artistic competencies to solve problems at work and in other settings.
3. Perceives self as expressive, original, intuitive, nonconforming, introspective, independent, disorderly, having artistic and musical ability, and ability in acting, writing, and speaking.
4. Values esthetic qualities.

Because the Artistic person possesses these preferences, competencies, self-perceptions, and values, the Artistic person is apt to be:

Complicated	Imaginative	Intuitive
Disorderly	Impractical	Nonconforming
Emotional	Impulsive	Original
Expressive	Independent	Sensitive
Idealistic	Introspective	Open

The Social Type

The special heredity and experiences of the Social person lead to a preference for activities that entail the manipulation of others to inform, train, develop, cure, or enlighten; and an aversion to explicit, ordered, systematic activities involving materials, tools, or machines. These behavioral tendencies lead in turn to an acquisition of human relations competencies such as interpersonal and educational competencies and to a deficit in manual and technical competencies.

This development of a Social pattern of activities, competencies, and interests creates a person who is predisposed to exhibit the following behavior:

1. Prefers social occupations and situations in which one can engage in preferred activities and competencies and avoid the activities demanded by realistic occupations and situations.
2. Uses social competencies to solve problems at work and in other settings.
3. Perceives self as liking to help others, understanding others, having teaching ability, and lacking mechanical and scientific ability.
4. Values social and ethical activities and problems.

Because the Social person possesses these preferences, competencies, self-perceptions, and values, the Social person is apt to be:

Ascendant	Helpful	Responsible
Cooperative	Idealistic	Sociable
Patient	Empathic	Tactful
Friendly	Kind	Understanding
Generous	Persuasive	Warm

The Enterprising Type

The special heredity and experiences of the Enterprising person lead to a preference for activities that entail the manipulation of others to attain organizational goals or economic gain; and an aversion to observational, symbolic, and systematic activities. These behavioral tendencies lead in turn to an acquisition of leadership, interpersonal, and persuasive competencies, and to a deficit in scientific competencies.

This development of an Enterprising pattern of activities, competencies, and interests creates a person who is predisposed to exhibit the following behavior:

1. Prefers enterprising occupations or situations in which one can engage in preferred activities and avoid the activities demanded by investigative occupations and situations.
2. Uses enterprising competencies to solve problems at work and in other situations.
3. Perceives self as aggressive, popular, self-confident, sociable, possessing leadership and speaking abilities, and lacking scientific ability.
4. Values political and economic achievement.

Because the Enterprising person possesses these preferences, competencies, self-perceptions, and values, the Enterprising person is apt to be:

Acquisitive	Energetic	Flirtatious
Adventurous	Exhibitionistic	Optimistic
Agreeable	Excitement-	Self-confident
Ambitious	seeking	Sociable
Domineering	Extroverted	Talkative

The Conventional Type

The special heredity and experiences of the Conventional person lead to a perference for activities that entail the explicit, ordered, systematic manipulation of data, such as keeping records, filing materials, reproducing materials, organizing written and numerical data according to a prescribed plan, operating business machines and data processing machines to attain organizational or economic goals; and to an aversion to ambiguous, free, exploratory, or unsystematized activities. These behavioral tendencies lead in turn to an acquisition of clerical, computational, and business system competencies and to a deficit in artistic competencies.

This development of a Conventional pattern of activities, competencies, and interests creates a person who is predisposed to exhibit the following behavior:

1. Prefers conventional occupations or situations in which one can engage in preferred activities and avoid the activities demanded by artistic occupations or situations.
2. Uses conventional competencies to solve problems at work and in other situations.
3. Perceives self as conforming, orderly, and as having clerical and numerical ability.
4. Values business and economic achievement.

Because the Conventional person possesses these preferences, competencies, self-perceptions, and values, the Conventional person is apt to be:

Careful	Inflexible	Persistent
Conforming	Inhibited	Practical
Conscientious	Methodical	Prudish
Defensive	Obedient	Thrifty
Efficient	Orderly	Unimaginative

ASSESSMENT OF TYPES

The types have been given empirical definitions so that the validity of their formulations can be examined and so that the typology can be applied to everyday problems. Several related methods have been used to assess a person's resemblance to the types.

We can assess a person's personality type by *qualitative* methods. A person may express vocational preferences for or hold employment in an occupation that is characteristic of a type; he or she may express preferences for or be engaged in educational training that is characteristic of a type. For example, a person may want to become a physicist, or be employed as a physicist, or plan to major in physics, or be enrolled as a physics major. Any one of these four kinds of information results in being classified as an Investigative type. This classification is accomplished by comparing a person's educational or vocational interests with vocations assumed to be typical of each personality type (see Appendix A). In the preceding example, "physicist" is one of the occupations that define the Investigative type. To take another example, a social worker would be classified as a Social type because "social worker" is one of the vocational criteria of this type.

Various *quantitative* methods have also been used to assess a person's resemblance to the types. The Realistic, Intellectual, Social, Conventional, Enterprising, and Artistic scales of the Vocational Preference Inventory (Holland, 1977) provide a simple procedure for typing a person. First, a person indicates the vocations that appeal to him or her and those that do not from a list of 84 occupational titles (14 occupations for each of the six scales). The six scales are scored and profiled. The higher a person's score on a scale, the greater the resemblance to the type that scale represents. The highest score represents a person's personality *type;* the profile of scores (obtained by ranking the scale scores from highest to lowest) represents the *personality pattern.*

The Self-Directed Search (Holland, 1979), a career guidance device explicitly derived from the theory and the correlates of the Vocational Preference Inventory, is another useful way to determine a person's resemblances to the types. The SDS uses a broad range of content—activities, competencies, occupations, and self-ratings—to assess the person's resemblance to each type. The subscales of the SDS can be used to define many of the undefined terms in the formulations of the types. For example, Realistic activities, competencies, self-concepts, and occupations correspond to the Realistic activity, competency, self-rating, and occupation scales of the SDS, and so on (the SDS is shown in Appendix B). The six theme scales of the Strong-Campbell Interest Inventory (SCII; Campbell and Hansen, 1981) were also developed to assess a person's resemblance to each of the personality types. In short, a person's resemblance to each type may be defined by vocational interest as manifested in vocational and educational preferences, current employment, or scores on certain interest scales. The different definitions for a given type in Table 1 are positively intercorrelated measures of the same type, since different methods of assessment have usually produced similar results.

Although there seems to be no one best method to assess a person's personality type, the Vocational Preference Inventory, The Self-Directed Search, and the use of current preference or occupation have either produced more coherent results or have special advantages by virtue of their simplicity or theoretical construction. The VPI scales were also used to create a comprehensive occupational classification (Holland, 1966a; Holland, Viernstein, Kuo, Karweit, and Blum, 1972) that has led to the most recent and most comprehensive classification. Gottfredson, Holland, and Ogawa (1982) developed the Dictionary of Holland Occupational Codes (DHOC) to characterize the work environments of the 12,099 occupations in the Dictionary of Occupational Titles (DOT; Department of Labor, 1977). Chapter 6 contains a complete account of the development of the classification system from 1959 to 1982.

Defining types according to a person's vocational preferences or present occupation has also proved useful, because these definitions yield the most substantial predictions (Holland and Lutz, 1968; Holland and Whitney, 1968; Frantz and Walsh, 1972). However, these methods lack the flexibility provided by the VPI or the SDS. For instance, a new occupation can be classified by administering the SDS or VPI to representative samples of people employed in the new occupation. Average scores for a particular occupation can then be profiled and coded to indicate that occupation's specific category in the classification.

At this time, no single assessment technique stands out as being the most advantageous for all purposes. This situation exists because a type is a construct that we can only assess by a variety of fallible (unreliable and partially valid) measures. No single measure can capture the essence of an ideal type, because we will always have fallible measures. It seems strategically valuable to continue to use several methods and to select methods according to the practical or research problems at hand. For example,

TABLE 1 Personality Types and Their Definitions

PERSONALITY TYPES

	Realistic	Investigative	Artistic	Social	Enterprising	Conventional
Self-Directed Search	Realistic	Investigative	Artistic	Social	Enterprising	Conventional
Vocational Preference Inventory	Realistic	Intellectual	Artistic	Social	Enterprising	Conventional
Theme scales for Strong-Campbell Interest Inventory	Realistic	Investigative	Artistic	Social	Enterprising	Conventional
Choice of major field	Industrial Arts Agriculture	Physics Biology	Art Music	Education Social science	Business administration Marketing	Accounting Business education
Choice of vocation*	Surveyor Mechanic	Chemist Physicist	Artist Writer	Teacher Counselor	Salesman Executive	Accountant Clerk
Current occupation or work history						

*See Gottfredson et al. (1982) for a complete list of the occupations defining each type.
Note: For example, persons with high scores on any of the following scales are assumed to resemble the realistic personality type: Realistic scale (Vocational Preference Inventory); Realistic scale (Strong-Campbell Interest Inventory); Realistic scale (SDS); choices of major fields such as agriculture and engineering and of occupations such as mechanic, farmer, or firefighter.

sometimes only occupational data are available; other times, only interest inventory and vocational aspirations are available. Ideally, it is desirable to secure both inventory and occupational data.

SUBTYPES OR PERSONALITY PATTERNS

A person's *personality pattern* is the profile of resemblances to the personality types. *Subtype* is a name for a particular personality pattern. Personality patterns and subtypes may consist of two to six variables or types. The number of variables used is a matter of convenience, number of subjects, and judgment. Table 2 illustrates how the six scales of the Vocational Preference Inventory or the Self-Directed Search define a person's personality pattern and how that pattern is coded for research or clinical use. A person's personality pattern can also be obtained directly by noting the three-letter code associated with his or her current occupation (see Chapter 6 and Appendix A).

A personality pattern may be psychologically *consistent* or *inconsistent*. The pattern is consistent if its related elements have common characteristics. For example, a pattern such as Realistic-Investigative has many traits in common—unsociability, an orientation toward things rather than people, self-deprecation, and traditional masculinity. However, a pattern such as Conventional-Artistic is inconsistent because it entails such oppositions as conformity and originality, control and expressiveness, and business and art. Table 3 (p. 28) shows three levels of consistency for all permutations and combinations of a two-variable pattern.

The *differentiation* of a personality pattern is expressed as a numerical value that equals the absolute difference between a person's highest and lowest VPI scores for the Realistic, Intellectual, Social, Conventional, Enterprising, and Artistic scales. These scale scores can range from zero to 14. Well-differentiated patterns have sharp peaks and low valleys, whereas poorly differentiated patterns are relatively flat. Figure 2 (p. 28) illustrates how differentiation is profiled.

Although differentiation is determined by an explicit and simple technique, it is a complex concept. My purpose was to create a concept that would capture what clinicians mean by a well-defined profile. To some degree, a differentiated profile will resemble a consistent profile, but differentiation is concerned more with the range of scores in the whole profile than with the consistency of the highest scores.

In the extreme case, a differentiated personality pattern would represent a person who resembles a single type and no other. The opposite case would be a person with a flat profile, or a person who resembles each type to the same degree. In the first example, the person would be unusually predictable; in the second example, the person would be very unpredictable—so much so that he or she would be characterized more by unpredictability than any other trait.

TABLE 2 The Coding of Interest Inventory Scales for the Study of Types and Subtypes*

SUBJECT	REALISTIC	INVESTIGATIVE	ARTISTIC	SOCIAL	ENTERPRISING	CONVENTIONAL	PERSONALITY PATTERN
A	4	2	8	13	14	12	ESC
B	9	12	2	3	6	5	IRE
C	1	4	10	7	6	2	ASE

*Vocational Preference Inventory scale scores.
Note: The coding of profiles can be elaborated by coding all scales and by indicating the elevation of various scales, but these elaborations require extremely large samples for empirical study. For this example, we have coded subjects by their three highest scores on the VPI.

TABLE 3 Levels of Consistency

LEVEL OF CONSISTENCY	PERSONALITY PATTERNS
High	RI, RC, IR, IA, AI, AS, SA, SE, ES, EC, CE, CR
Middle	RA, RE, IS, IC, AR, AE, SI, SC, EA, ER, CS, CI
Low	RS, IE, AC, SR, EI, CA

Because both differentiation and consistency are complex and indirect estimates of how well a person defines himself or herself, a direct and more interpretable estimate of identity has been added. In this instance, *identity* equals a person's score on the 18-item Identity Scale of *My Vocational Situation* (Holland, Daiger, and Power, 1980). This scale measures the clarity of a person's vocational goals and self-perceptions and is positively associated with having a small number of occupational goals that belong to a small number of main categories. Persons with low scores have many goals belonging to many main categories.

Finally, it is useful to think of consistency, differentiation, and identity not only as estimates of the clarity or definition of a personality, but also as estimates of the variety of personality repertoires (Staats, 1975, 1981) that a person will exhibit. For example, a clear sense of identity accompanied by a consistent and well-defined interest profile implies a person with predictable goals and repertoires of coping behaviors. In constrast, a low identity score accompanied by an inconsistent and poorly defined profile implies a person with poorly defined goals and coping behaviors, or with a diffuse, wide-ranging, and unpredictable repertoire for solving impersonal and personal problems.

The Identity Scale is intended to provide an alternate assessment that may be more useful than either consistency or differentiation. In applying the theory it is not necessary to employ all three concepts at the

FIGURE 2 Identical Personality Patterns with Different Degrees of Differentiation

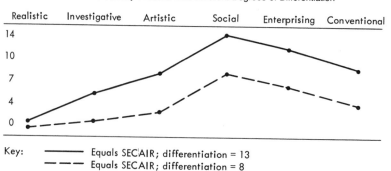

Key: ———— Equals SECAIR; differentiation = 13
      ------ Equals SECAIR; differentiation = 8

same time. Depending on the available data, a counselor or researcher can use one, two, or all three concepts.

Typological Relations

The relations among types, or the psychological resemblances among types, are assumed to be inversely proportional to the distances among types shown in Figure 3. The shorter the distance between any two types, the greater their similarity or psychological resemblance. For example, Realistic and Investigative are close together in Figure 3; therefore, they resemble one another. In contrast, Investigative and Enterprising types are far apart; therefore, they are very different. Investigative and Social types are at an intermediate degree of resemblance.

The hexagonal model serves three purposes in the theory: (1) It defines the degree of consistency in a person's personality pattern. Using a person's VPI profile, the two highest scale scores can be labeled as having one of three levels of consistency. Profile patterns composed of adjacent types on the hexagon are most consistent (for example, Realistic-Investigative, Investigative-Artistic, and so on). Profile patterns composed of opposite types on the hexagon are least consistent (Realistic-Social, Investigative-Enterprising, and Artistic-Conventional). And profile patterns composed of every other type on the hexagon form an intermediate level of consistency (for example, Realistic-Artistic, Investigative-Social, Artistic-Enterprising, and so on—see Table 3); (2) The hexagon defines the consistency of an environment in the same way. In this case, the percentage of types (real people) in each of the six categories is used to form an environmental profile; and (3) The hexagon defines degrees of congruence between person and environment. The most congruent situation for a Social person would be to be in a Social environment. The most incongruent situation for a Social person would be to be in a Realistic

FIGURE 3   A Hexagonal Model for Defining the Psychological Resemblances Among Types and Environments and Their Interactions

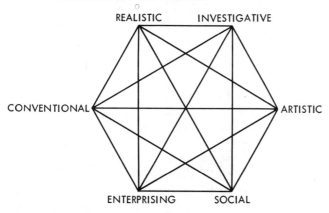

environment. By using the hexagon, several intermediate degrees of congruence can be defined.

The hexagonal model, then, provides a calculus for the theory, an abstract model for linking the main ideas so that the theory can be applied to practical or theoretical problems. For instance, after the user assesses a person's type and his or her environment, the hexagon can be used in conjunction with the formulations for the types and environments to define degrees of consistency and congruence and to predict the expected outcomes—satisfaction, achievement, and change in jobs.

TYPES AND EXPECTED PERFORMANCE

The formulations for the types imply a number of hypotheses as logical consequences. A person's resemblances to the types should predict a large portion of his or her behavior. The following sections summarize the major hypotheses about behavior that appear to follow from the formulations. These hypotheses are expanded and reexamined in Chapter 4. All hypotheses should be read as if the "other things being equal" cautions elaborated earlier preceded every hypothesis—especially sex, social class, intelligence, and educational level. In addition, the provisos elaborated in Chapter 4, "People in Environments," should also be observed.

Career Pathways

1. A person's dominant type or "the personality type" determines the primary direction of vocational choice. Primary direction equals the choice of one of the six main groups of occupations in the classification (see Appendix A). Example: A person with an enterprising personality type will tend to choose an enterprising occupation.

2. The types that the person resembles secondarily and thirdly determine the secondary and tertiary directions of vocational choice. Here, *secondary* and *tertiary* refer to the second and third letters in a person's code, and to the second and third letters that define a particular subgroup. These concepts identify the direction of a person's choice in a more specific manner. For example, a person may aspire to social occupations, or more specifically to subgroups of Social-Investigative (SI) or Social-Investigative-Artistic (SIA).

3. The specific nature of a person's occupational performance (what a person prefers to do on a particular job) comes from his or her personality pattern. Or, the personality pattern will predict characteristic work performance, working style, and preferred roles, including successful and unsuccessful attempts to reshape a particular position to make it more fitting.

4. High levels of personal consistency, differentiation, and identity will increase the probability that hypotheses 1 to 3 will hold.

5. Stability of successive career aspirations or jobs held over the life span will be positively associated with high levels of consistency, differentiation, and identity.

Level of Aspiration and Achievement

6. High vocational aspirations will be positively associated with the types in the following order: Enterprising, Social, Artistic, Investigative, Conventional, and Realistic.
7. Vocational achievement will be positively associated with the types in the following order: Enterprising, Social, Artistic, Investigative, Conventional, and Realistic.
8. The likelihood of creative performance increases the more a personality pattern resembles the following order from high to low: Artistic, Investigative, Social, Enterprising, Realistic, and Conventional.
9. Level of accomplishment in a field is positively associated with consistency, differentiation, and identity when the person's type is congruent with that field. In addition to the necessary talent, a differentiated C will probably make a better accountant than an undifferentiated one; a differentiated A will make a better artist than an undifferentiated one; and so on.

Career Involvement and Satisfaction

10. Career involvement and satisfaction will be positively associated with congruence.
11. Men whose interest patterns are more common among men generally will have more work involvement, less unemployment, and more job satisfaction.
12. Women whose interest patterns are more common among women (especially if their interest code resembles the code for homemaker, SAE or SAC) will have less work involvement, longer periods of unpaid employment in the home, and less job satisfaction outside the home.

    The assumption in hypotheses 11 and 12 is that the traditionality or commonness of a person's interests (see Holland, 1979, pp. 71–75, for distributions of codes by sex and age) is positively correlated with work *outside* the home for men and positively correlated with work *inside* the home for women. There is a substantial literature about this hypothesis for women but not for men. Briefly, working in or outside the home can be viewed as another kind of vocational choice.
13. High levels of consistency, differentiation, and identity will increase the probability that hypotheses 10 to 12 will hold.

Job Shifts and Unemployment

14. Other things being equal—job opportunities, personal resources, and so on—effective coping with job changes and unemployment goes with the following personality pattern order: Social, Enterprising, Artistic, Investigative, Conventional, and Realistic. The closer a person's resemblance is to this pattern order, the greater the competence. The assumption is that social and enterprising types have more interpersonal skills for dealing with these problems.
15. Effective coping with voluntary and involuntary job changes (layoffs and firings) and with unemployment will be positively associated with high levels of consistency, differentiation, and identity.

Educational Behavior

16. The choice of, stability in, and satisfaction with a field of study follow the same rules outlined for vocational behavior.

17. High educational *aspirations* go with the following personality pattern order: Investigative, Social, Artistic, Conventional, Enterprising, and Realistic.

18. Educational *achievement* follows the same order: Investigative, Social, Artistic, Conventional, Enterprising, and Realistic.

19. Persons with different personality patterns respond to instructors, teaching methods, and styles according to the formulations for the types. For example, a Social person should benefit from a Social teacher or a Social subject using personal teaching methods. See formulations for personality types for other hypotheses.

20. High levels of consistency, differentiation, and identity increase the likelihood that hypotheses 16 to 19 will hold.

Social Behavior

21. Personality pattern determines a person's participation and leadership in social affairs. The Social and Enterprising types will participate more than other types.

22. Personality pattern determines a person's choice of nonvocational activities and recreations (see formulations of types).

23. Personality pattern determines a person's orientation and responsiveness to others (see formulations of types). Persons with the same or closely related personality patterns will be attracted to one another. Conversely, people with dissimilar personality patterns will be more likely to dislike one another and come into conflict. "Similarity" can be assessed by the hexagonal model, the Zener-Schnuelle Index (Holland, 1979), or the Iachon Index (Iachon, 1984).

24. Competence in interpersonal relations goes with the following personality pattern order: Social, Enterprising, Artistic, Investigative, Conventional, and Realistic. The closer a person's resemblance to this pattern order, the greater his or her competence.

25. High levels of consistency, differentiation, and identity increase the likelihood that hypotheses 21 to 24 will hold.

Environmental Responsiveness

26. Persons with consistent, differentiated personality patterns and a high level of identity are more resistant to external influence than persons with inconsistent, undifferentiated personality patterns and a low level of identity. The former would also be expected to be more apt to restructure their jobs and other environments.

27. A person's characteristic reaction to environmental stresses is predictable from his or her personality pattern. Specifically, a Realistic type should find dealing with people in helping, teaching, or supervisory ways to be stressful; a Conventional type should have difficulty in coping with ambiguous tasks or problems—planning or playing charades; and an Artistic type should have difficulty following prescribed work routines. The various types will be expected to cope with stress in the same way that they cope with everyday problems (see formulations of types).

SUMMARY

The formulations for the types are models for assessing people, for discovering how they may have grown up, how they can be identified, how they can be expected to perceive and behave, and how types are related to one another. The types, subtypes (personality patterns), and the secondary concepts of consistency, differentiation, and identity are used to derive hypotheses about a person's career path, level of aspiration and achievement, job shifts, educational behavior, social behavior, and environmental responsiveness. The personality types and subtypes are also models for organizing knowledge and conceptualizing personality.

CHAPTER 3
THE ENVIRONMENTAL MODELS

Because human behavior depends upon both personality *and* the environment in which a person lives, the personality types must be supplemented by environmental information. To accomplish this task, six model environments have been proposed to characterize the common social and physical environments in our culture. The model environments correspond to the personality types.

Just as we can assess real people by comparing them with the personality types, we can assess real environments by comparing them with the models—that is, with the descriptions of hypothetical environments. The personality type reflects vocational preferences. An environmental model may be defined as the situation or atmosphere created by the people who dominate a given environment. For instance, a Social environment would be an environment dominated by Social types.

Because the personality types and the environmental models share a common set of constructs, it is possible to classify people and environments in the same terms and thus to predict the outcome of pairing people and environments. More explicitly, we can predict what will happen when a particular person is put into a particular environment by characterizing the person and his or her environment in terms of the types and models and reviewing the appropriate formulations in order to discover the congruities and incongruities the models suggest. For example, the interaction of a Conventional type and a Conventional environment should produce a number of desirable outcomes, such as work satisfaction, achievement, and vocational stability. This chapter and the next provide a complete account of the explanatory values of the theory for these purposes. The typology gives us a tremendous advantage both in planning research and in interpreting results. Without it, we would have to deal with a formidable number of possible person-environment interactions; with it, we have relatively few variables to juggle and an explicit rationale to guide us.

DEVELOPMENT OF MODELS

The construction of the model environments rests mainly on the suggestion made by Linton (1945) and others that most of our environment is transmitted through other people. This implies that the character of an environment reflects the nature of its members and that the dominant features of an environment reflect the typical characteristics of its members. If we know what kind of people make up a group, we can infer the climate that the group creates. For example, an office full of engineers would be expected to have a different atmosphere from that of an office full of accountants. An informal gathering of salespeople would differ in atmosphere from an informal gathering of ministers.

The formula—types flourish in congruent environments—needs some qualifications about the environment and the position of the person in the environment in order to be successfully applied. First, environments rarely have a homogeneous character, so where a person is located in a particular environment will determine the kind and amount of stimulation he or she will receive. For instance, students attending different classes in the same school or college undergo different experiences; employees working in different departments of a large organization undergo different experiences; and students attending the same college but living at home or in dorms are subject to different experiences. It is therefore important to assess the subenvironmental unit that makes up the largest or most influential portion of a person's environment. Second, it is equally important to estimate the psychological field or the environment that people perceive as theirs. A mother may want her daughter to become a physician, but unless the daughter is aware of this hope, it will have no effect. Third, the institutional demands of jobs, schools, or churches must be distinguished from the influences of the people who populate these institutions. Institutional influences such as job descriptions and rules and regulations may exert one kind of influence, but the network of personal relationships may exert another kind. Fourth, because power over others is not usually distributed evenly, it is important to assess what types have the most power. For instance, in a small, family-owned business, a father and son (according to type) may create a distinct and influential environment so that other types in the environment have only minor influence. Finally, the size and complexity of an environment—especially size—appear to have influences that are often independent of the distribution of types or other forces.

At this point, there is no simple or clear resolution of these practical and theoretical difficulties. At the same time, this summary of the complexities involved in describing the environment and how persons and environments interact suggests some useful courses of action for practice and research. They include the following: (1) Estimate the time spent in an environment; (2) check to see if the person is in a special subunit that can be isolated and assessed; (3) characterize the distribution of power and determine whether power should be taken into consideration; (4) ascertain the person's perception of his or her environment; and (5) control for size of environment or organization if at all possible. In short, examine and control for the influences that a simple census of types in an environment cannot hope to deal with.

In this revision, the definition of a particular environment has been supplemented with some concepts from the work on behavior settings (Barker, 1968), manning theory (Wicker, 1979), and occupations (Gottfredson, Holland, and Ogawa, 1982). These supplementary ideas are assumed to reduce some but not all of the deficiencies reviewed earlier.

FORMULATIONS

The descriptions of the model environments parallel the formulations for the personality types: Both kinds of formulations focus on activities, competencies, perceptions, and values.

The Realistic Environment

The Realistic environment is characterized by the dominance of environmental demands and opportunities that entail the explicit, ordered, or systematic manipulation of objects, tools, machines, and animals, and by a population dominated by realistic types. These demands, opportunities, and Realistic people create a characteristic atmosphere that operates in the following way:

1. It stimulates people to perform realistic activities such as using machines and tools.
2. It fosters technical competencies and achievements.
3. It encourages people to see themselves as having mechanical ability and lacking ability in human relations; it encourages them to see the world in simple, tangible, and traditional terms.

4. It rewards people for the display of conventional values and goods, money, power, and possessions.

These environmental experiences lead to secondary effects. People become:

1. More susceptible to pragmatic and traditional influences.
2. More attracted to realistic occupations and roles in which they can express themselves in realistic activities.
3. Less adept at coping with others. They have instead simple, direct, natural coping methods and repertoires.

People acquire or are reinforced for the following traits:

Asocial	Materialistic	Self-effacing
Conforming	Natural	Inflexible
Frank	Normal	Thrifty
Genuine	Persistent	Uninsightful
Hardheaded	Practical	Uninvolved

The Investigative Environment

The Investigative environment is characterized by the dominance of environmental demands and opportunities that entail the observation and symbolic, systematic, creative investigation of physical, biological, or cultural phenomena, and by a population dominated by Investigative types. These demands, opportunities, and Investigative people create a characteristic atmosphere that operates to produce the following outcomes:

1. It stimulates people to perform investigative activities.
2. It encourages scientific competencies and achievements.
3. It encourages people to see themselves as scholarly, as having mathematical and scientific ability, and as lacking in leadership ability; it encourages them to see the world in complex, abstract, independent, and original ways.
4. It rewards people for the display of scientific values.

These environmental experiences lead to secondary effects. People become:

1. More susceptible to abstract, theoretical, and analytic influences.
2. More attracted to investigative occupations and roles in which they can express themselves in investigative activities.
3. More apt to cope with others in rational, analytic, and indirect ways.

People acquire or are reinforced for the following traits:

Analytical	Independent	Rational
Cautious	Intellectual	Reserved
Critical	Introspective	Retiring
Complex	Pessimistic	Unassuming
Curious	Precise	Unpopular

The Artistic Environment

The Artistic environment is characterized by the dominance of environmental demands and opportunities that entail ambiguous, free, unsystematized activities and competencies to create art forms or products, and by the dominance of Artistic types in the environment. These demands, opportunities, and Artistic people create a characteristic atmosphere that operates to produce the following outcomes:

1. It stimulates people to engage in artistic activities.
2. It fosters artistic competencies and achievements.
3. It encourages people to see themselves as expressive, original, intuitive, nonconforming, independent, and as having artistic abilities (acting, writing, and speaking). It encourages people to see the world in complex, independent, unconventional, and flexible ways.
4. It rewards people for the display of artistic values.

These environmental experiences lead to secondary effects. People become:

1. More susceptible to personal, emotional, and imaginative influences.
2. More attracted to artistic occupations and roles in which they can express themselves in artistic activities.
3. More likely to cope with others in personal, emotional, expressive, and unconventional ways.

People acquire or are reinforced for the following traits:

Complicated	Imaginative	Intuitive
Disorderly	Impractical	Nonconforming
Emotional	Impulsive	Original
Expressive	Independent	Sensitive
Idealistic	Introspective	Open

The Social Environment

The Social environment is characterized by the dominance of environmental demands and opportunities that entail the manipulation of others to inform, train, develop, cure, or enlighten, and by a population dominated by Social types. These demands, opportunities, and Social people create a characteristic atmosphere that operates to produce the following goals and outcomes:

1. It stimulates people to engage in social activities.
2. It fosters social competencies.
3. It encourages people to see themselves as liking to help others, understanding of others, cooperative, and sociable; it encourages them to see the world in flexible ways.
4. It rewards people for the display of social values.

These environmental forces lead to secondary effects. People become:

1. More susceptible to social, humanitarian, and religious influences.
2. More attracted to social occupations and roles in which they can express themselves in social activities.
3. More apt to cope with others by being friendly, helpful, cooperative.

People acquire or are reinforced for the following traits:

Ascendant	Generous	Responsible
Cooperative	Helpful	Sociable
Empathic	Idealistic	Tactful
Patient	Kind	Understanding
Friendly	Persuasive	Warm

The Enterprising Environment

The Enterprising environment is characterized by the dominance of environmental demands and opportunities that entail the manipulation of others to attain organizational or self-interest goals, and by the dominance of Enterprising types. These demands, opportunities, and Enterprising people create a characteristic atmosphere that operates to produce the following goals and outcomes:

1. It stimulates people to engage in enterprising activities, such as selling, or leading others.
2. It fosters enterprising competencies and achievements.
3. It encourages people to see themselves as aggressive, popular, self-confident, sociable, and as possessing leadership and speaking ability. It encourages people to see the world in terms of power, status, responsibility, and in stereotyped, constricted, dependent, and simple terms.
4. It rewards people for the display of enterprising values and goals: money, power, and status.

These environmental experiences lead to secondary effects. People become:

1. More susceptible to social, emotional, and materialistic influences.
2. More attracted to enterprising occupations and roles in which they can express themselves in enterprising activities.
3. More prone to cope with others in an enterprising manner—by dominance, talkativeness, and so on.

People acquire or are reinforced for the following traits:

Acquisitive	Energetic	Flirtatious
Adventurous	Exhibitionistic	Optimistic
Agreeable	Excitement-	Self-confident
Ambitious	seeking	Sociable
Domineering	Extroverted	Talkative

The Conventional Environment

The Conventional environment is characterized by the dominance of environmental demands and opportunities that entail the explicit, ordered, systematic manipulation of data, such as keeping records, filing materials, reproducing materials, organizing written and numerical data according to a prescribed plan, operating business and data processing machines, and by a population dominated by Conventional types. These demands, opportunities, and Conventional people create a characteristic atmosphere that operates to produce the following goals and outcomes:

1. It stimulates people to engage in conventional activities, such as recording and organizing data or records.
2. It fosters conventional competencies and achievements.
3. It encourages people to see themselves as conforming, orderly, nonartistic, and as having clerical competencies; it encourages them to see the world in conventional, stereotyped, constricted, simple, dependent ways.
4. It rewards people for the display of conventional values: money, dependability, and conformity.

These environmental experiences lead to secondary effects. People become:

1. More susceptible to materialistic influences: money, position, and power.
2. More attracted to conventional occupations and roles.
3. More prone to cope with others in a conventional manner—to be controlling, conforming, and practical.

People acquire or are reinforced for the following traits:

Careful	Inflexible	Persistent
Conforming	Inhibited	Practical
Conscientious	Methodical	Prudish
Defensive	Obedient	Thrifty
Efficient	Orderly	Unimaginative

ASSESSING THE ENVIRONMENT

Because many of the psychologically important features of the environment consist of or are transmitted by the people in it, we can characterize an environment by assessing its population. The Environmental Assessment Technique (EAT) was developed for this purpose, and it can be used to assess the population of a college, a hospital, a business, a community, or of any other institution or group. The technique entails taking a census of the occupations, training preferences, or vocational preferences of a population. These preferences or occupations are categorized according to the criteria for class membership as belonging to one of the six environments. This classification results in a six-variable profile. The absolute numbers for each type are then converted to percentages of the total population for the particular environment or institution.

For example, a business with two hundred employees might have the distribution of types shown in Table 4. The environmental pattern of this business would be represented by the code CERSIA, because the dominant type in this environment is the Conventional, followed by the Enterprising, and so on. Such an environment would be expected to emphasize, among other factors, orderliness, social status, and conservative economic and political beliefs. Similar codes can be obtained for colleges by a census and categorization of the proportion of students in different major fields, or for neighborhoods by a census of the occupations of households.

Recent work (Gottfredson, Holland, and Ogawa, 1982) has provided a *Dictionary of Holland Occupational Codes* (DHOC) for the entire *Dictionary of Occupational Titles* (U.S. Department of Labor, 1977) so that the EAT technique can be based not only on one-letter occupational codes but also on two- and three-letter codes. For example, different Realistic environments can be assessed and compared by their distributions of two- or three-letter codes. And organizations with identical or similar one-letter code distributions can be compared for differences in two- or three-letter codes *within* each of the six main codes or occupational groups. The DHOC also provides the general educational development level (GED, an estimate of the education required to perform a particular occupation) for every occupation. The GED index (ranging from one to six) provides a useful estimate of the intelligence required and the prestige of an occupation (L. Gottfredson, 1980, Table 8)—a measure that can be used either as a control or explanatory variable.

TABLE 4   The Environmental Assessment Technique

TYPE	NUMBER	PERCENTAGE
Realistic	20	10%
Investigative	8	4
Artistic	4	2
Social	12	6
Enterprising	28	14
Conventional	128	64
Total	200	100%

Consistency

The *consistency* of an environmental pattern is defined by the same patterns and relations given in Table 3 and Figure 3. Consistent environments provide similar rewards and demands; inconsistent environments provide divergent rewards and demands. For instance, realistic and investigative environments are consistent because they are adjacent on the hexagon and involve similar activities, competencies, and rewards. In contrast, Realistic and Social environments are inconsistent because they are opposites on the hexagon and demand different interests, competencies, and values. The environments of the skilled tradesperson versus the teacher illustrate this opposition.

Differentiation

The *differentiation* of an environment is also defined following the same principle given for defining the differentiation of a personality pattern. In this case, the percentage difference between the most and least common personality types in a given environment equals the degree of differentiation of that environment. In the example in Table 4, the differentiation is 64 minus 2, or 62.

Differentiated environments encourage a narrow range of behavior in explicit ways; undifferentiated environments stimulate a broad range of behavior and provide ambiguous guidance. The differentiated environment is analogous to the person who resembles only one personality type; the undifferentiated environment is analogous to the person with a flat profile who resembles each type to the same degree.

Identity

Just as the defining of personality types has been supplemented with the secondary concept of identity, it appears helpful to prop up the EAT with a similar measure of identity. The empirical definition of an environment's identity can be obtained by a rational analysis of the goals of a family, educational institution, or business—an ambiguous and difficult process. An environment with a high identity would have a limited set of consistent and explicit goals; and an environment with a diffuse identity would have a large set of conflicting and poorly defined goals.

A more objective but indirect definition of environmental identity can be obtained by the following formula; *environmental identity equals the inverse of the number of its behavior settings.* Here it is assumed that a position or occupation usually has most of the structural and dynamic attributes outlined by Barker (1968) such as a special physical setting, some common expectations for the participants, time limits, a degree of independence from the surrounding environment, and so on. In addition, behavior settings are influenced by physical forces, social forces, learning, selection by persons (people choose settings), selection by behavior settings (selection and entrance requirements), and influence of behavior and the milieu (people and other forces change jobs).

To illustrate, a small store with three settings or different occupations would have an identity of 1/3 or .333. An elementary school with five occupations would have an identity of 1/5 or .200. A large industrial organization with 200 occupations would have an identity of 1/200 or .005. In short, environments with a small number of occupations would have high indices of identity; whereas environments with a large number of occupations would have low indices or a diffuse identity. These indices could be multiplied by 100 to eliminate the decimals and provide easily interpreted values.

This index of identity is expected to lessen the neglect in earlier formulations of two important organizational characteristics—size and structure. High identity is expected to be positively correlated with simple structure and small size; whereas low identity is expected to be correlated with complex structure and large size.

The index of identity can be supplemented with Barker's (1968) theory of manning or staffing and its extension by his associates (Wicker, 1979; Willems, 1967). Settings may be undermanned (have too few people to carry out a setting's program), optimally manned (have the right number of people), or overmanned (have more people than are needed).

The manning theory assumes that undermanned settings put pressure on people to make the settings function. Tests of under-manned settings (Wicker, 1979)—students in small high schools—have demonstrated that these settings encouraged more participation and have made students feel that they were serving in important and valued roles. Students have also reported more satisfaction. This satisfaction led, in turn, to an interest in maintaining the existence and structure of the settings.

For the present theory, it appears desirable to start with the simplest use of manning theory; namely, estimate under-, optimal-, and overmanning by dividing the total number of employees in an organization by the number of distinct behavior settings. Here the number of behavior settings equals the number of distinct three-letter occupational codes at a given GED level—not the sheer number of different occupational titles. For example, an accounting firm of 100 employees might have only five behavior settings, or 20 people per occupation or setting, because it is populated largely by accountants and secretaries, plus a few executives. In contrast, a small manufacturing company of 100 might have ten behavior settings, or ten people per occupation, because it requires a wider range of occupations at more levels of training (GED).

Whether or not this extension of the typology to manning theory will be advantageous is untested. Empirical work may show that the index of identity on page 42 incorporates much of the contribution of the concept of manning or staffing.

INTERNAL RELATIONS

The relations among the six kinds of environmental models are defined by the hexagonal model given earlier (Figure 3). The closer two environmental models are in the hexagon, the greater the similarity. The farther apart they are, the more divergent are their reinforcing properties. The formula provided by the use of the hexagon makes it possible to describe the relations of the six model environments within a single natural environment or the relations between two natural environments that may impinge on one another: one company versus another, one neighborhood versus another, one school versus another.

All of these assumptions should be amended in terms of the definition for the environments being compared. Well-defined environments (clear or high identity, high differentiation, small proportion of behavior settings, consistent EAT) will be more likely to demonstrate the hypothesized relations. In contrast, poorly defined environments will usually fail to demonstrate the expected relations.

EXPECTED INFLUENCES

Like the personality types, the model environments imply many hypotheses about a person's vocational, personal, educational, and social behavior. The following hypotheses are derived from the model formulations; they are regarded simply as axiomatic statements from which some inferences can be drawn.

Vocational Behavior

1. Each model environment attracts its associated personality type. Realistic environments attract Realistic types; Investigative environments attract Investigative types, and so on. Also, each environment repels some types more than others (see Figure 3).
2. Consistency of the environmental pattern promotes stability of vocational choice—affects the number and degrees of change.
3. Differentiation of an environment promotes stability of vocational choice.
4. Identity of an environment will promote stability of vocational aspiration and career.
5. The consistency, differentiation, and optimal staffing of an environment promote involvement, satisfaction, and stability of vocational choice.

Personal Effectiveness

6. Each model environment reinforces a characteristic group of activities, competencies, predispositions or behavioral repertoires.

7. Each model environment reinforces its own characteristic achievement. The Realistic environment promotes Realistic achievement; the Investigative environment promotes Investigative achievement, and so on.

8. The consistency, differentiation, identity, and manning of an environment interact to increase both the stability and the level of vocational achievement.

9. The model environments promote creative performance in the following descending order: A, I, S, E, R, C.

10. Creative performance will also be related to the number of behavior settings, diffuse identity, and lack of differentiation. This hypothesis is the instrumentation of Koestler's (1964) formulation of the ingredients of the creative process—a creative event results from seeing an old problem in one or more divergent contexts. Here it is assumed that an environment with many behavior settings is more likely to stimulate a variety of contexts for understanding problems. Likewise, the incorporation of Staats' (1981) behavior repertoires in the personality types implies that the acquisition of diverse repertoires is more likely to occur in diverse settings—a complex way of saying that a wide range of experience is helpful in problem-solving.

Educational Behavior

11. Each model environment reinforces a characteristic group of educational behaviors. See the formulations for the environments.

Social Behavior

12. Each model environment reinforces a characteristic group of social behaviors. See the formulations for the environments.

Sensitization

13. Each model environment sensitizes people or makes them more responsive to special stimuli such as characteristic attitudes, values, roles, and so on. See the formulations for the types. To illustrate, tell a social scientist about a very positive finding and his or her first reaction will be a recitation of a standard litany of potential deficits. In short, he or she won't believe—a good example of another powerful ghetto. The exceptions are test authors and theorists who are ready to believe any positive outcome of their work.

Organizational Behavior

14. Organizations with similar characteristics (EAT, identity, differentiation, and manning) will be more likely to interact with mutually satisfying relationships.

15. Well-defined organizations will be more likely to have members with higher levels of involvement and satisfaction.

16. Well-defined organizations will be more likely to be economically productive.

17. Organizations that are extremely well-defined or extremely diffuse will be expected to have shorter lifetimes than organizations between these extremes.

SUMMARY

The environmental models were developed to provide a more complete model for understanding human behavior. They have been revised by incorporating some new techniques and information and by incorporating Barker's (1968) concept of behavior setting and manning or staffing. These revisions are assumed to increase the usefulness of the environmental models. The environmental formulations are patterned after the personality types and can be applied to natural environments by categorizing the occupations or vocational interests of the inhabitants according to the classification scheme summarized in Chapter 6 and elaborated in Appendix A.

CHAPTER 4
PEOPLE IN
ENVIRONMENTS

The formulations for the personality types and the model environments provide the tools to describe and comprehend what happens when a particular kind of person lives in a particular environment. To illustrate, a person's career or development over the life span can be visualized as a long series of person-environment interactions and their outcomes that everyone experiences as they grow up and age. And some interactions are more important, public, and stressful than others: deciding on an initial job, deciding if or when to change jobs, getting divorced, being fired, deciding on or being forced to develop new competencies, changing one's undesirable habits or behavior, and deciding to continue the same line of work indefinitely.

The implications of the formulations for person-environment interactions have been divided into two main topics: (1) definitions and processes in person-environment interactions and (2) applications of the definitions and formulations to vocational life, personal effectiveness, educational behavior, social behavior, and environmental responsiveness.

DEFINITIONS AND PROCESSES

The following paragraphs define and illustrate five methods for characterizing the pairing of person and environment. Like the definitions of the types and environments, the definitions of interactions are needed to apply the theory to practical problems.

Degrees of Congruence

A person's relationship to the environment can be assessed according to the degree of congruence or compatibility. This assessment is defined by the hexagonal model. The most extreme degree of congruence is the situation in which a personality type is in a matching environment—for example, a Realistic person in a Realistic environment. The next degree of congruence is that of a personality type in an adjacent environment, such as a Realistic person in an Investigative or Conventional environment. A Realistic person in an Artistic or Enterprising environment represents a third and lesser degree of congruence. Finally, the most extreme degree of incongruence is the situation in which a personality type is in an opposite environment, such as a Realistic person in a Social environment. By using the hexagonal model in Figure 3, four levels of congruence can be obtained for each of the six types. More levels can be derived by using two- or three-letter codes for types and environments—for example, an RI type in an RI environment, an RI type in an IR environment, an RI in an RA or RC environment, and so on.

The personal and situational characteristics that create a particular degree of congruence can be made explicit by reviewing the formulations for the type and the environment involved. For instance, social types in social environments are an extreme case of congruence for many reasons. Social persons are provided an opportunity to engage in social activities, to use social competencies, to perform services they value, to see themselves as understanding and helpful, and to exhibit personality traits of generosity, friendliness, and sociability. In turn, the Social environment reinforces the self-images social types bring to the environment and rewards them for social values and social personality traits such as generosity, friendliness, and sociability. Of perhaps equal importance, Social types in social environments can also avoid the activities they dislike, the demands for competencies they lack, the tasks and self-images they do not value, and the situations in which their personality traits are not encouraged.

The content and structure of incongruent interactons can be elaborated in the same way. The formulations, then, serve to show how people and environments affect one another. For example, Conventional types in Artistic environments would discover the following kinds of oppositions or incongruities: they like structured activities, but the environment provides unstructured activities; they possess Conventional competencies, but the environment demands Artistic competencies; they look at the world in conservative ways, but the people in the Artistic environment look at the world in unconventional ways; their personal traits such as orderliness and inhibition are deprecated by Artistic types who tend to be the opposite, who are disorderly and impulsive. Taken together, these negative interactions should result in gross dissatisfaction, ineffective coping behavior, and probably leaving the environment.

The incorporation of the concepts of behavior repertoires (Staats, 1981) and behavior settings (Barker, 1968) in the personality types and environmental models provides a succinct summary of what is meant by congruency. Persons in congruent environments are encouraged to express their favorite behavior repertoires in familiar and congenial settings. In contrast, persons in incongruent environments find that they have behavior repertoires that are out of place and unappreciated. Or, they feel like the speaker who realizes that his or her favorite talk is going badly, and it is too late to find a more appropriate audience.

Degrees of Consistency

The outcomes of an interaction are influenced by the consistency of a person's personality pattern and the consistency of the environmental pattern. This assumption comes from the definitions of consistency (three levels) given earlier. For the person, a more consistent personality pattern represents an integration of similar interests, competencies, values, traits, and perceptions. Presumably such people are more predictable as well as more resistant to influence. For the environment, a more consistent pattern represents an integration of similar demands and rewards. Consequently, a more consistent environment usually exerts pressure for similar behavior.

Inconsistent people are less predictable because they combine more diverse interests, competencies, values, and perceptions. As a result, they have a more extensive repertoire of possible behaviors. Inconsistent environments are less influential, because they provide a wide rather than a narrow range of demands and rewards. With this background, it is reasonable that the interactions of consistent people and consistent environments will result in more predictable outcomes, and that these outcomes will influence both the people and their environments to a greater degree.

Degrees of Differentiation

Other things being equal (congruence, consistency, and identity), interactions are also affected by the differentiation of types and environments. Differentiation means the magnitude of the difference between highest and lowest scores on the six variables used to determine a person's or an environment's degree of resemblance to a personality type or an environmental model. The greater the difference between the highest and lowest of the six scores is, the greater the differentiation is. Graphically, the profile of a differentiated pattern will have high peaks and low valleys; the profile of an undifferentiated pattern will appear relatively flat. Figure 2 shows two identical personality or environmental patterns that have different degrees of differentiation.

The interaction of a differentiated person and a differentiated environment will be most predictable and intense because a well-defined (predictable, and therefore understandable) person is interacting with a well-defined environment that has a focused influence. The interaction of an undifferentiated person and environment will be least predictable, because undifferentiated persons and environments are composed of diverse elements and forces and so have a diffuse influence. When the person and environment are differentiated and undifferentiated or vice-versa, the interaction falls between these two extremes of predictability and intensity. To summarize, the differentiation of the personality or environmental pattern increases both the possibility that the hypothesized behavior in the formulations will occur and the magnitude of the hypothesized behavior.

Degrees of Identity

Interactions are also affected by the identity of types and environments. For types, identity is a person's score on the Identity Scale of *My Vocational Situation* (MVS; Holland, Daiger, and Power, 1980). And, for environments, identity equals the inverse of the number of behavior situations (distinct three-letter occupational codes). A high index equals high identity.

The interaction of a person with a clear sense of identity and an environment with a limited number of behavior situations will be more predictable than the interaction of a person and environment with diffuse or unclear identities.

Level of Education (GED)

Other things being equal, interactions are also affected by the degree of congruence as estimated by a person's GED level and the average level of GED of the environment in which he or she lives or works. Discrepancies (for example, person is at level two and job is at level three) make for poor performance and dissatisfaction or both. Such discrepancies work in both directions. A person may have too much training (GED level five) for an occupation (level three) or vice-versa.

Combinations of Congruence, Consistency, Differentiation, Identity, and Educational Level

Interactions involving different degrees of congruence, consistency, differentiation, identity, and educational level will result in different kinds and degrees of outcomes. At one extreme, the interaction of a type and model environment that are congruent, consistent, differentiated, focused (high identity), and at the same level of education will intensify and make more predictable the hypotheses about vocational life, personal effectiveness, educational behavior, social behavior, and environmental responsiveness. The outcomes are usually desirable. At the other extreme, incongruence, inconsistency, undifferentiation, diffuse identity, and divergent educational levels make the same hypotheses less predictable, and these characteristics usually lead to less desirable outcomes: poor performance, dissatisfaction, and change in job or self.

The relative influence or importance of these characteristics seems to be as follows: Congruence of the person-environment interaction is most influential; differentiation of person or environment is next; and consistency of person or environment is least influential. The relative influence of the identity and education or GED measures is in doubt. The Identity Scale for types has a promising beginning (Holland, Daiger, and Power, 1980), but the index of identity for the environment is untried in the present context, although the behavior setting and manning research has a positive research history (Wicker, 1979).

At this time, it is important to recall that consistency, differentiation, and identity are simply three techniques for defining the clarity, focus, or definition of a person or environment. They are positively correlated and intellectually similar, and I have at times been tempted to dump one or more of these definitions. Unfortunately, the evidence for each measure is uneven and mixed (see Chapter 5). Each measure has led to a string of negative studies, but each has also led to some striking positive results. It seems like a good idea to wait a little longer for the winner or winners to become obvious in new research.

The use of educational level to define the discrepancy of a particular interaction is a clear exception to these reservations. GED (educational level) and its correlates are well studied. It is strongly related to prestige, intelligence, educational level, and social class. Too much or too little of these variables result in a poor person-job fit (Kahn, 1981), a finding with a long and positive research history in industrial psychology. For instance, unemployed professionals who become cab drivers illustrate a poor fit that usually results in job dissatisfaction and turnover.

Table 5 summarizes how a particular interaction can be structured and analyzed by using the formulations for types and environments. Any interaction can be examined by using this cross-sectional plan for reviewing the main forces involved.

THEORETICAL APPLICATIONS

This section applies the definitions of person-environment interactions to vocational, educational, and social behavior. In addition, the definitions and processes outlined earlier are used to develop a comprehensive plan for explaining stability and change in personal behavior.

TABLE 5   The Structure of Person-Environment Encounters

PERSON ———————➤	ENVIRONMENT (BEHAVIOR SITUATIONS) ———————➤	OUTCOMES
Activities	Opportunities	Interests and Satisfaction
Competencies and GED	GED and Special Skill Demands	Achievement and Satisfaction
Disposition	Encouragement	Stability
Perceptions	Encouragement	Outlook
Self		
World		
Values	Encouragement	Values
Traits	Encouragement	Traits
Personality		
Repertoires	Encouragement	Repertoires
Resources	Sufficiency and	Increase all of
(Economic, Educational, Social)	Flexibility	above outcomes

Note: In career counseling, counselors and counselees can compare the congruence between a person's preferred activities, competencies, disposition, and resources with the opportunities in one or more potential occupational choices. In this way, a concrete understanding of the fitness of a particular occupation can be obtained. The same procedure can be followed for clarifying the nature of a person's job dissatisfaction and for finding a more congruent job or environment.

Career and the Life Course

The definitions of the personality types and model environments and the formulations about their interactions make it possible to trace a person's development and examine his or her principal environments from the time a person can express a vocational preference to the time of death. People can be assessed by their vocational preferences at different times in their lives. Environments—family background, school, work situations, and so on—can be assessed using the Environmental Assessment Technique (see page 41). By applying the theory with its classes and subclasses and relatively simple sets of definitions to an entire life span, we can use a great range of information about human behavior and environments, and thus more easily study person-environment interactions and their outcomes.

In the theory, development over the entire life course can be understood as a long series of person-environment interactions in which people are modified and stabilized as they select, pass through, or avoid behavior situations that reject, select, and encourage some behavioral or personality repertoires more than others.

Figure 4 illustrates this comprehensive, longitudinal model for explaining a person's life history. The formulation can be elaborated in many ways: by assigning single-letter codes to the person and each envi-

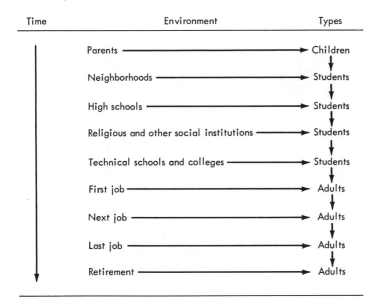

FIGURE 4   The Interactions of Persons and Environments

ronment and then, on the basis of the formulations for the personality types and the environmental models, making predictions about interactions and outcomes; or by assigning two- or three-letter codes to each type and environment in the life span. In this way, a person's movement from vocational preference to vocational preference, major field to major field, field of training to job, or job to job can be studied and interpreted in the context of the theory as vocational, educational, or social behavior.

Stability and Change

The comprehensive plan requires some supplementary formulations to cope with the problems of stability and change in human behavior: Why do some people continue to choose the same kind of occupation; why do others move between markedly different kinds of jobs? The following hypotheses have been derived from the previous formulations and are proposed to explain the processes of stability and change:

1. People find environments reinforcing and satisfying when environmental patterns resemble their personality patterns. This situation makes for stability of behavior because persons receive a good deal of selective reinforcement of their behavior. The greater the discrepancy between people's personality patterns and environmental patterns, the more dissatisfying, uncomfortable, and destructive these interactions become. Discrepancy is assessed by the hexagonal model and by the GED levels of the person and the environment.
2. Friendships and therapeutic and teaching relationships depend upon the same formulation given in hypothesis 1.

3.   Incongruent interactions stimulate change in human behavior; conversely, congruent interactions encourage stability of behavior. Persons tend to change or become like the dominant persons in the environment. This tendency is greater, the greater the degree of congruence is between person and environment. Those persons who are most incongruent will be changed least. Or, the closer a person is to the core of an environment, the greater the influence of the environment.

4.   A person resolves incongruence by seeking a new and congruent environment, by remaking the present environment, or by changing personal behavior and perceptions.
   A.   Differentiation and consistency of personality pattern as well as identity usually make for a change of environment in the face of an incongruent environment.
   B.   Persons with differentiated and consistent personality patterns and clear identity are more apt to remake the environment itself, if they cannot leave it, to achieve greater congruence. For example, people usually hire people whom they like or see as congenial.
   C.   Persons with undifferentiated and inconsistent personality patterns and diffuse identity tend to adapt to incongruence by changing their own behavior and personality pattern to achieve greater congruence with their environment.
   D.   A person's tendency to leave an environment increases as the incongruity of the interaction increases (see hexagon, Figure 3, for degrees of congruity and compare GED levels).

5.   Continuity in careers is the rule rather than the exception, because careers tend to snowball over the life course. The reciprocal interaction of person and successive jobs usually leads to a series of success and satisfaction cycles (Hall and Hall, 1976) that focus a career. The identity, consistency, and differentiation of a person's interests are indices of this focusing. In addition, continuity is perpetuated by other enduring properties of the person (demographic, genetic, and other aspects of personality; Costa and McCrae, 1980) and by the inflexibilities in work environments (credentialing, biases of age, race, sex, education, and appearance). The focusing of career also appears to be supported by the evidence about searching behavior, career patterns, and person-environment interactions in Chapters 5 and 6.
   A.   Snowballing provides partial but plausible explanations of the stability of personality; namely, stability occurs because most people select or are allocated to compatible environments where their current abilities, dispositions, and traits are exercised and rewarded, and where other abilities, dispositions, and traits are neglected. And in the process, a person acquires a more focused self-view.
   B.   Snowballing provides a plausible explanation of how a person will cope with problems on the job, in changing jobs, and perhaps other nonwork problems; namely, the current effects of snowballing (assessed by a current interest profile, and the related concepts of consistency, differentiation, and identity) will be used in problem-solving on and off the job. In short, a person will act like the type he or she resembles most in dealing with work and nonwork problems.
   C.   Snowballing suggests why change in careers or personality is so difficult, and why many interventions have so little impact. The typical interventions—talking to a counselor, therapist, employer, or friend—must contend with a person whose behavior and thinking is imbedded in a focused life history or a chaotic one, and in an environment that is pushing

for the maintenance of the status quo, unless the person is in an incongruent environment. The rapid development of self-help groups, career courses, and family therapy is an acknowledgment of the need to create more wide-ranging therapeutic environments or to change the social systems in which people are enmeshed.

The processes of snowballing (the interaction of individuals and jobs over the lifespan) provide a partial but plausible explanation for the long-term stability of traits, values, competencies, interests, perceptions, and other characteristics. In short, the present theory is congenial with both interactionist (Endler and Magnusson, 1976; Wachtel, 1973) and trait views (Block, 1977; Epstein, 1979) of personality. The evidence for the stability of vocational interests over long time spans (Campbell, 1971) supports the snowballing conception of career development.

These general formulations are most applicable to vocational behavior, because that kind of experience has been the major source of stimulation and support for these ideas. At the same time, they also appear applicable to other phenomena—to educational and social behavior.

Vocational Behavior

When the main hypotheses about personality types are seen in the context of interactions with the environment, these additional hypotheses follow:

1. The direction of a person's vocational choice is stabilized or maintained when he or she lives in a congruent environment. Conversely, the direction of a person's vocational choice tends to change when he or she lives in an incongruent environment. (The stability or change in a person's work history follows the same principle.)
2. The "level" of a person's vocational choice is stabilized by a congruent environment. Conversely, an incongruent environment tends to change a person's level of vocational aspiration.
3. The "level" of a person's occupational achievement is encouraged by the congruence of his or her work environment.
4. A person's vocational satisfaction is encouraged by the congruence of his or her work environment.

These hypotheses are conditioned by the clarity of a person's personality—consistency, differentiation, and identity—and by the degree of congruity according to the hexagonal model and GED level.

Educational Behavior

The hypotheses derived from the personality types about educational behavior resemble those for vocational behavior. The choice of, stability in, satisfaction with, and achievement in a field of training or study follow the identical rules outlined for vocational behavior. In the same way, people respond positively to instructors whose personality patterns resemble their own and when the intelligence levels of each do not involve gross discrepancies. For example, teachers like to teach bright students because it is easier to communicate and get positive outcomes. Student attrition and delinquency—especially in elementary and secondary schools—is probably a function not only of the failure to achieve minimal skills but also a failure in empathy or understanding, for teachers are largely Ss and dropouts are largely Rs—opposites in the hexagonal model and usually females versus males in the classroom. In higher education, the situation is usually reversed—many male faculty, but few female—so that female students receive less empathy and support than males.

Personal Development and Effectiveness

Biological differences aside, emotional stability is initiated by a person's early experiences, particularly those of childhood. The stable individual probably has parents whose individual personality patterns are consistent in themselves and are congruent with the other parent's personality pattern. Consequently, the parents' values and childrearing practices are harmonious and free of major conflict. These attributes foster consistent, integrated behavior in the child. Because children perceive themselves and the world accurately, they are more likely to select congruent environments for training and eventual vocation. This selection leads to achievement, reinforcement, and satisfaction.

If, however, one or both parents has inconsistent personality patterns and diffuse identities, or if the father's pattern is incongruent with the mother's, then children are likely to develop an inaccurate picture of themselves and the world, inconsistent values, inconsistent interests and competencies, and little self-confidence. Consequently, children will tend to vacillate, make poor choice of environments, and function ineffectively even in compatible environments.

In short, personal stability is the outcome of passing through a series of consistent environments that strengthen one's ability to cope with the world in an integrated way. Instability, in contrast, results from living in a succession of inconsistent environments that create and perpetuate inaccurate perceptions of self and world, divergent interests and competencies, and conflicting values. The hypotheses concerned with personal effectiveness (creative performance, style of work, interpersonal competence) are all more likely to occur when the person locates or is placed in a congruent environment.

The more congruent the environment and the personality pattern are, the more likely it is that people will exhibit particular social and avocational behavior hypothesized from their personality patterns: (1) amount of participation and leadership in social affairs, (2) choice and maintenance of interest in nonvocational activities and recreations, and (3) interest in and responsiveness to others in the environment. In contrast, the more incongruent the environment is, the greater the likelihood is that the person will not participate or exhibit these behaviors.

Environmental Responsiveness

Other things being equal (consistency, differentiation, identity, intelligence, and social status), types resist the influence of their environment the more divergent their personality pattern is from the environmental pattern. And the closer the resemblance of personality and environmental patterns, the more sensitive and pliable the person becomes. For example, athletic facilities receive marked financial support because several popular types (Realistic, Enterprising, Social) like athletics. In sharp contrast, the arts receive little support because Artistic types are uncommon, and because artistic activity is low on the agenda of the remaining types.

SUMMARY

Some methods for explaining the processes in person-environment interactions have been outlined. The application of these methods to vocational, educational, and social behavior has been illustrated, and the formulations about the types and environments have been used to derive some expected outcomes. The types, subtypes (personality patterns), and the secondary concepts of consistency, differentiation, and identity are used to derive hypotheses about a person's career path, level of aspiration and achievement, job shifts, educational behavior, social behavior, and environmental responsiveness. The personality types and subtypes are also models for organizing knowledge and conceptualizing personality.

CHAPTER 5
SOME EVIDENCE

The purpose of this chapter is to summarize the evidence for the usefulness of the personality types, environmental models, and their interactions. Chapter 6 summarizes the evidence for the usefulness of the classification system.

The review for the period 1959 through 1983 focuses on direct evidence (correlational or experimental tests of hypotheses) rather than indirect evidence, although some related or indirect evidence has been included. Because there are more than 400 studies to review, only the most important are summarized in any detail. I have tried to provide an accurate characterization of the strengths, weaknesses, and ambiguities of the evidence. I have emphasized the findings from well-designed, large-scale investigations that follow the theory in explicit fashion. I only mention, and sometimes ignore, the poorer studies (those that were poorly planned and executed with ambiguous results). At the same time I have included *all* investigations in the references so that others can review my interpretations. A few valuable reports arrived too late for incorporation in the text, but they are included in the references.

The evidence has been organized according to the following topics: personality types and patterns, environmental models and patterns, people in environments (interactive studies concerned with careers, career interventions, and personal relations) and cross-national comparisons of assessment devices and theoretical tests. Last, the interpretative summary is my evaluation of the evidence: the strengths and weaknesses of the theory; what kind of work might be neglected and what work needs more attention.

PERSONALITY TYPES

Hypotheses about the personality types have attracted the most research interest. Using the definitions suggested in the first, second, or third statement of the theory (Holland, 1959, 1966b, 1973) or special definitions of their own, investigators have assessed elementary, high school, college, and graduate students, as well as employed adults, to test hypotheses about the types. To make the studies more amenable to summary and analysis, they have been grouped according to the kind of hypotheses they test: (1) characteristics of the types, (2) personality patterns and identity, (3) life history or development of the types, (4) personal and occupational outcomes, and (5) typological definitions—what we have learned from the use of a wide range of inventories and techniques to define a person's type or personality pattern.

Distinctive Qualities

The many attempts to show whether or not the characteristics attributed to types have validity are difficult to categorize. Only a few studies use a single set of theoretical definitions and a single set of criteria and test only concurrent or predictive relationships; many studies are elaborate mixtures of tests of concurrent and longitudinal relationships and use multiple measures to determine the characteristics of types. For convenience and comprehension, they have been reviewed here as comprehensive tests, personality inventories and scales, self-descriptions, values, abilities, and competencies.

Comprehensive tests.   Most of the early studies of the types, which were done by Holland and his colleagues, are characterized by the use of multiple dependent variables and multiple methods for the definition of types. In short, these exploratory studies usually capitalized on almost any readily available data in an attempt to develop fuller knowledge. Because these shotgun studies produced a large number of analyses, only the principal findings will be summarized.

In one early monograph, Holland (1962) assessed two large samples of bright high school graduates (National Merit finalists) over one- and two-year intervals (N = 1,177 and 994). Using VPI scale scores, vocational choice, or choice of major field to define a student's type, Holland found that a broad range of personal characteristics, usually bearing out the theory, was associated with the types. These included academic aptitudes, self-ratings, extracurricular activities, academic interests, nonacademic achievements, and personality variables (16 PF).

Although this first study was generally positive, it revealed two major deficiencies. The findings for a particular type often overlapped those for a similar type, and the formulations at that time (Holland, 1959) were not sufficiently explicit or comprehensive to cope with the myriad results dredged up by this data-rich study. On the positive side, most analyses were statistically significant and were moderately efficient.

In a second monograph, Holland (1963) again used a sample of National Merit finalists (N = 592). This longitudinal study differed from the first in two ways: the time interval was longer (first to fourth year of college) and six scales of the Strong Vocational Interest Blank were selected to assess the types. Using the Strong scales and the choice of vocation and major field to define a student's resemblance to the types and a similar array of dependent variables (choice of field at graduation, self-ratings, extracurricular achievements, and so on), Holland produced findings that approximated those obtained in the first study. A similar pattern of success and failure was observed. On the one hand, the use of the Strong scales demonstrated that the types could be defined by different instruments to yield similar results. On the other hand, the overlapping among types persisted in some analyses, and the deficiencies of the 1959 formulations were observed again—lack of clarity and comprehensiveness.

In a third report, Holland and Nichols (1964) studied changes in major field plans for a one-year period (high school senior year to end of freshman year in college). They assessed a sample of National Merit finalists (332 boys and 181 girls) in high school with interest, personality, originality, self-rating, achievement, and aptitude measures; they then assessed the students again in college and compared their pre- and post-college plans. Remaining in a given field (classified according to the typology) appears to be related to having personal attributes commonly associated with those of the typical student; leaving a field is related to dissimilarity between a student's attributes and those of the typical student. For example, boys who left realistic fields (largely engineering in this instance) appeared to be irresponsible, original, tolerant of ambiguity, and complex in outlook. In contrast, boys who remained in realistic fields were responsible, unoriginal, intolerant of ambiguity, and simple in outlook.

These and other findings are tenuous because a much larger sample would have been necessary to produce reliable findings. Large samples are required because the categorization according to type and sex reduces the usable portion of a sample to one-twelfth of its total, and the typical sample attrition decimates these subcategories even more.

In a fourth report, Holland (1963–64) used another sample of bright students (360 boys and 278 girls) to test some hypotheses about types. Students filled out a questionnaire that included items about their vocational choices, an adjective checklist, self-ratings, multiple-choice questions about how they cope with problems, and sentence stems about vocations.

The cross-sectional analyses of these data indicated that students classified as different types according to their VPI scores described themselves in expected ways. For example, boys categorized as investigative characterized themselves as analytical, curious, hard-headed, imaginative, intellectual, mechanical, not popular, quiet, reserved, scholarly, scientific, and so on. The majority of adjectives associated with the other types yielded similar positive evidence, although a few adjectives appeared either inconsistent with or unanticipated by the formulation for a given type. Similar results were obtained when types were studied for their characteristic reactions to stress, competencies in various fields, and most enjoyable activities. For example, boys with high scores on the Realistic scale of the VPI said that they "most enjoy working with their hands, tools, or instruments"; that they would find it most frustrating to "take patients in mental hospitals on recreational trips"; that they believe their "greatest ability lies in the area of mechanics"; and that they are "most incompetent in the area of human relations."

The fifth report (Holland, 1964), a one-year longitudinal study like four of five earlier reports, replicated many previous findings about the characteristics of types and extended the range of personal characteristics found to be related to the types. Using a sample of 1,437 National Merit finalists, the investigator correlated VPI scores with self-ratings, life goals, and achievements. Again, student characteristics were usually associated with appropriate types. For example, boys with many social preferences (high social scale on VPI) rated themselves high on understanding of others, cooperativeness, and interest in religion.

The sixth monograph in this series (Holland, 1968) is perhaps the most valuable, since a large sample of college freshmen from 28 colleges with a wide range of academic talent and social status was employed (1,576 men and 1,571 women). Although the sample was not a representative one, it did allow a large-scale test of the theory with a relatively normal group (in contrast to National Merit finalists).

Students were categorized as types and subtypes according to their VPI profiles and then compared on twenty-two dependent variables including competencies, life goals, self-ratings, and personality and attitudinal variables. Simple analyses of variance usually showed substantial differences across the types. Comparisons across subtypes such as RI, RS, RC, RE, and RA were also significant, and even comparisons across closely related subtypes yielded some differences—for example, RIS, RIC, RIE, and RIA.

The results of this study extended those of previous studies, with some differences: (1) The results for women were more positive than those for men—in all earlier studies, it had been the other way around; (2) the results were more explicit and substantial. A count of the theoretically expected high mean scores for types and subtypes is as follows: For men, 76 percent of the predictions are correct for comparisons across types, 75 percent are correct across two-letter subtypes, and 64.1 percent are correct across three-letter subtypes. For women, these percentages are 84.0, 75.4, and 72.7, respectively; (3) The overlapping among types remained but seemed less pronounced than before, although no statistical tests were performed; and (4) These statistical tests strongly suggested that people with similar codes have similar characteristics, which means that as we move from comparisons across types to comparisons of subtypes, there will be an obvious increasing similarity of personalities. This is implied by the F tests, which decrease dramatically in size from comparisons across types to comparisons within types (see Tables 2 to 7, Holland, 1968).

Abe and Holland (1965a) assessed 12,432 college freshmen in thirty-one colleges and universities for their interests, favorite activities, attitudes, life goals, and vocational aspirations. Students were classified by vocational aspiration and compared on 117 variables. In general, many comparisons resulted in large mean differences that were consistent with the formulations for the personality types (see Tables 4 to 15, Abe and Holland, 1965a). Abe and Holland (1965b) also used a student's choice of major field as the independent variable in place of vocational choice and repeated the analyses just described. The results closely resembled those obtained by the use of vocational choice.

Williams (1972) selected a sample of 145 male graduate students from eighteen departments and sorted them according to type. Students were assessed by the VPI, the 16 PF, the Allport-Vernon-Lindzey Study of Values (AVL), and the Miller Occupational Values Indicator. Comparisons among types indicated that a student's field of study (type) and his or her VPI, AVL, Miller Occupational, and 16 PF scores were usually consistent with the characteristics attributed to the types.

This complex and cleanly executed study is perhaps the best of its kind. The results are not only typically significant, but often of practical value. To illustrate, the application of discriminant analysis to the independent variables results in relatively efficient classifications of students. Using the VPI scales, 93 of 145 students are correctly classified according to fields of study. In the case of the AVL, 67 of 145 students are correctly classified, and the 16 PF scales correctly classify 83 of 145. The latter finding is especially important because it is strong evidence that field of study is partially dependent upon personality. These and other results replicate earlier findings and extend the characteristics associated with types to new variables.

In another large sample of 20,369 college freshmen in 37 institutions, Baird (1970) assessed the relation of six vocational interests (VPI) to 35 life goals, 31 self-ratings of ability and personality traits, and 22 scales measuring potential for academic and nonacademic achievement. Separate canonical analyses for each of the three domains and for each sex resulted in canonical correlations that ranged from .20 to .70. In short, vocational interests were significantly related to life goals, self-ratings, and potentials for achievement, and some patterns of these variables are consistent with the formulations for the types.

In a similar analysis, Schmitt and White (1978) performed a canonical analysis of the relation between the SCII theme scales (Campbell and Holland, 1972) versus the Job Description Inventory, the Job Diagnostic Survey (Smith, Kendall, and Hulin, 1969), and the Need Scales (Alderfer, 1972). The results for a sample of 860 recent high school graduates yielded canonical correlations of only .22, .37, and .44 for three variates. Generally, the results lend only a low level of support to the relation of vocational interests to job satisfaction and job need variables.

Most recently, the *Dictionary of Holland Occupational Codes* (Gottfredson, Holland, and Ogawa, 1982) provides indirect but persuasive evidence about the distinctive qualities of each type. That dictionary, which is a reorganization of the *Dictionary of Occupational Titles* (Department of Labor, 1977), provides abundant evidence that the six types of occupations require workers with special clusters of skills, interests, values, and aptitudes. (See Tables 11 to 14 in Gottfredson, Holland, and Ogawa, 1982. Table 15 from that volume, which summarizes the most discriminating variables between adjacent or closely related types, is reproduced here as Table 6.)

Personality inventories and scales. The evidence from correlational studies of the relation of the VPI or SDS to a wide range of personality inventories supports the descriptions of the types. The best single summary is in the manual for the VPI (Holland, 1977); see Tables 8 to 12 for the correlations between the VPI and the Guilford-Zimmerman Temperament Survey (Guilford-Zimmerman, 1949), the California Psychological Inventory (Gough, 1957), the 16 Personality Factor Questionnaire (Cattell et al., 1970), and the Edwards Personal Preference Schedule (EPPS, Edwards, 1959).

Taylor and Kelso's correlation matrix (1973)—shown as Table 10 in the VPI manual—provides a typical set of correlations for the VPI versus a personality inventory. They assessed 188 college males with the VPI and California Psychological Inventory (CPI), tested the ability of the VPI to discriminate across fields of study, and correlated VPI and CPI scale scores. The results indicated that students usually select courses consistent with their type and that types tend to have many of the personality traits attributed to them. At the same time, the highest correlation (VPI vs CPI scales) was only .36.

The relation of the VPI to the 16 PF provides the most substantial evidence for characteristics of the types (Table 11 of VPI manual). And more recently, Ward, Cunningham, and Wakefield (1976) compared the VPI and 16 PF in a canonical analysis of the data obtained from 425

Table 6   Variables Discriminating between Adjacent Occupational Types

REALISTIC VERSUS INVESTIGATIVE (*N*=72)

Realistic rated higher than Investigative in:
  Strength
  Stooping
  Hazards
  Activities involving processes, machines, or techniques versus social welfare
  Activities involving tangible productive satisfaction versus prestige, esteem
Investigative rated higher than Realistic in:
  Intelligence
  Verbal aptitude
  Numerical aptitude
  General educational development
  Scientific and technical activities versus business contact

INVESTIGATIVE VERSUS ARTISTIC (*N*=62)

Investigative rated higher than Artistic in:
  Intelligence
  Numerical aptitude
  Measurable or verifiable criteria
  Seeing
  Scientific and technical activities versus business contact
Artistic rated higher than Investigative in:
  Feelings, ideas, or facts
  Influencing people
  Talking, hearing
  Communication of data versus activities with things
  Abstract and creative versus routine, concrete activities

ARTISTIC VERSUS SOCIAL (*N*=58)

Artistic rated higher than Social in:
  Data
  Spatial perception
  Feelings, ideas, or facts
  Abstract and creative versus routine, concrete activities
  Activities involving processes, machines, or techniques versus social welfare
Social rated higher than Artistic in:
  People
  Clerical aptitude
  Dealing with people
  Variety and change
  Talking, hearing

SOCIAL VERSUS ENTERPRISING (*N*=59)

Social rated higher than Enterprising in:
  Scientific and technical activities versus business contact

TABLE 6 (cont'd)

Enterprising rated higher than Social in:
  Numerical aptitude
  Activities involving processes, machines, or techniques versus social welfare

ENTERPRISING VERSUS CONVENTIONAL ($N=59$)

Enterprising rated higher than Conventional in:
  Data
  People
  Dealing with people
  Talking, hearing
  Abstract and creative versus routine, concrete activities
Conventional rated higher than Enterprising in:
  Finger dexterity
  Repetitive or continuous processes
  Set limits, tolerances, or standards
  Seeing
  Scientific and technical activities versus business contact

CONVENTIONAL VERSUS REALISTIC ($N=68$)

Conventional rated higher than Realistic in:
  Clerical aptitude
  Dealing with people
  Repetitive or continuous processes
  Communication of data versus activities with things
Realistic rated higher than Conventional in:
  Specific Vocational Preparation (SVP)
  Spatial perception
  Measurable or verifiable criteria
  Strength
  Stooping

Note: This table shows significant differences ($p < 0.05$) for up to five variables. When more than five variables significantly discriminate, only the five largest differences are shown.

Source: Gottfredson, G. D., Holland, J. L., and Ogawa, D. K. *Dictionary of Holland Occupational Codes*. Palo Alto, California: Consulting Psychologists Press, 1982. Copyright 1982 by Consulting Psychologists Press and reproduced by special permission of the publisher.

undergraduates. Their analysis yielded three significant canonical correlations (.56, .50, and .37) that were easily interpreted and consistent with the descriptions of the types involved—especially the Enterprising, Artistic, and Conventional types. In a related but indirect assessment of the formulations about the types, Bachtold (1976) compared female psychologists, scientists, artists, writers, and politicians on the 16 PF through a multiple discriminant analysis. "Politicians were more sociable, conscientious, self-controlled, and group dependent; artists and writers were more affected by their feelings, spontaneous and natural, and inclined to follow their own urges; scientists were more reserved, serious, and tough-minded; and psychologists were more flexible, liberal, and accepting."

The relation of the VPI to the EPPS has also provided some evidence for the characteristics of types. Wakefield and Cunningham (1975) related the VPI and EPPS in a canonical analysis of the data for 372 undergraduates (juniors). Their analysis produced canonical correlations of .42, .40, and .34. They conclude that the VPI and EPPS measure the same three orthogonal dimensions of personality. Selected characteristics attributed to the Investigative, Artistic, Enterprising, Conventional, and Social scales were supported by interpretable weights.

Kristjanson (1969) investigated the relation of the SVIB to the EPPS scales for a sample of 255 college males. Student SVIB scores were reduced to the six type scores by averaging student scale scores that had been assigned to the types. Three different analyses (analyses of variance using raw scores, ranked scores, and cutting scores of the EPPS) yielded similar results—the majority of findings were in the predicted direction, but the magnitude of relations between interest type and EPPS scales was small but consistent with findings in related studies.

For example, the significant results in two or three analyses imply that Realistic types are self-deprecating, enduring, and passive; Investigative types are achieving and enduring but not affiliative; Social types are intraceptive, nurturant, dominant, but not independent, succorant, or orderly; Conventional types are orderly and achieving; Enterprising types are dominant, aggressive, and succorant, but not enduring, self-deprecating, or intraceptive; and that Artistic types are achieving and independent, but not orderly or enduring.

Two related studies using the SVIB (six or two scales to represent the types) and the EPPS (Bailey, 1971; McMullin, 1973) have also produced weak and less interpretable results.

Nord's (1976) study of undecided students (N = 80) indicates that the scales of the Myers-Briggs Type Indicator (MBTI) are correlated with the SDS scales in predictable directions. For example, Artistic correlates −.46 with Sensing, .26 with Intuition, −.41 with Judgment, and .38 with Perception. In contrast, Conventional correlates .34 with Sensing, −.20 with Intuition, and −.20 with Perception. These results are especially impressive because the SDS often yields relatively flat and unpredictive profiles among undecided students.

In another study, Folsom (1969) assessed a sample of 1,003 college students with the College Student Questionnaires (CSQ, Peterson, 1965) and then compared student types (defined by their choice of major field) on seven scales of the CSQ. The results lend support to the type formulations, except for the Enterprising category. Besyner, Bodden, and Winer (1978) found that the VPI and the needs scales of the Personality Research Form (PRF, Jackson, 1967) are only weakly and inconsistently related in a sample of 217 female and male undergraduates. In a related study, Bohn (1966) related a student's psychological need scores from the

Adjective Check List (Gough and Heilbrun, 1965) to scales on the Strong (R = printer, I = chemist, A = artist, S = social science teacher, E = sales manager, and C = accountant). Although Bohn used only 75 college counseling clients, about one-third of his results were statistically significant. The expected associations between types and needs, however, were only occasionally found.

Another investigation (Gentry, Winer, Sigelman, and Phillips, 1980) suggests that a person's VPI scores (99 females and 99 males—all undergraduates) have some expected correlation with Thorne's Life Style Analysis (Thorne, 1965). Among males, the Enterprising scale correlates significantly with Individual Stylistic (.22), Exploitative (.23), Domineering-Authoritarian (.29), Conforming (.19), One-upmanship (.25), Aggressive-Domineering (.31), Amoral-Sociopathy (.18), and Resistant-Defiant (.17). For females, only the Individual Stylistic (.18) and Aggressive-Domineering (.20) scales are significantly correlated with the Enterprising scale. And Dolliver and Mixon (1977) found that when students (N = 350) sorted occupations, SCII, or VPI test items by following descriptions of the six ego state functions, the results indicated a moderate correspondence between Berne's ego state descriptions and Holland's types.

In an analysis of the VPI and the Orientation and Motivation Inventory (OMI) scores obtained from 281 high school and 121 college students, Lorr and Stefic (1978) employed a discriminant function analysis to predict a student's highest VPI score from the OMI scores. The results were statistically significant and accounted for 80 and 91 percent of the variance of the VPI scores of high school and college samples. In addition, an examination of the mean scores of the OMI for each VPI type implies some support for the characterization of the types. For example, Realistic types (high school students) are characterized as risk takers, having an interest in the present (high scores), but not theoretical, psychologically minded, and orderly or concerned with personal relations (low scores). Realistic types (college students) are highest on casual style of approach and lowest on personal and psychological orientation.

Most recently, Costa, McCrae, and Holland (in press) examined the relation of the Self-Directed Search (SDS) to the Neuroticism-Extraversion-Openness Inventory (NEO; Costa and McCrae, in press) in a sample of men (N = 217) and women (N = 144) aged 21 to 89. Correlations indicated that Investigative and Artistic interests had strong positive associations with Openness to Experience and that Social and Enterprising interests had strong positive associations with Extraversion. Neuroticism was only inconsistently and weakly related to the SDS scales. Of special importance, differentiation scores based on the SDS were unrelated to age for females and males—more evidence for the stability of interests or types from young adulthood to old age.

Others have applied the hypotheses about types to a single or very homogeneous population. Patterson, Marron, and Patterson (1971) tested some of the hypotheses about the social type. Occupational therapy students (N = 109), representing the social type, were administered the Edwards Personal Preference Schedule (EPPS), the 16 PF, the Minnesota Multiphasic Personality Inventory (MMPI), the Tennessee Self-Concept Scales, and the Firo-B. The results indicated that the occupational therapy student resembled the description for the social type.

Self-descriptions. Several studies imply that people categorized as types by their aspirations, field of training, interest scores, or occupation describe themselves according to the typological formulations. The first study (Holland, 1963), in which self-descriptions (adjectives) were correlated with VPI scores for a large sample of high school students, resulted in characterizations that were supportive. This large-scale study was summarized on page 60. Later, Wall, Osipow, and Ashby (1967), using a sample of 186 male college freshmen, demonstrated that a student's ranking of six descriptions of the types according to his resemblance to each resulted in relatively clear and significant relationships between student rankings and SVIB group scores. In short, students see themselves in ways that correspond with their interest scores. In another analysis, Osipow, Ashby, and Wall (1966) showed a strong relationship between a student's choice of occupation, sorted according to type, and his typological ratings.

More recently, Westbrook and Molla (1976) and Molla (1978) have performed two explicit investigations of the self-descriptions for each type as well as factor analyses of the Self-Directed Search (SDS) and special adjective checklists. In the first study, Westbrook and Molla (1976) asked a sample of undergraduates (N = 191) to characterize six occupations representing the type by using the adjectives that are assumed to describe the types (Holland, 1973). They found that females and males of the same type used the same adjectives with some exceptions. They also developed a list of adjectives that were unique for each type and were the five adjectives most highly rated for a type (30 adjectives for six types). A six-week test-retest administration of this list (N = 175) produced correlations ranging from .69 to .79 with a median r of .74.

Molla (1978) then obtained a rectangular sample (evenly distributed across the types) of 293 undergraduates from diverse fields in a state university and performed eight separate factor analyses of the scales in each section of the SDS (activities, competencies, occupations, self-estimates) as well as analyses of three overlapping adjective checklists—Holland's adjective checklist (1973), the same list minus nine adjectives, and Molla's list of 30 unique adjectives. The factor analyses of the adjective checklist, the separate sections of the SDS, and a single analysis of all scales did approximate the hexagonal arrangement. The pattern of factor loadings was similar for related types and implied that the constructs (types) have some generality across multiple kinds of content and several methods of measurement. At the same time, these analyses, like older analyses (Edwards and Whitney, 1972), indicate that there' was considerable overlap among types and that the number of types may be fewer than six.

Values. The relation of values to types has often been consistent with the characteristics of the types. The life goal items (Astin and Nichols, 1964; Baird, 1970) and the Allport-Vernon-Lindzey scales (Williams, 1972; Laudeman and Griffeth, 1978) have suggested that the Investigative types have high scores on the theoretical scale and value scientific achievements, that Artistic types have high scores on the Esthetic scale and value artistic accomplishment, that Social types have high scores on the Social and Religious scales and value altruism and religion. The findings for the other types have usually been less distinct: the Enterprising and Conventional types have similar high scores on the Political and Economic scales, although they appear to value somewhat different life goals. Likewise, Realistic and Investigative types in college student samples usually value science.

The ability of values variables to discriminate among trainees or people in different occupations has also undergone an occasional test. For instance, Sweet (1982) has demonstrated that a vocational interest measure (VPI) accounts for most of the variance in discrimination among 1,255 technician-level students in 24 separate courses. In separate discriminant analyses, Super's Work Values Inventory (1968) accounted for 31 percent of the variance in group differences, whereas the Australian version of the VPI accounted for 62 percent of the variance. And the discriminant analyses based on both inventories accounted for 66 percent, or the work values scales provide only a little information on group differences beyond that provided by the VPI.

In this connection, it is important to note that Rokeach (1973) has provided a substantial volume of evidence about the values of females and males according to social class, race, occupation, occupational choice, and role. Even a casual review of this landmark publication shows that a person's occupation and values are moderately related and often consistent with the types. Another volume by Gordon (1975) using the Survey of Interpersonal Values (SIV) has provided another extensive summary of similar findings: values were associated with both occupational and sex differences in expected directions. Of special importance, the seven values in the SIV usually correspond to the types in expected ways.

Abilities and competencies.   Different types have developed different kinds of abilities and competencies, and these differences correspond in a diffuse way to the demands of the occupation a particular type engages in. The evidence for this interpretation is vast, so only some illustrative data are presented here.

Table 7 for a large sample of college freshman (Holland, 1968) demonstrates that students with different kinds of interests have developed somewhat characteristic competencies. Students interested in scientific occupations report more scientific competencies than students with any other kind of interests; students with Realistic interests report more technical competencies than other students. Like the relation of interests

TABLE 7   Correlations of VPI Scales with Self-Reported Competencies in College Freshmen

Competencies	REAL		INV		SOC		CONV		ENT		ART	
	M	F	M	F	M	F	M	F	M	F	M	F
Scientific	15	19	41	39	04	08	−02	01	00	05	07	11
Technical	36	25	18	18	−10	03	05	11	03	13	−07	07
Govt. & Social Studies	−06	05	13	13	20	11	06	−04	18	13	21	20
Athletic	08	09	11	10	06	07	01	−01	14	13	02	06
Business and Clerical	00	03	07	03	11	10	22	22	26	20	08	06
Social & Educ'l	−04	00	08	01	37	33	11	04	30	26	25	18
Homemaking	12	05	11	04	18	12	10	08	14	11	16	07
Arts Comp.	−03	06	14	11	25	18	06	−01	21	25	51	45
Leadership & Sales	−02	01	11	06	29	24	16	07	35	29	25	20
Foreign Language	−05	01	14	08	13	05	04	−05	10	08	18	16

Note: Males = 3771; Females = 3492. Underlined correlation coefficients indicate the expected relationships.

Source: From *Manual for the Vocational Reference Inventory*. Copyright 1965, 1975, 1978 by John L. Holland. Reproduced by permission of the publisher, Consulting Psychologists Press, Inc.

to personality, the correlations in Table 7 are usually small but consistent with the formulations for the types. In addition, closely related types (adjacent on the hexagon) tend to share similar competencies.

A related study suggests that self-ratings of abilities and reports of competencies are supported by objective aptitude measures. Kelso, Holland, and Gottfredson (1977) computed simple and canonical correlations between the scales of the Self-Directed Search and The Armed Forces Vocational Aptitude Battery (ASVAB) for a sample of 192 high school girls. Specific predictions about the relation of types to particular aptitudes received some weak support. Of special importance, self-ratings of ability and self-reports of competencies accounted for more variance in the ASVAB scales than did the other sets of SDS scales (Activities or Occupations).

The reorganization of the Dictionary of Occupational Titles according to the Holland classification (Gottfredson et al., 1982) indicates the aptitudes as well as the interests, temperaments, and working conditions that each occupation requires for satisfactory performance. (See Tables 12 and 13 in the dictionary for the aptitudes related to occupational types.) Taken together, these tables imply that there are small to moderate but consistent relations between the characteristics of the types and the requirements of the occupations that types seek or engage in.

Personality Patterns and Identity

The hypotheses about personality patterns (the differentiation or consistency of a person's interest profile) have received mixed support. The early investigations usually produced negative or negligible findings, but a few old and recent investigations have produced positive and substantial findings. The evidence for the value of vocational identity as a construct for defining the behavior of a particular type is largely untested but encouraging. A brief review of the studies that focus primarily on the person follows. The investigations of differentiation, consistency, or identity that focus on the environment or person-environment interactions are with a few exceptions reported in other sections.

Differentiation.   Only a few successful tests of hypotheses about differentiation have been made. Holland (1968) categorized students as having profiles of high, middle, or low differentiation (the difference between the highest and lowest VPI raw score), and then compared students for stability of vocational choice. For men, the results clearly support the hypothesis: Differentiation is positively related to stability—that is, spiked profiles are stable, and flat profiles are unstable ($P < .05$). The results for women were not significant. Another test of the differentiation hypothesis in the same study examined the stability of vocational choice for students whose VPI profiles had (1) "no ties"—a single scale was higher than any other scale; (2) the two highest scales were "tied"—both had equal scores; or (3) the three or more highest scales were tied. The results of these analyses were also significant and according to expectation for men, but not for women. In the successful analysis, differentiation increased the efficiency of prediction about 8 to 15 percent in a linear fashion.

A recent longitudinal investigation (Taylor, Kelso, Longthorp, and Pattison, 1980) provides the most comprehensive and persuasive evidence for the validity of the hypotheses about differentiation. The authors first administered the VPI and a questionnaire to 406 female and 501 male high school students, and one year later students filled out the SDS and another questionnaire.

In the first analysis—a comparison of well- and poorly-differentiated students (upper and lower 20 percent)—nine of eleven comparisons on self-knowledge, occupational knowledge, and spare-time interests were statistically significant ($P < .001$), all of them in a direction that was consistent with the definition of differentiation (see Table 8). Further comparisons, using followup and initial assessment data, show that the high differentiation group made vocational choices that were more stable than those of the low differentiation group. In addition, using all students (N = 896) at both times, differentiation increased significantly from time one to time two—a one-year interval.

In a second analysis, a stepwise discriminant analysis was performed

TABLE 8   Comparisons between Low Differentiation (1 or 2) Group (N = 185) and High Differentiation (10 to 14) Group (N = 171) on Self-Knowledge, Occupational Knowledge, and Spare-time Interest Variables

VARIABLE	GROUP	MEAN	SDs	t[a]
Self-Knowledge				
Consistency[b]	LD	1.91	1.24	−5.84*
	HD	2.52	.65	
Congruence	LD	2.87	.78	−4.45*
	HD	3.21	.67	
VPI Self-Control[b]	LD	7.41	5.12	1.54
	HD	6.66	4.04	
VPI Masculinity	LD	4.83	3.05	−4.15*
	HD	6.18	3.07	
VPI Status	LD	4.60	2.83	−6.10*
	HD	6.50	3.04	
VPI Infrequency[b]	LD	5.50	3.58	1.11
	HD	5.12	2.88	
VPI Acquiescence[b]	LD	3.35	3.10	−16.95*
	HD	9.80	4.04	
Occupational Knowledge				
Jobs Listed[b]	LD	4.21	1.79	−8.03*
	HD	5.92	2.20	
People Consulted	LD	4.25	1.90	−4.03*
	HD	5.10	2.07	
Spare-time Interests				
Leisure Differentiation	LD	2.69	1.10	−6.10*
	HD	3.42	1.18	
Leisure Consistency	LD	1.85	.84	−3.31*
	HD	2.15	.82	

[a]One-tailed t-test, df = 354
[b]Calculations of t used separate variance estimates.
*$p < .001$

Source: Taylor, K. F., Kelso, G. I., Longthorp, N. E., and Pattison, P. E. Differentiation as a construct in vocational theory and a diagnostic sign in practice. Melbourne Psychology Reports, No. 68, 1980 ISBN 0–86839–362–2, University of Melbourne. Reproduced by permission.

using only the nine variables obtained at time one. The discriminant function was not only significant but also very efficient. Eight variables correctly classified 87 percent of all students in these extreme groups.

A final analysis estimated how well the nine initial variables were able to predict the differentiation scores of the 896 students who completed the VPI. A regression analysis predicted one-third of the variance.

One other investigation has provided clear support for differentiation. Holland, Gottfredson, and Nafziger (1975) found that differentiation (as well as consistency) predicted scores on a decision-making task more efficiently than any rival predictors. The simple correlations were small, but the results—good decision makers had differentiated profiles— held for samples of high school students (N = 1,005), college students (N = 692), and employed adults (N = 140).

The positive results in these three large-scale studies are in sharp contrast to the negative or negligible findings obtained in most studies (W. E. Werner, 1969; Bates, Parker, and McCoy, 1970; Kernen, 1971; Villwock, Schnitzen, and Carbonari, 1976; O'Neil, 1977; Nafziger et al., 1975; Schaefer, 1976; Frantz and Walsh, 1972; Florence, 1973; Spokane et al., 1978). In some instances, the negative results may be due to poor designs or small samples. For example, it is important to control for SES, intelligence, and type in testing hypotheses about differentiation. In addition, large samples are required to secure stable and significant results, because the expected relations are small.

Finally, several investigators and statisticians have been dismayed by the naiveté of the definition of differentiation and have derived more complex mathematical definitions. Aul (1979) has provided an explicit analysis of the deficiencies in the Holland index, but in the only empirical test of the Aul index it proved to be no better or worse than the old index. More recently, Iachon (in press) has developed still another index that appears closely related and mathematically superior to both the Holland and the Aul indices. The Iachon index correlated .88 with the Holland index in a small sample. At this time, it appears useful to try out both the old and new indices on larger samples. It is likely that the old index could be retained for clinical work because of its practicality and that the Iachon index could be the preferred index for research purposes when the computation of a more precise formula would be effortless.

Consistency. Like differentiation, consistency has had a checkered research career—about as many negative as positive results. However, well-designed studies that closely follow the theory have produced nearly all of the positive evidence. To illustrate, Wiley and Magoon (1982) used a sample of 211 Social types (defined by SDS high point code as college freshmen) and grouped by consistency level (78 high, 79 medium, and 54 low) to forecast persistence (graduation) and cumulative GPA. They found that high- and medium-consistency students persisted at a higher rate than low-consistency students, and that students with higher levels of consistency achieve higher GPAs than students with lower levels of consistency.

Three predictive studies for single types have also shown that consistency has strong relations with stability of a college student's vocational aspiration. O'Neil and Magoon (1977) and O'Neil, Magoon, and Tracey (1978) followed a sample of Investigative types (N = 171), at three levels of consistency (defined by SDS codes as college freshmen), from freshman to senior year and from freshman year to current occupation three years after graduation. Consistency of freshman SDS yielded substantial positive predictions four and seven years later. At graduation, 76 percent of the Investigative types with high consistent SDS codes had an occupational plan in the Investigative area; but only 34 percent of the Investigative types with low consistent codes had an occupational plan in the Investigative area. Middle levels of consistency were similar (not significantly different from high levels of consistency). Three years after college or seven years after the initial assessment, the hit rate for the current occupation of an Investigative type with high consistency was 54 percent but only 13 percent for a type with a low level of consistency. In a similar study, Touchton and Magoon (1977) used a sample of female Social types (defined by high point code of freshmen SDS) and obtained similar results: consistency of aspirations (first and second aspirations as a freshman belonged to the same category) was an efficient predictor of vocational plan three years later (76 percent).

Aiken and Johnston's (1973) study of undecided students implies how consistency leads to more predictable behavior. Undecided counselees with consistent VPI profiles were more likely to increase information seeking than counselees with inconsistent profiles. A similar study (Miller, 1982), using the differentiation of GOT scales of the SCII (Campbell and Hansen, 1981), indicated that differentiation and information seeking were positively associated.

Other striking results have been obtained by creating still another definition of consistency or by using the consistency of a person's occupational code. For example, Barak and Rabbi (1981) used a college student's first two major field aspirations to create four levels of consistency and found that "consistent" students tended to persist in college, did not change majors, and had high grades. The results were not only significant but occasionally substantial. Earlier work (Holland, Sorensen, Clark, Nafziger, and Blum, 1973) has shown that the consistency of the occupational code of a man's first job predicts the category of his job five years and ten years later. In contrast, men with inconsistent occupational codes are not as predictable and become even less predictable over a ten-year interval. These findings seem important, for they are based upon a large subsample of a national representative sample of men in the United States. More recently, Gottfredson (1977), using a sample that represented the 1970 working population, obtained the most impressive results. When the occupational codes of females and males were used to sort people into three levels of consistency, consistency had a strong relation with occupational stability for the entire age range. People with consistent codes change the kind of work they do much less frequently than people at the lower levels of consistency.

In another study, Gottfredson (1975) found that the stability of a parolee's or probationer's employment was related to the consistency of a man's claimed occupation. The significant correlation was low but as efficient as any other predictor.

In contrast, Erwin (1982) and others have found little or no support for the value of consistency. The Erwin longitudinal study was well designed, but the use of a map of college majors to define consistency may have been a poor measure of consistency. A reanalysis with a standard measure might clarify the results.

Combinations. The use of consistency and differentiation in combination has been examined only occasionally and again with mixed results. Perhaps the most dramatic results for the concepts of differentiation and consistency are given in Table 9 (Holland, 1968). These simple analyses were performed to learn if the effects of consistency, differentiation, and vocational role (ability to name a specific role in one's future occupation) are cumulative—that is, if their combined occurrence results in more efficient predictions. All possible combinations were tried. The results suggested that consistency, differentiation, and vocational role preference cumulate to improve the prediction of vocational choice over 8- to 12-month intervals, but their relative contributions appear unequal. Explicit role preference contributes most to the prediction, followed by differentiation and then by consistency. However, when these analyses were repeated by controlling for VPI high-point code of the largest subsample (Investigative men), the results became clearer—so much so that they appeared contrived.

The results suggest a way to define vocational maturity or vocational adaptiveness in terms of the present theory. Vocationally mature people have consistent and differentiated profiles and can enunciate a role within their future occupations. The results also reinforce some common notions about vocational counseling clients, particularly the notion that the row at the top of Table 9 describes the people vocational counselors rarely see, whereas the bottom row describes the typical client. In other words, most

TABLE 9   Prediction of Final Vocational Choice from Student's VPI Profile and Role Preference

VPI PROFILE						SAMPLES (MALES ONLY)					
Consistency	Homogeneity			Preferred role		Fall % Hits	f	Spring % Hits	f	Fall-Int % Hits	f
C	+	Hi	+	Explicit	=	51.8	305	53.4	509	68.2	107
I	+	Hi	+	Explicit	=	52.2	115	53.0	185	54.4	49
C	+	Lo	+	Explicit	=	44.2	330	45.0	420	51.2	63
I	+	Lo	+	Explicit	=	45.0	160	37.3	233	47.5	56
C	+	Hi	+	Ambiguous	=	33.3	126	39.5	124	46.4	13
I	+	Hi	+	Ambiguous	=	26.2	42	32.1	56	30.0	10
C	+	Lo	+	Ambiguous	=	31.8	195	39.1	156	27.1	13
I	+	Lo	+	Ambiguous	=	25.6	86	28.9	90	19.4	6

Source: Holland, J.L. Explorations of a theory of vocational choice: VI. A longitudinal study using a sample of typical college students. *Journal of Applied Psychology,* 1968, 52. Table 27, 30. Copyright 1968 by the American Psychological Association, and reproduced by permission.

clients are those who produce confused interest profiles and who are unclear or uncertain about the vocational role they want to play.

On the other hand, Villwock, Schnitzen, and Carbonari (1976) found that differentiation and consistency added no significant variance to congruence in predicting the stability of choice of major field for 167 college students. Likewise, Danek (1971) found that differentiation and consistency singly or in combination were unrelated to self-actualization measures and were generally not in accord with theoretical predictions for a sample of 84 college students.

Identity. The evidence for the usefulness of this new construct is promising but sparse. The evidence for the reliability and validity of the Identity Scale has been summarized by Holland, Daiger, and Power (1980). The scale was developed using a sample of 496 high school sophomores and validated on a new sample of 824 high school, college, and adult workers. The 23-item Identity Scale had a KR 20 of .89 and the construct validity of the scale was supported by external ratings, factor analysis, item content, item process analysis, correlational analysis, and earlier research (Holland and Holland, 1977).

Subsequent research has also been supportive. Taylor (1980a) reexamined the reliability of the Identity Scale (214 male and female college students) and obtained a KR 20 of .87 and found that the Identity Scale correlated .48 with a Decidedness Scale (Taylor, 1980b). In another investigation, Grotevant and Thorbecke (1982), using 41 male and 42 female high school students, showed that the Identity Scale was significantly correlated with occupational commitment (assessed by a revision of the Marcia Identity Status Interview) for females (.42) and males (.49). And Henkels, Spokane, and Hoffman (1981) have reported that for a sample of 92 college students high identity was related to high scores on the Capacity for Status and Sense of Well Being scales of the California Psychological Inventory (Gough, 1957). Most recently, Olson (1982) reported that the Identity Scale discriminated homemakers from displaced homemakers and that the Identity Scale correlated .48 with a "satisfaction with life" rating and .64 with a "satisfaction with homemaking" rating for the total sample (N = 338).

All of these studies lend support to the construct validity of the Identity Scale, but no study has investigated the ability of this scale to forecast vocational stability in a career, its value in combination with consistency, differentiation, and type, or whether or not this scale could serve as an estimate of vocational adaptation. Earlier work by Stevens (1973) on placement readiness implies that the ability to cope successfully with career transitions may be predicted by the Identity Scale. Many of the career problems compiled by Campbell and Cellini (1981)—problems in decision making, implementing career plans, and in organizational performance and institutional adaptation—appear to be problems in which one's identity plays an influential role.

Life History

The general formulations about the development of types assume that children, adolescents, and adults become different types with different degrees of consistency, differentiation, and identity because they begin life with different patterns of biological and social heredity, and because different types have different life histories. The research tests of these ideas are incomplete, but they clearly suggest that different types do have different life histories and imply how aspirational and work histories become more stable with age. Further, different types have different life histories because they live in families with divergent interests, competencies, income, and opportunity, and because children, adolescents, and adults also become active and selective users of environmental opportunities and deficits.

Family influence. Multiple investigations imply that types produce types. They indicate in simple or complex analyses that various parental variables are usually related to a child's type in adolescence. In an early study, Holland (1962) showed that a student's high-point VPI code was significantly related to the values and goals that fathers held for their sons and daughters. For example, a father who wanted his son to be "popular" was more apt to have a son with a peak on the Enterprising scale; fathers who wanted their sons to be "curious" were more likely to have sons who peaked on the Investigative or Artistic scales. In another analysis using a different sample of bright students and their parents, additional small but significant relationships were obtained between a child's vocational interests and his or her mother's attitudes about child rearing as assessed by the Parental Attitude Research Instrument (Schaeffer and Bell, 1958). The most obvious interpretation of the results (Holland, 1962, Table 18) is that Conventional types (male and female) have mothers with the most authoritarian attitudes. Because fathers and sons had been administered VPIs (short and long forms), it was possible to test whether or not fathers and sons tended to have the same high-point codes or to be of the same type. Six by six chi-square tests were significant (P < .001), and the positive relationship is readily observable in the table based on 768 father-son pairs (Holland, 1962, Table 18). Finally, the effects of consistent attitudes between father and mother were analyzed for their relation to the child's vocational aspirations classified according to the typology. The analyses suggested that boys with realistic choices are more likely to have both parents with authoritarian attitudes, whereas boys with investigative choices are more likely to have both parents with democratic attitudes. These and other findings are significant, but the relationships are small and sometimes ambiguous. At best, they are only suggestive.

In an unpublished paper, Whitney (1970) successfully classified students as types using parental variables. Whitney used a sample of bright students (N = 295) to develop weights for classifying students according to centour scores. The weights derived from the first sample were then applied to a cross-validation sample (N = 575). The classification of students according to parental variables was only partially successful. The efficiency of the classification procedure was very low but significant. At the same time, small parent-child relationships are par for the course. Stronger relationships were found for child and same-sex parent (as opposed to opposite-sex parent).

And, Barclay, Stilwell, and Barclay (1972) found that parental occupation was associated with a broad range of student behaviors. Barclay assessed 1,386 elementary school children with the Barclay Classroom Climate Inventory (Barclay, 1983) and classified children as types and subtypes using parental occupation. The simple analyses of variance for 29 variables for each subtype strongly suggested that parental type (occupation) may encourage special outcomes in children, including their vocational interests, their sociometric choices of other children, and the teacher expectations they generate.

In a large-scale study of 127,125 students entering 248 four-year colleges, Werts and Watley (1972) compared paternal occupations with children's nonacademic scientific, artistic, oral, leadership, musical, and literary achievements in high school. The results imply that children excel at their fathers' occupational skills. For example, sons of scientists tended to win science contests, whereas sons of entrepreneurs had essentially zero probabilities of such success. These and other findings are impressive because they suggest the strong influence of family on a student's activities.

Several more recent studies indicate that a college student's type is predictable from a few parental and demographic variables. For example, Grandy and Stahmann (1974a), using a random sample of college freshmen (N = 603) and a discriminant analysis, predicted student type (one of six) with moderate efficiency (45 percent), or as well as the average interest inventory agrees with the category of a person's vocational aspiration. The variables in these predictions included: father's occupation (Realistic, Investigative, or Artistic), mother's occupation (Investigative or Conventional), student sex, and father's politics. This study was replicated by DeWinne, Overton, and Schneider (1978) who used a larger sample (713 males and 839 females) and a more stringent statistical criterion. Comparisons of the occupational codes of parents and offspring again produced positive results. This study suggested that fathers influenced both sons and daughters; whereas mothers influenced only a son's type (occupational aspiration).

In a closely related study, Schneider, DeWinne, and Overton (1980) examined in a small sample the relation of a student's occupational choice to parental occupation when both parents were categorized as the same type (had occupations classified in the same category). Only students who had parents classified as the same type were studied. The Kolmogorov-Smirnov one-sample tests for sons and daughters indicated that congruent fathers and mothers had a significant effect on the occupational choices of daughters but not on sons. Nafziger et al. (1972) also examined the effect of parental congruency on an offspring's occupation. Using a national representative sample of females and males, the investigators obtained significant relations between father-son and mother-daughter, but of special importance, when father and mother shared the same occupational category (one of six), the relation of parental occupation to child's occupation was increased about ten percent.

In a complex and ingenious investigation of sexual identity, Hazanovitz-Jordan (1982) found, regardless of sex, that Social-Artistic interests were associated with an identification with mothers, that Realistic-Investigative interests were associated with an identification with fathers, and that individuals highly identified with both parents were apt to have Enterprising interests.

Finally, Viernstein and Hogan (1975) found parental occupational type to be significantly related to the *level* of a child's occupational aspiration in a sample of bright seventh and eighth graders. For instance, girls with high level occupational aspirations had codes that resemble their father's occupational code. In a related study of high aptitude students (275 females and 544 males), Nichols and Holland (1963) found that parental interests, attitudes, and goals for their children often had small but significant relations with a child's achievement in academic and nonacademic areas. When 12 criteria of achievement were categorized according to type, the data implied that parents encourage achievements that are similar to their own interests and attitudes and discourage achievement in areas they dislike or devalue. And like many earlier investigations, variables obtained from the father were more highly related to the criteria than were those obtained from the mother.

Generally, the foregoing studies indicate that a child's type is somewhat predictable from parental type or other parental variables. Such investigations are helpful, but they are unknown mixtures of biological and social inheritance. The following studies imply that a small portion of parental influence is due to the biological inheritance of vocational interests.

Grotevant, Scarr, and Weinberg's (1977) large-scale investigation of families with biological and adopted children implies that vocational interests have a small inherited component. They even imply that the shape of the profile is inherited. Parents and children (N = 870) were administered the SCII and scored on the six theme scales. The data suggest that biologically-related family members resemble each other on the six theme scales, but at a low level. In contrast, adoptive family members are, on the average, no more similar than parents and children paired randomly from the population. The data from this landmark study are consistent with earlier findings from identical and fraternal twin studies (Osborne, 1980; Roberts and Johansson, 1974) in which the interests of identical twins are more closely related than those of fraternal twins.

In another analysis of the earlier family data (Grotevant et al., 1977), Grotevant (1979) has also reported that the environment created by parent interest similarity (a parent-parent difference score or the sum of the absolute differences on the six theme scales) affects the degree to which the interests of children come to resemble those of parents. In short, similarity of parental interests increases the resemblance between children's interests and both parents. Grotevant also reviews how the degree of parental similarity may influence children in different ways and affect family interactions.

Developmental history. A small group of studies implies that people who have different vocational aspirations, different interests, or work in different occupations have characteristic life histories (Mumford and Owens, 1982; Kuhlberg and Owens, 1960; Barry and Bordin, 1967; Frantz, 1969; and Laurent, 1951) and that different life histories lead to different levels of achievement (Brown, 1978; Ritchie and Boehm, 1977; Baird, 1976; Loughmiller, Ellison, Taylor, and Price, 1973).

Three of these biographical or developmentally oriented investigations have used explicit estimates of the six types. Kelso (1976) has perhaps provided the most impressive evidence for the similarity of males and females of the same type and, at the same time, demonstrated that a student's vocational aspiration can be efficiently predicted from personal and environmental data. Using a sample of 11th grade girls (N = 523) and boys (N = 386), Kelso first sorted their vocational choices according to type. Then he used both regression and canonical analysis to explore the relations of type to personality, family, and peer data. Canonical correlations of .69 and .75 were obtained for boys and girls; their cross-validation resulted in small shrinkages—correlations of .58 and .66. Finally, he substituted the data for each sex in the opposite-sex equation. The correlation for girls, using the boys' equation, was .60, and the correlation for boys, using the girls' equation, was .41—strong signs that the variables that predict typological outcomes are similar for the two sexes. And when the predictors are classified—family background, parental attitudes and values, peer characteristics, or individual characteristics—the individual characteristics are the most efficient and the family background variables are the least efficient.

Eberhardt and Muchinsky (1982) administered the Vocational Preference Inventory and the Owens Biographical Questionnaire (Owens and Schoenfeldt, 1979) to 437 female and 379 male undergraduates. Multiple discriminant analysis, regression analysis, and analysis of variance were used to determine the relation between life experiences and vocational preferences or type. Cross-validated multiple correlations between biographical factor scores and interest inventory scores account for two to 35 percent of the variance in interests. The Investigative scale is most predictable for both females (35 percent) and males (21 percent), and the Conventional scale is least predictable for both females (six percent) and males (two percent). Of equal importance, biodata factor scores were usually associated with the interest scales according to the formulations for the types. In the multiple discriminant analyses, a total of 40 percent of the variance in RIASEC group membership (assessed by high-point code of VPI) was explainable by the life history information for males. For females, 52 percent of the variance in IASEC group membership was explainable by the life history information. Three female Realistic types were omitted from this analysis.

This elaborate investigation suggests that a person's dominant interest type is shaped, in part, by his or her life-history experiences. In addition, these experiences "play a substantial role in the development of one's interests, for life experiences account for as much as 35 percent of the variance in vocational interests."

In a comprehensive and complex exploration of manifest interests and career development, Cook and Alexander (1979), using the ETS Growth Study data, assessed the types with six ad hoc leisure activity scales. Their study produced mixed results. Leisure activities were stable over the school years and produced marked sex differences that closely resemble those found for adults (Holland, 1979). On the other hand, the leisure interest scales had only weak or no relation to subsequent employment in congruent jobs.

Personal and environmental constraints.   An extensive literature indicates that vocational aspirations, careers, and personalities are constrained and limited by environmental events and relevant personal characteristics. The present theory assumes that these influences are expressed in the types a person comes to resemble. The life history data reviewed earlier illustrates how gender, school grades, social class, occupational opportunity, and other life events lead to different types. The theory has been useful (hypotheses receive empirical support) in these and other studies because researchers have typically used relatively homogeneous samples of students or adults in which the range of values for intelligence, social class, education, and age is restricted and thus crudely controlled. Nevertheless, the explicit use of age, sex, education, intelligence, social class, and occupational prestige as control or moderator variables should improve empirical testing and understanding especially in large samples with diverse characteristics.

Unfortunately, there are no precise estimates of the relative influence of constraining personal and environmental variables because economists, sociologists, and psychologists use their favorite variables rather than comprehensive sets, and because they are interested in different outcomes. There is, however, considerable evidence that the following variables are major influencers of vocational aspirations and careers: perceptions of job-self compatibility, sex type, prestige, and required effort associated with a job (L. Gottfredson, 1981); intelligence, education, and social class (Blau and Duncan, 1967; L. Gottfredson and Brown, 1981; Schmitt et al., 1978; Flanagan et al., 1973; Husen, 1968); school grades (D. Gottfredson, 1982); and the influence of significant others (Sewell, Haller, and Portes, 1969).

Occupational and Personal Outcomes

The family and life history studies support the assumption that different types have histories that are to some degree consistent with the type a person resembles. The studies in this section summarize the outcomes associated with different types and their special life histories. In short, different types search for different kinds of work, see the world in different ways, attain different levels and kinds of achievements, and have different life styles.

Searching behavior. Earlier statements of the theory suggested that types "search" for congenial environments, but the hypotheses about types were not concerned with the actual searching activity. Now we do have a few studies that suggest how types search for environments. These studies imply that types are not passive victims of the environments they encounter but are rather active seekers and avoiders of potentially compatible and incompatible situations.

Holland and Nichols (1964) found that people leave fields for which they lack interest and aptitude and seek fields for which they possess interest and aptitude. These are old conclusions, but this study documents them with a comprehensive assessment that provides both an objective and subjective picture of the process. In another study, Holland (1964) observed that students tended to be attracted to students like themselves. Subjects were asked to list the major fields of their three best friends. When a student's field was compared to the field of his or her best friend (listed first), the resulting 6 × 6 table was significant by chi-square test (P <001 for men; P < .10 for women). In general, best friends shared the same major fields or were attracted to the same field where they met and interacted. Identical analyses for each of the remaining friends produced similar 6 × 6 tables.

Later, Hogan, Hall, and Blank (1972) extended the similarity-attraction hypothesis to activities and vocational interests. Using a standard experimental design for testing this hypothesis, they clearly demonstrated that students expect to like people who have interests similar to their own rather than people with divergent interests. This simple experimental study used a sample of 122 college students who were administered a brief interest and activities inventory to assess their resemblance to each of the types. The answer sheets were first sorted randomly into three groups, and then special answer sheets were constructed so that five weeks later each student received one of three kinds: (1) an answer sheet that was a copy of his or her own, (2) an answer sheet that agreed with half of his or her original responses, or (3) an answer sheet that was the opposite of his or her own. The students were asked to rate the person represented by the answer sheet on three items, using a seven-point scale. Three one-way analyses of variance were all significant (P < .001), and the mean ratings were in the expected order from high to low, without exceptions. In short, the subjects liked those who most resembled them in interests. The subjects also believed that people with interests similar to their own would be "enjoyable to work with," as well as "well adjusted."

Apostal (1970) has shown that students prefer those subcultures in their college that are consistent with their personality type. In a related study, Kipnis, Lane, and Berger (1967) found that "impulsive and restless" college students are attracted to business majors, whereas more controlled students are attracted to science and mathematics. These results imply that people search for environments that demand or support their more salient traits. For example, science and mathematics require day-to-day persistence and study; well-controlled people should therefore find science fields more congenial than business fields, which often demand risk taking. Other analyses indicate that bright science students with high-impulsiveness scores get poorer grades and are less satisfied than bright science students with low-impulsiveness scores. A related study suggests that people are attracted to "familiar" jobs. Norman and Bessemer (1968) have shown that high school boys (N = 100) prefer familiar job titles to unfamiliar ones, regardless of the occupational prestige level. This "clinging to the familiar" persisted even when descriptive statements were used instead of job titles.

Andrews (1973) used a sample of 81 adults (aged 21 to 55) to demonstrate that there is a closer relationshp between a man's future job and his current VPI code than between his current job and current VPI code (P < .05). Andrews developed an elaborate procedure for measuring relatedness of personality pattern (VPI profile) and environment (job) by using the hexagonal model in Figure 3. Finally, Kunce and Kappes (1976) have suggested that college males who preferred structured environments resembled the Realistic and Conventional types more and the Artistic and Social types less. The results for females were not significant.

Occupational perceptions and cognitive styles. The assumption that people search for satisfying occupational environments implies that a person has a library of occupational stereotypes with a useful degree of reliability and validity. If stereotypical perceptions of occupations had no validity, people would have to devote enormous amounts of time to the acquisition of information so that they could cope successfully with the selection of their first and subsequent jobs.

Fortunately, a few investigators have made rapid progress with work that supports this assumption. In two major studies, O'Dowd and Beardslee (1960, 1967) showed that a sample of fifteen occupations are perceived in much the same way by a variety of large samples of faculty, college students, high school students, men, and women. They also demonstrated that although occupational stereotypes are complex, they can be organized in terms of a few factors which represent some of the common dimensions of occupations, especially status. They also showed that demographic differences make only small differences in the perception of occupations, and they found little change in stereotypes over four years of college.

Other studies support these findings and fill in more information about occupational stereotypes. Schutz and Blocher (1960), using a sample of 135 high school seniors, found that a student's vocational preference was significantly related to the "vocational sketch" (occupational stereotype) a student had selected as self-descriptive one week earlier. They then suggested how the process of vocational choice might operate and why such stereotypes should have validity. In another study of 679 high school senior boys, Banducci (1968) found that a student's social status, academic potential, and vocational interests have a small rather than a large influence on the accuracy of his occupational stereotypes. At the same time, Banducci extended the work of O'Dowd and Beardslee (1967) and Grunes (1957) by suggesting how several personal characteristics operate in expected ways. For example, bright students had more accurate stereotypes of higher-level jobs, and poor students had more accurate stereotypes of lower-level jobs. In addition, students tended to have more accurate perceptions of occupations that corresponded to the dominant scale in their vocational interest profile (VPI). In short, Banducci's work illustrates how selective perception functions in a person's occupational search according to type and demographic characteristics.

In a persuasive study, Marks and Webb (1969) demonstrated that students entering the fields of industrial management or electrical engineering possess "a fairly accurate image of the typical incumbent of the intended occupation." Their elaborate study was of two occupational titles by three levels of experience—freshmen, seniors, and professionals before, during, and after training. The earlier study by Banducci (1968) contained a Range of Experience Scale that was unrelated to the accuracy of a student's occupational stereotypes when the effects of social status and academic potential were held constant.

In other studies, Holland (1963–64) has shown that students perceive occupational titles representing the types in stereotypical ways and that students rate the typical person in their future occupation in accordance with the formulations for the types (Holland, 1964). In an elegant study, Hollander and Parker (1969) had 54 high school students describe six occupations (one per type) using the Adjective Check List (Gough and Heilbrun, 1965). A single-factor analysis of variance with repeated measures was used to determine the validity of the student descriptions. Every ACL need scale (15) was significant across the six occupations, and student stereotypes were generally consistent with the formulations for the types.

Related work (Shinar, 1975) has shown that sexual stereotypes of occupations are pervasive and similar for females and males rating occupations according to their feminine or masculine qualities. These findings hold for female and male college students using vague instructions, estimated proportion of men and women employed in an occupation, or the sex-related attributes linked with an occupation. Likewise, the sexual stereotyping of occupations and activities has been observed in young children (Schlossberg and Goodman, 1972), adolescents (Cook and Alexander, 1980), and workers (Nolan and Bakke, 1949).

Other surveys (Braunstein, Haines, Leidy, and Starry, 1970) demonstrate that high school students (N = 4000) have stereotyped ideas about organizations—large corporations, federal government, college, small business, or nonprofit service agency—as well as about different careers—business executive, lawyer, college professor, research scientist, or counseling psychologist. For instance, the paired comparison technique revealed that large corporations are preferred for salary and advancement, but small business is preferred for "lasting friendship." These and other findings indicate how young and old probably use a complex system of occupational, sexual, and organizational stereotypes (generalizations) in vocational decision making. And the experiments by Jackson, Peacock, and Smith (1980) on impressions of personality in the employment interview suggest that personnel workers and lay persons share and use a common network of ideas about occupations and personal characteristics. In short, the system of stereotypes is extensive and complex, and it is not limited to inexperienced and untrained young people.

Two other lines of research imply that different personality types perceive and process information differently. Bodden and his colleagues have used several modifications of Kelly's Repertory Grid Technique to assess the complexity-simplicity dimension. Briefly, subjects rate occupations in terms of a standard set of characteristics such as much or little education, high or low income, influences or doesn't influence people, and so on. People with high levels of complexity rate different occupations differently, whereas people with low levels of complexity make fewer distinctions among occupations.

In successive articles, Bodden and Klein (1973) and others found that cognitive complexity was positively associated with congruency of aspiration and potential work environment. Winer, Haase, Glenn, Cesari, and Bodden (1979) reported that three VPI scales (S, E, and A) were weakly correlated with cognitive complexity. And of special interest, Winer, Warren, Dailey, and Hiesberger (1980) reported that cognitive simplicity characterizes the perceptions of occupations associated with one's personality type (assessed by major field) and that the perceptions of occupations in other categories are more complex. These investigators suggest "that the more complex individual is more able than the simple individual to make a congruent decision because he or she can think of logical reasons to reject many different occupations as disliked or dissimilar to oneself." This interpretation appears to be another definition of identity, or perhaps it is a negative definition of identity—"I can tell you what I have rejected in considerable detail, and by implication, my present option or type lacks these characteristics."

Other investigators (Crutchfield, Woodworth, and Albrecht, 1958; Osipow, 1969) have shown that vocational interests (SVIB and VPI scales) are correlated with objective perceptual tests, associative flexibility, word-sorting, extreme response sets, and closure flexibility. Most of these early studies failed to attract the interest of researchers or simply failed to produce positive and consistent results. Witkin's (1978) work on field independence-dependence is an exception. Field independent college students are attracted to the natural sciences and mathematics—fields that call for cognitive restructuring skills—whereas field dependent students find fields like elementary school teaching and social work more congenial. In a direct assessment of the relations between field independence-dependence and the types, Cleveland (1979) found that selected types (assessed by the VPI) and field independence-dependence (assessed by the Group Embedded Figures test) were correlated in the expected directions.

Harren and Biscardi (1980) explored the relation of cognitive style (Conceptual Level, CL; Decision-Making Styles, DMS) and sex-role attitudes to type (choice of major field and occupation) for a large sample of college students. Selected sex-role attitudes and cognitive styles predicted major field but the results often differed by sex. Other investigators (Chase, 1980) have also reported that Conceptual Level is related to types and in about the same way. Realistics are usually at the lowest level of cognitive development and Socials are usually at the highest level.

To summarize, there is some consistent evidence that different types perceive and think about occupations and the world in different terms. The strongest and clearest generalization is that occupational perceptions are stable over time, have validity, and to a lesser degree are selectively perceived according to social status, intelligence, and degree of involvement in the occupation in question. Equally important, occupations seen as representing particular types are seen in ways that appear consistent with characteristics attributed to the types. The evidence for the relation of cognitive styles to types is weak and often inconsistent.

Kind of training or work.   Predictions of what kind of training or work a person will select or remain in when his or her type is assessed by the VPI, SDS, SVIB, SCII, or similar inventories have always been statistically significant and usually moderately efficient. Predictions from VPI scales (high-point codes) have ranged from 21 to 64 percent correct identification, depending on the type and occupational category in question and the time interval for the prediction—one to seven years (O'Neil, Magoon, and Tracey, 1978; O'Neil and Magoon, 1977; Touchton and Magoon, 1977; Gottfredson and Holland, 1975b; Power, 1981; McGowan, 1982; Holland, 1968; Wiggins and Weslander, 1977).

Other investigators have used discriminant analysis, analysis of variance, and other statistical techniques to estimate how efficiently a person's field of training can be predicted from the SDS, the SCII Theme Scales, or sketches of the types. These studies usually indicate that college students in different fields and in some specialties within fields have codes, interest profiles, or other characteristics that are consistent with the formulations for the types (Abe and Holland, 1965a, 1965b; Scott and Sedlacek, 1975; Holland, 1966a, 1968; Brue, 1969; Wall, 1969; Williams, 1972; Osipow, Ashby and Wall, 1966; Wall, Osipow, and Ashby, 1967; Utz and Hartman, 1978). Although these investigations have usually yielded statistically significant results, the efficiency or magnitude of these discriminations varies greatly from chance to 85 percent correct classification. This great range of results appears partly a function of the educational field selected for study. For example, discriminating engineering students from social workers is much easier than discriminating among students in different engineering specialties.

A large group of relatively simple studies indicates that employed and retired workers have interest codes or profiles that are usually, but not always, in accord with theoretical predictions for particular occupations. Walsh and his students (Walsh, Horton, and Gaffey, 1977; Fishburne and Walsh, 1976; Benninger and Walsh, 1980; Matthews and Walsh, 1978; Ward and Walsh, 1981; Gaffey and Walsh, 1974; Spokane and Walsh, 1978) have assessed small samples of employed workers (females and males, blacks and whites at different levels of education) with the VPI, SDS, or both and found that the majority of high-point codes obtained by these inventories are consistent with theoretical predictions. Discrepancies between actual and expected codes and differences between females and males and blacks and whites appear ambiguous—it is not possible to clearly attribute these anomalies to sampling, reality, or theoretical failure. The VPI (Holland, 1977) and SCII (Campbell and Hansen, 1981) manuals also provide extensive data for the codes of employed workers. Other investigators (Weil, Schleiter, and Tarlov, 1981) have demonstrated that a short form of the VPI (42 items) distinguished residents in internal medicine who wanted to become generalists from those interested in a subspecialty, and residents who preferred clinical practice to academic medicine. Future generalists were more interested in social occupations; whereas future subspecialists were more interested in investigative and artistic careers. This national study and a closely related one (Weil and Schleiter, 1981) entail comprehensive and elaborate analyses of life histories and employment preferences that also appear consistent with the VPI data.

Warren, Winer, and Dailey (1981) had 65 females and males, aged 50 to 88, complete the VPI and respond to a work history questionnaire. In general, the one-letter codes of a person's first, longest, and last job are congruent with the VPI taken at a later time (between age 50 to 88). Or, most participants pursued careers that are consistent with the theory. Wiggins (1982) has performed a similar investigation of retired teachers.

He discovered a strong correspondence between three-letter VPI codes and the former occupation of 102 retired secondary teachers for five occupational groups.

Another line of research has demonstrated that predictions of the kind or direction of vocational choice or actual work can be increased dramatically by using the codes of a person's vocational aspiration *and* the high-point code of the VPI, SDS, or SVIB. This kind of investigation was stimulated by earlier studies that discovered that the category of a person's vocational aspiration was as efficient as the high-point code of an interest inventory or a similar comparison using a discriminant function analysis (Holland and Lutz, 1968; Dolliver, 1969; Whitney, 1969). In these and other longitudinal studies, researchers (Bartling and Hood, 1981; Borgen and Seling, 1978; Touchton and Magoon, 1977) have learned that combinations of vocational aspiration and interest inventory scales yielded predictions as high as 85 percent correct identification (Holland and Gottfredson, 1975). The range of correct identification was from 60 to 85 percent for time intervals of one to eleven years for the VPI, SDS, or SVIB. In all studies, predictions are substantially higher when expressed choice and interest inventory share the same category or are in agreement. Other work (Holland, Gottfredson, and Nafziger, 1975) implies that congruency of aspiration and interests is an alternative measure of identity and may be a useful predictor of career stability.

Once a person is employed, the current occupation usually becomes a more efficient predictor of subsequent occupations than do any other variables (Gottfredson and Becker, 1981). The application of the classification to work histories demonstrates that careers have substantial continuity or that the *direction* (kind of work engaged in) of the average career is predictable both from earlier aspirations or earlier employment. The data for this interpretation are summarized later in Chapter 6.

Finally, a small group of studies implies that a person's or a group's working style—especially the values, goals, and activities preferred—are influenced by the types they resemble. Smart and his colleagues have demonstrated in several large-scale assessments of college faculty that the goals of six groups of academic departments were often predictable from the types they resemble (Smart and McLaughlin, 1974), that faculty effort (instruction, research, public service, institutional-professional activity) varied significantly according to type (Hesseldenz, 1976), that chairpersons of academic departments devote different amounts of time to selected dimensions of their job and that these differences are usually in accord with the directional hypotheses of this theory (Morstain and Smart, 1976).

Level of training and work.   The first formulation for the level of occupational choice or achievement (Holland, 1959) was that occupational level equals intelligence plus self-evaluation. This formulation has been used by several investigators, and in every instance it has led to positive and often efficient results. Stockin (1964), Hughes (1972), Schutz and Blocher (1961), Holland (1962), and Fortner (1970) have substituted different measures in the formula and employed different statistical analyses.

To simplify the theory, the formula for the level of occupational choice was reformulated in terms of personality patterns (Holland, 1966b). In that formulation, the more a person resembles Enterprising and Social types, the more likely he or she is to have higher aspirations, to achieve more, and to be occupationally more mobile. The next formulation (Holland, 1973, p. 25) is more explicit: The closer a person's resemblance is to the personality pattern ESAICR, the greater is his or her expected vocational aspiration and eventual achievement.

The first test of the 1973 formulation produced substantial results. The initial *occupational* code for a national, representative sample of men was used to predict their occupational status five and ten years later (Holland, Sorensen, Clark, Nafziger, and Blum, 1973). Occupational status was defined as job prestige. The rank-order correlation between the expected and observed level of occupational prestige was .52 and .61 for five- and ten-year intervals.

Two other tests of the 1973 formulation produced clear and significant results. Wiggins and Weslander (1979) in a study of 320 high school counselors found that counselors given high ratings by their supervisors had a mean code of Social-Artistic-Investigative for the VPI, whereas counselors rated as ineffective had a Realistic-Conventional-Enterprising code. Or, resemblance to the counselor code in the occupational classification (SAI or SAE) was positively associated with supervisory ratings. Multiple regression analyses indicated that the Social (+), Realistic (−), and Enterprising (+) scales were more salient than experience or any other variable in the prediction of job performance. A similar study (Weslander and Wiggins, 1982) of 104 social studies teachers also produced clear and substantial results. In this instance, the Enterprising (+), Social (+), and the Conventional (−) scales (VPI) were among the five most influential variables in the regression formula.

The prediction of academic achievement has resulted in negative, weak, or ambiguous findings. These results are difficult to evaluate. Some studies (Aderinto, 1974) may have failed because the investigator used everything but the most relevant hypothesis—the rank order of a person's interest profile, because the investigator was unable to use the most desirable variables (Lee, 1970), or because the 1973 formulation is not useful.

The present formulation for occupational achievement incorporates the 1973 formulation (the closer the resemblance is to the profile of ESAICR, the higher the level of occupational attainment is) plus level of educational attainment or intelligence. No tests of this more comprehensive formulation have been made, although there is considerable evidence that the individual variables have moderate relations to occupational achievement.

Avocational endeavors and preferences. The general hypothesis that a person's type or personality pattern will determine a person's choice of nonvocational activity or recreation has received some explicit support.

Taylor, Kelso, Cox, Alloway, and Matthews (1979) developed a Leisure Checklist (LC), consisting of 36 items keyed to Holland's six occupational categories, and administered the LC, an Australian form of the VPI, and some questionnaire items to 907 high school students. The results are characterized by a "consistent but weak association between adolescents' use of their leisure and (a) the kind of school subjects which most interest them, (b) their inventoried preferences among a wide range of occupations, and (c) their expressed vocational preferences."

In a related study, Melamed (1976) found that the leisure activities of adult workers—two occupations for each Holland category—had a high degree of similarity between group personality patterns on the VPI and group leisure patterns. Later Melamed and Meir (1981) performed a closely related study of the effect of interest-job congruity and avocational activity. Taken together, both studies imply that "people tend to select leisure activities congruent with their personality pattern, that people in congruent occupations saw their preferred activities as an extension of the kind of activities they engaged in at work, and that people in incongruent occupations compensate for this situation by selecting compensatory leisure activities." Their integration of the present theory and recreational theory provides some helpful clarification of the interaction of person, job, and recreation.

Perhaps the most impressive study is a longitudinal investigation of vocational and avocational interests. Varca and Schaffer (1982) administered the SVIB and a questionnaire about avocational activities to 1,944 college freshmen. Nine years later, 376 males and 338 females responded to a similar questionnaire. No significant differences were observed between respondents and nonrespondents. The SVIB data were used to assign students to types. The adolescent and postcollege data were analyzed separately using a 6 (Holland type) × 2 (sex) MANOVA followed by univariate F tests. Both MANOVAs were significant (P < .001). The authors' hypotheses about the relation of type to avocational activities were supported for five of six types in adolescence and for six of six types in young adulthood. They also indicate that the results support the notion that individuals self-select a variety of situations. This work provides, then, more evidence that types are sometimes active, not passive, recipients of environmental events.

Typological Definitions

The use of different interest inventories and techniques to define types and personality patterns has produced similar, but not identical, positive research outcomes. The use of multiple assessment devices has served to clarify the meaning of the types because more multi-method and multi-trait correlational matrices have become available, and to demonstrate that the formulations for the types are not limited to the special characteristics of the VPI—the first and most researched inventory for the typological definitions.

Interest inventories. The use of the VPI to define types and personality patterns has extended the meaning of the VPI scales, and by inference the meaning of the types, to many unanticipated variables and personal characteristics. Consequently, the use of the VPI for typing persons is supported by an extensive base of validity evidence as the following paragraphs show.

Several investigators have correlated the VPI and the SVIB scales using simple or canonical correlations or both. For example, Haase (1971) correlated six VPI scales and 47 scales of the SVIB and found six canonical correlations for a sample of 176 male college students that ranged from .66 to .86. Haase concludes that the VPI and the SVIB measure similar dimensions. Other researchers (Lee, 1970; Cockriel, 1972) have correlated the VPI and Strong, scale by scale, and obtained positive evidence that these inventories cover similar ground and do so almost precisely according to expectation. And Rezler (1967) found that the VPI and the Kuder (1960) intercorrelate according to expectations.

Campbell (1971) and Campbell and Holland (1972) developed an alternate male form of the VPI by selecting Strong items in accordance with the definitions of the types. These six a priori scales of equal length were then used to rescore the occupational samples in the Strong archives. The classification of 76 occupations according to the mean scores of employed adults on this alternate form of the VPI and according to the actual mean VPI scores of aspirants to the same occupations (Holland, Whitney, Cole, and Richards, 1969) resulted in 84 percent agreement among the six main categories. This outcome is clear evidence that aspirants to occupations closely resemble incumbents, that the definitions of the types are not dependent upon the idiosyncrasies of the VPI, and that the Strong data strengthen the formulations for the types and their associated classification.

Hansen and Johansson (1972) developed an alternate form of the VPI for scoring the women's Strong blank. Their scale-construction method parallels the method used by Campbell and Holland (1972). The application of the six typological scales to 92 criterion samples of employed women (median sample size, 200) arranges occupations "in a common sense and meaningful sequence over a range of about two standard deviations."

Other indirect tests of the definition of types have been made by several researchers. Lee (1970) classified 432 male college freshmen according to the high-point code of their VPI profile and then treated these six subsamples as separate populations. For each sample, Lee used canonical correlations and a multiple linear regression to predict grades and achievement scores from the SVIB and the VPI scores. The outcomes suggested that appropriate Strong or VPI scores (physicist for Investigative, accountant for Conventional, and so on) only occasionally predict according to theoretical expectations. The results of this elaborate study are, however, especially difficult to interpret. At best, they appear to give some weak support to the definition of types in VPI terms, for Lee reports more negative than positive results.

In a similar study using the same sample, Lee and Hedahl (1973) obtained significant and substantial results. When students were categorized according to their VPI high-point code and compared on the Basic Interest (BI) scales of the SVIB, the BI scales discriminated among the types with moderate efficiency: "Twenty-one of the 22 F tests and 19 of the Scheffe multiple comparisons among the means were significant." In particular, BI scales usually peaked according to the formulations for the types; for instance, Enterprising students had the highest mean on public speaking.

Recent research indicates that the VPI has moderate and predictable relations with the Milwaukee Academic Interest Inventory (Rosen and Baggaley, 1982). And Lowman and Shurman (1982) have shown that a short form of the VPI (six scales of five items each), administered to 2,621 federal employees from five organizations, had psychometric characteristics that resembled the 14 item scales of the full VPI. Factor analyses of the items yielded six factors. Only two items were misplaced. Intercorrelations resembled the hexagonal model with two exceptions. Coefficient alphas ranged from .65 to .84 for the total sample. The three-letter codes for 23 occupational groups closely resembled the codes for comparable occupations in the Occupations Finder of the SDS (Holland, 1979).

Gottfredson, Holland, and Holland (1978) developed the seventh revision of the VPI to improve the psychometric properties of the scales, to bring all occupational titles into accord with the appropriate category in the Holland classification, and to reduce sex differences without reducing validity. Despite the changes between the sixth and seventh revisions, little improvement in psychometric properties was obtained. The VPI may be close to the limit of what can be accomplished with 14-item scales.

The evidence for the reliability, validity, and effects of the SDS on the test taker is summarized in the manual (Holland, 1979) and in the articles cited earlier. The predictive study by Gottfredson and Holland (1975b) is of special importance because it demonstrates with large samples (894 and 989 college males and females) that each section—competencies, activities, self-ratings, occupations, and vocational aspirations—has predictive validity. These findings support the hypotheses about the salient characteristics of the types and indicate that divergent kinds of content can be used to assess the types.

The SCII manual (Campbell and Hansen, 1981) summarizes the

evidence about the six General Occupational Theme scales developed to assess the types. This positive evidence is another sign that the formulations for the types can be assessed in different ways.

Qualitative indices. The testing of hypotheses about the types from qualitative data—choice of field of study, employment status, expressed choice of occupation—categorized according to type has usually been more efficient than predictions from interest inventories. For example, the efficiency of the VPI rarely exceeds 45 percent—a gain of about 28 to 29 percent over chance. Over eight to twelve months, Holland (1968) found that a student's initial choice of occupation, categorized according to type, was about twice as efficient or about 63 to 86 percent for the different types. Elton and Rose (1970) studied the vocational migrations of university students over a four-year interval and obtained similar results. For a sample of 530 men, the percentage of hits per type or category ranges from 49 to 87 percent for predictions made from the category of a student's freshman choice. For the same sample, the percentage of hits per type or category ranges from only nine to 41 percent for the ACT Admission Tests and the Omnibus Personality Inventory organized by a stepwise multiple discriminant analysis. Taylor and Kelso (1973) and others have obtained similar results in comparisons of the predictive efficiency of the VPI versus expressed vocational choice.

These findings and the literature reviewed earlier strongly suggest that a person's intentions, current training, or occupational status are powerful indices of one's type. McLaughlin and Tiedeman (1974) and L. Gottfredson and Becker (1981) demonstrate that the predictive value of vocational aspirations increases with age. Predictions at older ages are more efficient than predictions at younger ages. In addition, predictions from vocational aspirations at any age fade as the time interval increases. At the same time it is important to reiterate that the use of expressed choice in tandem with an interest inventory results in substantial gains in predictive efficiency. The use of current occupation and an interest inventory for prediction has not been tested.

Race, sex, and social class. The application of the hypotheses about types to special groups has usually resulted in positive evidence. The results for females and males, blacks and whites, rich and poor are characterized by similarity of support for the hypotheses about types. This evidence needs to be distinguished from the differences in average scores and in the distributions of interest scores, types, aspirations or occupations in these and other populations. Those data and the associated controversies about inventory biases are discussed in the SDS Manual (Holland, 1979, pp. 51–55) and in a related paper (Holland, in press).

A few studies are of special value. Salomone and Slaney (1978) tested selected hypotheses about person-job congruence and the relation between self-descriptions and type in a sample of 470 male and 447 female *nonprofessional* workers (GED levels 1–4). For both female and male workers, interests (high-point code of the VPI) were moderately related to current occupation (categorized in the Holland classification) and self-descriptions were moderately related to the description for a person's type. The studies of black and white workers in high and low level jobs by Walsh and his colleagues (reviewed earlier) also suggest that the typing process by the VPI or SDS has as much validity for blacks and females as it does for whites and males. And, the application of the occupational classification scheme to the work histories of men and women in both lower and higher level jobs demonstrates that these work histories follow predictable patterns (Holland et al., 1973; Gottfredson, 1977).

Typological Structure

The hexagonal model has received relatively clear and positive support in a wide range of investigations using samples of elementary, secondary, and college students, and employed adults. These studies have also used a variety of configural and factor analytic techniques as well as a variety of assessment devices.

The hexagonal model was proposed by Holland, Whitney, Cole, and Richards (1969), and the first hexagonal arrangement of VPI scores was supported by a statistical analysis which located the six scales in a best-fitting plane. Cole and Cole (1970) published the mathematical formulation for obtaining the hexagonal configuration, and Cole, Whitney, and Holland (1971) demonstrated how the configural analysis could be used to locate occupations or groups, according to the hexagonal model. These initial analyses stimulated a series of related investigations.

Cole and Hanson (1971) found that the hexagonal model could be obtained from the correlational matrices of the SVIB, Kuder OIS, MVII, VPI, and the ACT VIP for large samples of males. When the same analyses were applied to large samples of females who had taken the same inventories (but not the MVII), Cole (1973) obtained configurations that were similar to those for males.

Edwards and Whitney (1972) applied the Cole and Cole (1970) configural analysis as well as factor analysis to correlational matrices obtained from the SDS (358 and 360 college males and females). The configural analyses approximated a hexagonal model for both males and females. Edwards and Whitney (1972) also performed several factor analyses—separate analyses for each of the four domains (activities, competencies, occupations, and self-ratings) and for the total 30 × 30 matrices. They usually found that the same main factors existed within each domain and that the patterns of factor loadings were similar from one domain to the next. Taken together, the multiple factor analyses imply that the personality types can be assessed in one or more of four domains and the first definitions of the type based on the VPI scales probably can be interchanged with definitions based on other domains with only minor errors. The clear patterns of convergent and discriminant validity in the original correlational matrices for men and women reinforce the same conclusion (see Edwards and Whitney, 1972, Table 1, p. 4). In a related study, Richards (1968) performed diagonal factor analyses to determine the degree to which each VPI scale is independent of what all the scales have in common. The results of separate analyses for large samples (3,771 men and 3,492 women) clearly demonstrated that each scale does measure something different. There are at least six kinds of people; there may be more, but there are not fewer.

Rachman, Amernic, and Aranya (1981) obtained similar results for the hexagonal model and the structure of the SDS. These investigators factor analyzed the *items* in each section of the SDS and the total inventory for 1,206 professional accountants in Canada. The results for the factor analyses of each section and the entire inventory support the hexagonal model, and the confirmatory factor analysis supports the hypothesis that the SDS measures six factors. However, the Social and Enterprising types are combined into one factor, and the sixth factor describes the general factor of the occupations section. Only the factor analysis of the occupations section (VPI scales) of the SDS discriminated among all six types. When the severe homogeneity of the sample is considered, the results are very supportive.

Crabtree and Hales (1974) administered the VPI to 759 male and 672 female high school seniors and applied the Cole and Cole configural analysis. The hexagons found for females and males were very similar to those obtained by Cole and Hanson (1971).

Wakefield and Doughtie (1973) applied the principal factors method to the VPI for 373 undergraduates. They then measured the Euclidean distances between each pair of the six types in the common factor space. Of the 54 possible comparisons, 45 were consistent with the hexagonal model. These and other investigators then applied this more precise testing procedure to other groups. Bobele, Alston, Wakefield, and Schnitzen (1975) had students (N = 174) describe themselves using 78 adjectives taken from the formulations of the types (Holland, 1973) and applied the Wakefield-Doughtie (1973) analysis. In this instance, 35 of 54 comparisons were in the predicted direction. Bobele, Alston, Wakefield, and Doughtie (1976) applied the same techniques to data for the VPI and the adjective checklist used earlier and obtained similar results. Last, Cunningham, Alston, Doughtie, and Wakefield (1977) applied the Wakefield-Doughtie analysis to the VPI data for a sample of high school dropouts in a special learning center (N = 252). Of the 54 distance comparisons 40 were consistent with the hexagonal model. A comparison of the results with those for college students strongly suggests that VPI is measuring the same constructs in both samples. And Lunneborg and Lunneborg (1975) applied the Cole and Cole (1970) spatial configural analysis and the

Wakefield and Doughtie (1973) distance analysis to the VPI and the Vocational Interest Inventory (VII) (Lunneborg, 1975) for 235 college students. These results were unusually supportive of the hexagonal model: "All adjacent scale distances were smaller than all intermediate distances, and all but one of the intermediate scale distances was smaller than the opposite distances." The factor analysis also demonstrates that the RIASEC model is similar to the Roe model as defined by the VII.

Attempts to derive the hexagonal model from a multidimensional scaling (MDS) of similarity judgments have produced mixed results. Shubsachs and Davison (1979) found no support for the hexagonal arrangement, although they found that occupations (three per Holland category) in five of the six categories were perceived as similar. In contrast, Rounds, Davison, and Dawis (1979) found that the theme scales (SCII) for males and females produced the hexagonal model in the same RIASEC order as did the VPI scales when the TORSCA solution (Young and Torgerson, 1967) was derived from correlational matrices for these inventories. The Euclidean distance analysis (Wakefield and Doughtie, 1973) for the SCII and VPI scales was also supportive but more so for males than females: For the SCII, 50 of 54, and 38 of 54, comparisons were in the predicted direction for males and females; for the VPI, the same comparisons were 48 of 54 and 43 of 54. In these and many of the earlier studies, the data for females form a misshapen polygon, but the ordering of the scales is usually the same.

In contrast, Eberhardt and Muchinsky (1984) obtained strong support for the hexagonal model by predicting a person's actual VPI score or type from life history data and then by examining the patterning of hits and misses to see if these patterns approximated the hexagonal model. They used the data from an earlier study (Eberhardt and Muchinsky, 1982) summarized earlier on page 80. Three analyses support the hexagonal model: VPI scale scores were regressed on biographical factor scores to obtain criterion scores for each person; then the predicted scores were correlated with the actual VPI scores. In every instance the highest correlations in separate analyses for females and males occurred for the actual and predicted score for the same personality type. In addition, the majority of correlations followed the ordering indicated by the hexagonal model. Next, multiple discriminant analyses of the biographical factor scores were used to classify persons according to type (highest score on VPI). For females and males, the hit rates were 51.8 and 40.4 percent. The distribution of errors for males and females followed the hexagonal model. Most errors were one step removed from the correct classification and followed in descending order by fewer errors for two and then three steps removed. Finally, Eberhardt and Muchinsky provide another table (actual group membership based on high-point VPI code by predicted classification based on biographical factors). This simple analysis provides a more explicit picture of hit rates, base rates, and predictive anomalies.

For example, the Conventional type for both males and females was least predictable from the biographical data. The Investigative and Enterprising types were most predictable among males; whereas the Social and Investigative types were most predictable among females.

Four other studies are germane to the hexagonal arrangement and the perceptions of the types. Edwards, Nafziger, and Holland (1974) factor analyzed VPI data for large samples (200 to 3,771) of male and female elementary school students, high school students, college freshmen, and employed workers. These analyses suggest that people become more differentiated with age: More factors are needed to account for the occupational perceptions (VPI) of older persons. Or, the hexagons formed by the matrix of VPI scores become more clearly defined with age. Cureton's (1970) factor analysis of the Project Talent interest inventories for national representative samples of high school students provides similar but stronger evidence for the differentiation hypothesis.

Finally, there is some evidence that high school students (N = 794) can identify the three types they resemble most (SDS scores) with some validity (Wilkinson, 1977). In addition, Kelso and Taylor (1980) discovered that 26 psychologists (provided with descriptions of the types) could agree significantly on the 18 CPI dimensions that would be associated with each type. An empirical assessment of the agreement between judges and actual CPI versus VPI data for a sample of college students was substantial, although judges had difficulty separating the Realistic and Investigative types. These analyses suggest that although "types, like syndromes, are fuzzy concepts," they do imply that adolescents and professionals can interpret descriptions of the types in a distinct and consistent way.

ENVIRONMENTAL MODELS

The hypotheses about the environmental models have attracted only a few researchers, and their efforts have been devoted mostly to educational environments. The evidence about environments (direct and indirect) has been categorized as educational or occupational. At this time, the environmental studies have used the 1973 (Holland, 1973) formulations. The revisions proposed on pages 41–43 have not been tested for their usefulness. Also, because investigations are sometimes hard to classify, some environmental studies are reviewed here, and others are found in People in Environments (pp. 105–119).

Educational Environments

In an extensive series of reports, Astin and his colleagues have tested the general hypothesis that the environment of an undergraduate institution can be known by the distribution of student types at that institution. Using the environmental assessment technique (EAT) described on page

41, Astin and Holland (1961) learned that the student description of a college obtained from the College Characteristics Index could be predicted from the percentages of the six student types attending the college. Such descriptions were reliable accounts over one to six years; reliability coefficients ranged from .54 to .97, with a median of .93.

In another test of the environmental assessment technique, Astin (1963) polled students in 76 colleges (15 to 216 students per college) for their perceptions of the college environment and its effects: "Mean responses to 14 of the 18 college environment items were significantly related to EAT variables in the predicted direction," and "15 of the 21 perceived effects of college were significantly related to at least one EAT variable." For example, "all items pertaining to the importance of social groups and interpersonal skills . . . tended to be negatively related to" the Investigative dimension of the EAT. The relationships between student perceptions and the remaining five EAT variables were less successful.

In other studies, Astin has been only peripherally concerned with validating the Environmental Assessment Technique, but he has accumulated substantial evidence that the EAT variables, principally in his weighted version, assess large portions of influential variance in the environment and correlate with many of its objective features. Astin (1964) has found that the characteristics of entering freshmen can be predicted with moderate efficiency from the EAT variables for a college and that the EAT variables are correlated with freshmen variables in expected ways. In another study, Astin (1965a) reports significant relationships between the popularity and selectivity of an institution and its EAT variables.

In a more analytical article, Astin (1965b) assessed classroom environments to learn whether or not consistent differences would be found among the different fields of study. Student ratings of introductory courses in 19 fields were obtained from 4,109 students at 246 institutions. Differences among the 19 fields on all 35 ratings were statistically significant, and the differences among fields were often large. These and other results strengthen the main assumptions underlying the EAT: (1) The environments in different fields are different; (2) The characteristics of instructors representing a field may resemble our theoretical expectations. In Astin's (1965b) study, "instructors in accounting ranked above instructors in all other fields in frequency of taking attendance, in having their classes meet at a regularly scheduled time and place, in following the textbook closely in their lectures, and in being judged as 'speaking in a monotone' "; and (3) The college environment is probably affected by the distribution of students and faculty in different fields of study.

In his book *The College Environment* (1968), Astin also indicates that the EAT variables have substantial and plausible relationships to numerous subjective and objective aspects of college environments. His guide to colleges, *Who Goes Where to College?* (1965a), also summarizes many relationships between the EAT variables and a wide range of students and institutional characteristics (see Astin, 1965a, Appendix E, p. 115).

In another group of reports, Richards and others have used the EAT variables (Astin and Holland, 1961) to assess two-year colleges, four-year colleges, and graduate school environments. In addition to classifying students according to field, Richards has extended the EAT concepts by using the number of faculty and the number of curricula, classified according to field, as methods for assessing environments.

In their first study, Richards, Seligman, and Jones (1970) obtained EAT profiles for undergraduate and graduate environments. For each environment, individual EAT profiles were obtained for curriculum (number of course offerings in each of six areas), faculty (number of faculty in each area), and students (number of students graduating in each area). To obtain comparable scores for curriculum, faculty, and students, the authors converted scores for each kind of assessment to normalized standard scores. The results revealed that these three methods for assessing a college environment produce similar findings. The profiles obtained from the curriculum and faculty are also relatively stable for a 20-year interval. The correlations between the faculty EAT scores for a college and the scores obtained from Astin's institutional factors, from his weighted EAT variables for students, and from the scores of Pace's College and University Environment Scales (CUES) support the construct validity of the faculty EAT measures: "More than half of the correlations are significant, and each of the other environmental measures is significantly correlated with several faculty, curriculum, and degrees profile scores." Table 10, taken from Richards, Seligman, and Jones (1970), summarizes these relationships. Similar analyses of 87 graduate school catalogs (Richards & Seligman, 1969) revealed that EAT profiles for graduate degrees, faculty, and curricula were positively intercorrelated, and that the CUES scales were usually related to graduate school EAT measures in consistent ways.

These studies are valuable not only because they extend the EAT concepts to new populations or sources of data, but also because the new techniques do not confuse student characteristics with environmental measures. Since the original EAT measures used students only, interaction studies employing the EAT variables based on student types may have been studies of only student characteristics, rather than studies of student and environmental variables. In addition, these new scoring procedures "make it possible to study new problems such as the history of college environments or international differences in college environments." In a related study, Richards, Bulkeley, and Richards (1971) characterized the faculty and curricula of 94 two-year colleges. Again, they obtained positive results. EAT scores based on faculty, curriculum, and student degrees for the six areas corresponding to the types were positively intercorrelated; correlations ranged from .27 to .82, with a median *r* of .52. In addition, the three techniques for assessing the EAT variables

TABLE 10 Correlations between Faculty Profile Scores and Environmental Measures Developed by Others

ENVIRONMENTAL MEASURES	FACULTY PROFILE SCORES							
	Elevation	Scatter	Realistic	Intellectual	Social	Conventional	Enterprising	Artistic
College and University Environment Scales[a]								
Practicality	26**	-25**	04	-43**	25**	06	-26**	12
Community	-65**	-28**	-38**	-18	12	33**	-11	38**
Awareness	16	-09	-22*	-11	17	-11	19*	19*
Propriety	-42**	-12	-32**	-29**	29**	36**	-27**	25**
Scholarship	-12	05	13	39**	-27**	-13	09	-15
Astin (1956)[b]								
Intellectualism	00	19*	35**	59**	-52**	-28**	21*	-31**
Estheticism	-03	20*	01	06	-08	-09	05	10
Status	-13	00	-24**	13	-13	-25**	54**	24**
Pragmatism	44**	09	68**	40**	-40**	-36**	-01	-55**
Masculinity	08	04	23**	40**	-42**	-20*	35**	-29**
Selectivity	09	31**	25**	44**	-39**	-23**	22**	-23**
Size	94**	23**	33**	-06	02	-33**	03	-18*
Realistic orientation	46**	05	72**	35**	-34**	-33**	-16*	-53**
Intellectual orientation	-24**	02	31**	57**	-48**	-18*	09	-28**
Social orientation	-08	-09	-48**	-59**	65**	31**	-27**	38**
Conventional orientation	31**	-17*	-08	-17*	05	-18*	36**	08
Enterprising orientation	-09	-09	-28**	-01	-04	-21*	53**	26**
Artistic orientation	-15	06	-57**	-39**	32**	20*	12	55**
Astin (1962)[c]								
Affluence	-10	17	24*	55**	-36**	-32**	24*	-22*
Size	88**	00	34**	-11	15	-26*	-16	-29**
Masculinity	27*	-24*	41**	30**	-31**	-27*	12	-35**
Homogeneity	-50**	28*	-07	22*	-30**	38**	-05	-06
Realistic	61**	13	66**	14	-14	-33**	-37**	-41**

[a]N = 106. *P < .05.
[b]N = 139. **P < .01.
[c]N = 78.

Source: Richards, J.M., Jr., Seligman, R., and Jones, P.W. Faculty and curriculum as measures of college environment. *Journal of Educational Psychology,* 1970, 61, 324–332. Copyright 1970 by the American Psychological Association, and reproduced by permission of the author.

correlated with environmental factor variables obtained in another study of two-year colleges (Richards, Rand, and Rand, 1966).

Richards (1971) has also characterized 124 Japanese colleges and universities by performing a factor analysis of their institutional characteristics and by classifying their faculty according to type. When the faculty scores representing the EAT variables are correlated with the factor analytic variables of institutional characteristics, the results are similar to those obtained in American institutions (Richards, Bulkeley, and Richards, 1971; Richards, Seligman, and Jones, 1970). Over half the correlations are statistically significant, and each environmental measure is correlated with several profile scores. Equally important, the correlations are, with few exceptions, consistent with the formulations for the environmental models.

Barclay (1967) developed a method for assessing the "teacher-press" or the teacher environment for eleven different high school curricula. Teachers nominated students who most and least conformed to their notions of ideal students. High- and low-rated students were then compared on 80 intellective, personality, motivational, and vocational variables. Using Holland's classification, Barclay found that the direction of environmental press in each curriculum was often predictable from Holland's formulations, but that there were many contradictions. For example, the students rated "high" by business education teachers were ESCs and the students rated "low" were SERs (as assessed by the VPI). Barclay's results also show that similar secondary and college curricula have similar VPI profiles or codes.

Hearn and Moos (1976) assigned college students in 42 living units to one of the types according to their expected or actual major field and assessed the social climates of each living unit with the University Residence Environmental Scale (URES). The correlations between the six environmental types (major field percentages of each environment) and the 10 ratings of the living group climate (URES) were generally in accord with theoretical expectations. For example, Investigative majors emphasized independence, student influence, and innovation and de-emphasized traditional social orientation, competition, academic achievement, order, and organization. On the other hand, living groups with a high proportion of Conventional majors emphasized traditional social orientation, competition, order, and organization and de-emphasized involvements, support, student influence, and innovation. At the same time, this correlational analysis produced some contradictory findings. For example, Investigative majors were high in involvement and low in academic achievement. In short, this field study gives moderate support to the environmental models.

In a similar study, Hearn and Moos (1978) assigned 207 high school classes in 19 high schools to Holland types and assessed class climates with the Classroom Environment Scales (CES). The analyses of variance indicated that class types and eight of nine CES subscales were significantly related. For the most part the results support the characteristics attributed to the environmental models. For example, Investigative classes such as mathematics and science emphasized task orientation and teacher control but de-emphasized involvement, affiliation, and innovation. At the same time, some findings were not supportive. In addition, a configural analysis yielded only weak support for the hexagonal model.

Occupational Environments

The construct validity of the EAT measures has been strengthened by showing that a great range of objective, environmental, and personal characteristics associated with individual occupations have strong and consistent relationships with groups of occupations when they are organized according to the model environments. The factor analytic investigations of the Dictionary of Occupational Titles and standardized job analyses (McCormick, Jeanneret, and Mecham, 1969; McCormick, Jeanneret, and Mecham, 1972) made it possible to learn how the EAT variables are related to both personal and environmental measures developed to characterize the full range of occupational environments.

This task was accomplished by categorizing each of 832 occupations as one of six kinds. Then simple analyses of variance tests were performed for each of 32 occupational factors (McCormick et al., 1972). The results provide clear evidence that the Holland environmental categories, developed almost entirely from psychological data, also encompass more objective, situational data about jobs (see Table 11).

More recently, Gottfredson, Holland, and Ogawa (1982) demonstrated that the ratings of occupational demands or requirements for 12,099 occupations are usually consistent with the characteristics of the six environmental models. (See Tables 11–14 in the Gottfredson et al. [1982] dictionary.) L. Gottfredson's (1980) investigation of the construct validity of the Holland occupational classification also demonstrated that the occupational categories "have considerable validity for describing work activities, general training requirements and rewards, particularly when it is supplemented by a measure of occupational prestige level." She also demonstrated that demands *within* Holland categories differ by level. For instance, low level social jobs require less complex coping with people than do high level social jobs. This study provides the strongest evidence for the value of adding prestige or educational level (GED) to all analyses of the classification and environmental models.

In a related study, Prediger (1982), using a small sample of DOT ratings (data, people, things) to create special scales, has demonstrated in a complex series of factor and planar analyses that a person's interests (high-point or three-letter code) have a strong correlation with the tasks which characterize a person's occupation. In short, the items in interest inventories (preferred activities, ratings of abilities, acquired competencies) are clearly correlated with the demands of an occupation. In theo-

TABLE 11 Relation of Holland Classification (Occupational Categories) to the Purdue Factored Dimension Scores for 832 Occupations

PURDUE OCCUPATIONAL DIMENSION		HOLLAND CLASSIFICATION					
		Real	Inv	Soc	Conv	Ent	F
JD 19. Staff-	X	−.06	.81	.40	.09	−.56	22.20
related activities	SD	.68	1.45	1.01	.88	1.36	
JE 22. Unpleasant hazardous	X	.38	−.48	−.32	−.53	−.31	50.78
physical environment	SD	1.09	.36	.44	−.42	.55	
*JE 23. Personally demanding	X	.42	−.51	−1.20	.26	−1.17	148.58
situations (-social)	SD	.54	.96	1.47	.61	1.04	
JF 26. Unstructured vs. structured	X	−.20	.62	.63	−.31	.75	44.83
work	SD	.96	.73	.76	.87	.64	
JF 25. Attentive-discriminating	X	.06	.66	−.19	−.32	.27	11.38
work demands	SD	1.09	1.02	.97	.94	.89	
*JF 24. Businesslike work	X	.55	−.60	−.16	−.63	−1.01	168.62
situations (realistic)	SD	.64	.71	.94	.72	.72	
JF 27. Variable vs. regular	X	.18	−.43	−.12	−.37	.05	13.31
work schedule	SD	1.12	.62	.81	.66	.96	
JO 1. Decision-communication-	X	−.40	.87	.76	−.30	1.45	198.01
social responsibilities	SD	.64	.60	.92	.60	.82	
*JO 2. Skilled activities	X	.30	.85	−.42	−.47	−.39	45.14
(investigative)	SD	1.07	.80	.70	.47	.59	
JO 3. Physical activities and	X	−.24	.45	−.10	.44	.19	22.97
related environment conditions	SD	1.08	.60	.69	.60	.67	
JO 5. Information-processing	X	.40	−.58	−.09	−.86	.08	85.93
activities	SD	.84	.80	.77	.88	.64	
JO 4. Equipment-vehicle	X	.16	−.14	−.07	−.33	−.06	10.05
operation	SD	1.12	.73	.59	.51	.68	
JA 2. Perceptual interpre-	X	.10	.52	.11	−.24	−.30	9.71
tation	SD	1.03	1.15	1.08	.72	.67	
JB 8. Decision-making	X	−.24	1.09	.26	−.33	1.20	91.51
	SD	.84	.64	.91	.72	.78	
JB 9. Information-processing	X	−.47	.85	.38	.78	.03	87.01
	SD	.79	1.04	1.05	.89	.82	
JC 10. Machine-process	X	.34	.05	−.37	−.36	−.51	36.36
control	SD	1.04	.89	.58	.67	.65	
JC 14. Handling-manipulating	X	.19	−.49	−.01	.08	−.79	25.29
activities	SD	1.02	1.03	.94	.75	.79	
JC 12. Control-equipment	X	−.15	.26	.36	.17	.03	7.35
operation	SD	1.27	.45	.52	.54	.59	
JC 16. Skilled-technical	X	.08	−1.26	−.29	.30	−.27	25.82
activities	SD	1.10	1.20	.88	.54	.65	
*JC 15. Use of finger device	X	.34	−.39	.15	−.87	.11	70.62
vs. physical work (-conv.)	SD	.83	.84	.65	1.10	.58	
JC 11. Manual control-	X	−.31	−.02	.43	.36	.35	29.23
coordinated activities	SD	1.14	.97	.57	.49	.46	
JC 13. General body	X	−.07	.12	−.22	.20	.10	4.14
activity	SD	1.13	.82	.99	.62	.63	
*JD 17. Communication of	X	−.41	.71	.76	−.30	1.55	219.98
decisions-judgments (ent.)	SD	.48	.65	.97	.66	1.05	
JD 18. Job-related informa-	X	−.36	.22	−.03	.59	.49	47.16
tion exchange	SD	.76	1.02	.95	.97	1.19	

TABLE 11 (cont'd)

PURDUE OCCUPATIONAL DIMENSION		HOLLAND CLASSIFICATION					
		Real	Inv	Soc	Conv	Ent	F
JD 21. Public-related	X	−.11	.28	−.05	.37	−.20	11.48
contact	SD	.86	.80	.88	.84	1.24	
JD 20. Supervisor-subordinate	X	−.16	−.14	.09	.22	.25	7.97
relationships	SD	.93	.77	.97	.93	1.13	
JA 3. Information from	X	−.50	.32	.75	.15	1.12	130.49
people	SD	.82	.66	.85	.65	.78	
JA 4. Visual input from	X	−.20	.26	.06	.36	.06	13.31
distal sources	SD	1.08	.55	.86	.66	.75	
JA 1. Visual input from	X	.31	.42	−.40	−.48	−.33	39.74
devices-materials	SD	1.04	.82	.68	.54	.67	
JA 5. Evaluation of information	X	−.01	.20	−.43	.31	−.17	11.19
from physical sources	SD	1.08	.80	.85	.41	1.01	
JA 6. Environmental awareness	X	.11	.37	−.33	−.15	−.04	6.26
	SD	1.04	1.28	.87	.76	1.08	
JA 7. Awareness of body	X	−.02	.08	−.25	.16	−.05	2.88
movement posture	SD	1.07	1.27	1.09	.64	.91	

*Purdue factors selected to create VPI profiles to add more occupations to Holland classification.

Note: For a complete account of the meaning of the Purdue Dimension scores, see Jeanneret and McCormick (1969) or McCormick, Jeanneret and Mecham (1972). The JO dimensions resulted from an overall components analysis of the Position Analysis Questionnaire, while dimensions labeled JA 1 through JF 27 resulted from separate analyses of each division in the PAQ. $F_{001} = 4.62$.

Source: Holland, J. L., Viernstein, M. C., Kuo, H., Karweit, N. L., and Blum, Z. D. A psychological classification of occupations. *Journal Supplement Abstract Service*, 1972, 2, 84.

retical terms, many of the characteristics attributed to particular environments in this theory are supported by these analyses, when interests and occupations are categorized as types and environmental models. In another group of factor and configural analyses, Prediger, using 27 sets of intercorrelations for the VPI, SDS, SCII, SVIB, and other inventories, has also demonstrated that the hexagonal model can be derived from "data/ideas" and "things/people" dimensions obtained from the DOT data. The hexagons derived from the DOT ratings are very similar to those from interest data. In short, Prediger has provided persuasive evidence that interest profiles and occupational environments have strong relations that are consistent with theoretical expectations—Realistic interests are related to the demands of Realistic occupations, Investigative interests are related to those of Investigative occupations, and so on.

Other attempts to find support for the hexagonal and environmental models in occupational data have produced a wide range of outcomes. Toenjes and Borgen (1974) applied discriminant function analysis to the data for the rated (supervisors) occupational reward characteristics of 148 occupations. Although the hexagonal shape was distorted, the occupational groups were arranged in the correct order (RIASEC). They also found "reward" differences among occupations when the 148 occupations were categorized into six environments (13 of 21 rewards were significant at .001 level). On the other hand, Rounds, Shubsachs, Dawis, and Lofquist (1978) found "only modest support for the environmental formulations" in analyses of the rewards and Position Analysis Questionnaire data for 181 occupations. Their attempts to derive the hexagon were not successful, although eight reward dimensions were significantly related to the six occupational groups in predictable orders.

The differences between the Toenjes and Borgen, and Rounds et al. studies may be due to different statistical methods and sampling. But Rounds et al. suggest that "occupational reinforcers and behavior requirements, as opposed to vocational interests, may describe different aspects of the occupational environment." On the other hand, L. Gottfredson's (1980) analysis of the same data led her to conclude that the classification "scheme predicts variance not only in work activities (on which Holland's theory focuses) but also in job requirements and rewards (about which the theory has as yet little to say)." "Rewards" refer to the occupational reinforcer data that both Rounds et al. and L. Gottfredson used.

Mount and Muchinsky (1978) have also obtained strong support for the correspondence between a worker's interests and occupational environment. When the SDS codes (high-point) for 362 workers were compared with the codes (one-letter) for current occupation, 76 percent of the workers were in occupational environments that matched their interests, abilities, and competencies.

Smart (1975) treated 15 sources of job satisfaction as reinforcers or predictors of the overall job satisfaction or department chairpersons classified as belonging to one of the six model environments. The regression analyses for a sample of 1,198 chairpersons in 32 universities suggested that the overall job satisfaction in different fields entails different combinations and weighting of the specific sources of satisfaction. However, the relation between specific facets of satisfaction and the environment in which a chairperson's field was categorized was only occasionally in a predictable direction. In a related article, Smart (1976) discovered that chairpersons (N = 935) in different occupational environments also devoted significantly different amounts of time to selected dimensions of their job.

PEOPLE IN THE ENVIRONMENTS

The theory has been applied to the person-environment interactions of high school and college students and to employed people. The results of studies before 1973 were initially disappointing, but some research since 1973 has been very positive—even exciting.

Aspirational and Career Studies

This section summarizes the outcomes of studies using high school and college students, and employed adults. The theme running through these investigations is a concern with the effect of person-environment interactions on a person's vocational aspiration or career, although most studies were also concerned with many other dependent variables.

High school students. Werner (1974) selected a sample of 527 boys and girls from a population of 1,445 students in seven occupational training centers. Students from six occupational areas were selected to represent each type: auto mechanics for Realistic, technical electronics for Investigative, practical nursing for Social, data processing for Conventional, distributive education for Enterprising, and commercial art for Artistic. An additional 67 students who had left these programs were available for analyses of attrition.

Students were assessed with the VPI, the Kuder, and questionnaires about occupational concerns and achievement. In this study, the special occupational training was treated as the environment. For example, auto mechanics training equaled a Realistic environment. A student who peaked on the Realistic scale of the VPI and who was training as an auto mechanic was in a congruent environment. Using this definition of congruence and the standard definitions of consistency and differentiation for a student's VPI profile, Werner obtained the following results:

1. Students in congruent environments had higher achievement scores than students in incongruent environments.
2. Congruence was related to satisfaction for boys but not for girls.
3. Congruence was related to remaining in a program.
4. Consistency and differentiation of a student's VPI profile yielded inconsistent and negative results.
5. Consistency, congruence, and differentiation were found to be additive for achievement but not for satisfaction.

In many ways, Werner's study reiterates many trends and problems found in the early studies—positive support for the general hypothesis about congruence of type and environment, but mixed results for most other hypotheses.

In a complex study, Cole (1975) found that for selected definitions of the environment, a student's satisfaction with high school environment correlated positively but weakly with school satisfaction. In addition, there was considerable evidence that three different measures of the school environment were strongly related: school reputation according to a school official, EAT measures, and student perceptions of the school. Consistency and differentiation measures produced negative results.

Perhaps the best single test of the congruency hypothesis was an experiment in which six types of high school students gave their reactions to six simulated work environments. Helms and Williams (1973) obtained a sample of 92 girls and 127 boys to represent each type (high-point code of SDS) at two levels of socioeconomic status by a stratified random sampling procedure from a pool of 2,933 students who had taken the SDS. The study sample was assigned at random to each of the six Job Experience Kits and asked to give their reactions to each simulated job by filling out a questionnaire. This standard form assessed a student's perception of the congruency of self and job or were the activities, competencies, interests, values, and personality traits implied by the simulation seen as compatible.

A two-factor, fixed-effects design with repeated measures over one dimension was used to test the hypothesis that different types would respond to different jobs in different ways. In addition, it was assumed that the degree of perceived congruency would be predictable from the hexagonal model. Both of these hypotheses were strongly supported for females and males. For example, both female and male Conventional types (SDS) found the Conventional Work Kit (Accountant) most compatible and the Artistic Kit (Designer) least compatible. Other work kits were arranged in intermediate degrees of congruency. In contrast, consistency and differentiation of student type produced only negative outcomes.

This experiment is of special value because students were put through a simulated random work history that would not be possible in real life; that is, despite some "floundering and trial" most people explore a limited range of occupations so that the potential degree of congruency or incongruency is reduced. Consequently, tests of the congruency hypothesis have a special cross to bear.

The findings of the Helms-Williams experiment resemble some of the findings in a large-scale evaluation of brief summer programs developed to introduce high school females and minorities to engineering. Richards, Williams, and Holland (1978) have reported that such programs of one to three weeks conducted by engineers on college campuses function like a typical job experience. The number of students planning to study engineering was increased—all participants (N = 1271) had expressed an interest in engineering—but the more potential a student had for engineering (assessed by an engineering potential scale composed of vocational aspirations and relevant competencies), the more likely a student was to plan on engineering. Conversely, students with less potential for engineering went away believing that engineering was not for them and that the experience was helpful.

College students.   Several investigators have studied the effect of congruence upon stability of vocational choice, satisfaction with college, achievement, personal adjustment, and other outcomes.

Holland (1968) used a sample of 2,347 college students at twenty-seven colleges and universities to test some hypotheses about stability of vocational choice and satisfaction with college. A student's initial choice of vocation was used to characterize her or him as a type, and the EAT was used to define the environment. Several analyses provided weak support for the congruence hypothesis—students tended to maintain their vocational choices when their college was dominated by students whose choices belonged to the same general class. Weak support was also obtained for the hypothesis that homogeneous environments are conducive to vocational stability. And conflicting findings were received for the hypothesis that students' satisfaction with college will be greater if their type is congruent with their college environment: The results were negative for men and positive for women. Finally, the average satisfaction score at a college was negatively correlated with the differentiation of the college environment: Students "are more likely to be satisfied in colleges characterized by their flat profiles—about equal percentages of personality types."

Posthuma and Navran (1970) tested the hypothesis that students whose interests were congruent with the faculty would get better grades than students with incongruent interests. The investigators administered the VPI to all available first year students (N = 110) and 88 percent of the faculty (N = 44) at a military college. A discriminant analysis indicated that the VPI could be used to discriminate student groups at four grade levels. Comparisons of faculty with students at each grade level were also significant, but the trends were not consistent with congruence. A comparison of the modal VPI profiles for faculty versus the modal profiles of students at four levels of academic achievement were generally as predicted, but not significant. Profiles for faculty and "top students" correlated (rank-order) .69; profiles for faculty and "failure students" correlated −.26.

Elton (1971) provided indirect evidence about the interaction of types and environments. Using small college student samples, Elton showed that students who left engineering underwent personality changes that made them different from students who remained in the engineering environment. In contrast to students remaining in engineering, "students transferring to arts and sciences become more realistic, nonjudgmental, intellectually liberal, and skeptical of orthodox religious beliefs." Comparisons of university students with students in two-year colleges implied similar expected environmental effects. For example, two-year college students showed the smallest change on the variable of scholarly orientation.

Privateer (1971) examined the effect of a college environment upon entering freshmen. Upon entry, Privateer assessed all freshmen (N = 600) with the VPI. Then an "established population" of administrative staff, randomly selected faculty, juniors, and seniors were administered the VPI and CUES. After an eight-month exposure to campus life, the freshmen were again administered the VPI along with a questionnaire and the CUES for the first time. A student's congruence with his or her environment (VPI versus EAT for the college) was not significantly different from fall to spring. Student profiles did not become more consistent, but the differentiation of student profiles did increase. These and other results were generally negative.

Although Astin (1965c) and Astin and Panos (1969) have been primarily concerned with estimating the effects of educational environments, their work also lends support to the present hypothesis about person-environment interactions because they use the Holland typology in some analyses to characterize students and college environments. In an early study of college influence, Astin (1965c) used 17 student (precollege) variables to control for student input, and found "some support for the hypothesis that the student's career choice comes to conform more and more to the . . . modal career choice in his college environment." In their major study involving 36,000 students at 246 institutions, Astin and Panos (1969) came to the same conclusion. Table 57 of their book gives a summary of the environmental characteristics that affect vocational choice. It shows that the EAT variables influence vocational choice, but that a host of other environmental variables are also potent influences and often more important.

Walsh and Lacey (1969, 1970), in separate studies of men (N = 151) and women (N = 157), examined how students change over four years of college by asking students to estimate how they have changed on rating scales of adjectives, traits, and abilities. The results suggest that students of a given type (defined by their field of study) become more like that type. Although their results hold only for three types for men and four types for women, the findings are consistent with the hypothesis that an environment dominated by a particular type reinforces the same type. In a similar study, Walsh, Vaudrin, and Hummel (1972) found that college seniors report more change consistent with their personality type than freshmen do. Another study (Walsh and Barrow, 1971) designed to test the personality differences between students who make congruent or incongruent choices of major field produced negative results. And Walsh and Russell (1969) found that students who had made a congruent choice of college major (student's high-point VPI code and choice of field belong to the same category) reported fewer personal adjustment problems than students who had made incongruent choices. This finding is consistent with the hypothesis that congruence encourages personal stability.

A related study by Walsh and Lewis (1972) reinforces some earlier findings and has a strong design. The investigators categorized a student's choice of field in college as congruent, incongruent, or undecided. Congruent students (37 males and 37 females) peaked on VPI scales that were congruent with their choice of field—for instance, high-point VPI code is "investigative" and choice of field is "physics." Incongruent students (37 males and 37 females) peaked on VPI scales that were incongruent with their choice—for example, "conventional" and "art." And undecided students had failed to make a choice. These three groups were administered the Omnibus Personality Inventory (Heist and Yonge, 1968) and then compared scale by scale using analysis of variance.

The statistically significant results imply that congruent males, as opposed to incongruent or undecided males, report "few attitudes associated with social alienation or emotional disturbance" (personal integration scale), "few feelings or symptoms of anxiety" (anxiety level scale), and many responses associated with making a good impression on the inventory (response-bias scale). These results appear consistent with the hypothesized effects of person-environment congruence—maintenance of personal stability and satisfaction—and they suggest that stability of vocational choice occurs through integration with others and subsequent reinforcement. These and other findings also imply that people with good judgment or who are psychologically healthy tend to make congruent choices. The results for women were sometimes statistically significant but often ambiguous. However, sex differences on single scales are usually in accord with past evidence and stereotypes about men and women.

Morrow (1971) used samples of college students (N = 323) majoring in mathematics or sociology to test the hypothesis that satisfaction with one's field depends upon the congruence of type and field. Morrow's results were mixed: Satisfaction with major was significantly related to personality type for mathematics students but not for sociology students.

Frantz and Walsh (1972) applied the theory to graduate student-institution interactions. These investigators tested the usefulness of different definitions of congruence, consistency, and differentiation, and the effects of these variables on satisfaction and achievement. Most findings were negative, ambiguous, or weak. The most important and clearest finding is that students who are congruent, consistent, and differentiated are more satisfied and achieve more than students who do not possess all these characteristics (see Frantz and Walsh, 1972, Table 4).

Nafziger, Holland, and Gottfredson (1975) discovered that congruency of student type (high-point code of SDS) and major field (categorized according to the Holland classification) was significantly related to satisfaction with that environment (students, professors, and activities in major fields), but congruency did not predict satisfaction with the total college environment. Likewise, the role of differentiation and consistency of personality type in interactions was not supported in this large-scale longitudinal study.

Most recently, Rose and Elton (1982) and Elton and Rose (1982, unpublished ms) have performed four-year longitudinal studies of the relation of congruence, differentiation, and consistency to interest (ACT VIP) and aptitude scores in men and women with stable and unstable vocational choices. Using large samples and canonical variate analysis in both investigations, they found some support for the importance of congruency in stable women but no support for the value of consistency and differentiation. In the case of males, no clear support was found for congruency, differentiation, or consistency.

It is not clear why this complex and elegant study produced so many negative outcomes, and why it contradicts many other tests of the congruency hypothesis. Rose and Elton (1982) suggest that these differences are due to "differences in methodology—time intervals, definitions of stability, instruments."

Three other studies imply that congruence of type and field of training is associated with persistence in a field or better academic adjustment. Spokane, Malett, and Vance (1978), using a sample of 324 male and 157 female liberal arts students who had taken the SCII, found that students whose SCII scores supported their expressed curricular choice (congruent) were more stable (fewer curricular changes), more differentiated, and more academically oriented than incongruent students over a five-semester period. The authors, however, indicate several methodological weaknesses—uneven sampling of types and ambiguities in the definition of congruence. In a study of current status, Spokane and Derby (1979) examined the congruence of major field choice and three-letter codes from the VPI for 129 undergraduates. Multivariate analysis of variance indicated that congruent females were more consistent (consistency of VPI code), reported higher levels of certainty, and perceived congruence. No differences between congruent and incongruent students were observed for satisfaction with choice, differentiation, ego strength, and other variables. In a similar study, Walsh, Spokane, and Mitchell (1976) explored the differences in academic adjustment between students who had made congruent, incongruent, and undecided college major choices. The congruent females and males tend to report more clearly defined educational and vocational goals, higher levels of aspiration, and greater satisfaction with their choice of college major than the undecided and incongruent groups.

Cartwright and Power (1982) examined the effect of a three-week teaching experience on the interests (SDS) of 125 education students. Students took the SDS one week before and one week after the teaching experience. The data were analyzed by a multivariate analysis of variance for repeated measures on the differentiation scores. The only significant outcome was an increase in the differentiation scores ($P < .001$), and this finding was, as predicted, due largely to an increase in social scores on the post-SDS administration. This study resembles the Taylor et al. (1979) longitudinal investigation in which the treatment was 11 months of high school, and the effect was a clear increase in differentiation. Together they imply the need to use real life experience or potent treatments to affect the differentiation of a person's interests.

Finally, Bruch and Krieshok (1981) have put the congruence hypothesis to a severe but successful test. Engineering freshmen in curricula that emphasized theoretical mathematics and science coursework were assumed to be in a congruent environment if their high-point VPI code was I. Students with a high-point VPI code of R or with a tied RI profile were assumed to be incongruent. The investigators tracked freshmen in three successive classes for two years. No differences in academic potential were observed for the two groups, but the I-types as opposed to R-types and tied RI's, persisted with significantly greater frequency in two of three classes and tended to get better grades.

Employed adults. The application of the interactive hypotheses to employed samples suggests that congruency of person and job leads to stability or continuity over long periods of time and to job satisfaction. In theoretical terms, continuity means moving between jobs that belong to the same occupational category. Continuity has also been elaborated to mean moving between jobs that belong to the same or a theoretically related category following the hexagon. Because most of the evidence for stability or continuity of aspirations or careers has been obtained in tests of the Holland classification, most of that research is contained in Chapter 6, "The Classification System." However, two outstanding examples of that work are summarized here, for they illustrate the phenomena that require explanation. These studies also have some explanatory value, but it is often ambiguous.

Gottfredson (1977) applied the Holland classification to a one in 1,000 sample of 21- to 70-year-old male and female workers in the 1970 census. He demonstrated that career stability in five-year intervals increases with age from 25 to 70 for both sexes. (See Table 12.)

Gottfredson performed similar analyses for only those people who changed occupations in the period 1965–70. These analyses also resulted in clear but weaker evidence for the categorical stability of careers of both sexes. In addition, Gottfredson performed an analysis of only those

TABLE 12   Agreement of 1965 and 1970 Occupational Category for Employed Civilians

AGE IN 1970	MEN			WOMEN		
	% same	K	N	% same	K	N
21–25	74.6	.37	1,915	72.3	.54	1,169
26–30	76.6	.57	3,547	79.4	.70	1,476
31–35	82.2	.70	3,760	83.2	.76	1,253
36–40	87.3	.79	3,883	85.5	.80	1,487
41–45	87.9	.80	4,271	86.8	.81	1,827
46–50	89.9	.82	4,165	89.1	.84	2,053
51–55	90.7	.83	3,664	89.2	.85	1,899
56–60	91.3	.84	3,162	90.3	.86	1,585
61–65	91.0	.83	1,937	90.0	.86	957
66–70	91.2	.84	781	90.9	.88	353

Note: The percentages of agreement and kappa's are derived from 6 × 6 tables in which a person's occupation in 1965 is compared with his or her occupation in 1970.

Source: Gottfredson, G. Career stability and redirection in adulthood. *Journal of Applied Psychology,* 1977, *62,* 436–445. Copyright 1977 by the American Psychological Association and reproduced by permission of the author.

workers who changed the general education development level of occupation. The results still demonstrated that about 50 percent of these workers remained in the same category (one of six) over a five-year interval.

Of special value, Gottfredson compared the career stability of workers at three levels of consistency (high, medium, and low) as defined by the two-letter code of a worker's job in 1965. These analyses were also successful. High levels of consistency were associated with a high degree of stability, medium levels with medium stability, and low levels of consistency with the lowest level of stability. These findings provide strong support for the hypothesis that the structure of an occupational environment, expressed in an occupational code, has merit and functions like consistency of an SDS profile (see Holland, 1968, and O'Neil, Magoon, and Tracey, 1978).

In a simple but dramatic study Lucy (1976) applied the classification to a person's major field at graduation and his or her high-point VPI code as an employed adult for a total sample of 884 female and male college graduates of a state university. The relation between field of training and VPI high-point code obtained ten to 35 years after graduation is substantial, ranging from 42.9 percent to 60.7 percent in the same category for 35- and 15-year intervals, respectively. This study illustrates that careers have marked continuity. Johansson and Campbell (1971) have summarized similar and more comprehensive data for the stability of vocational interests.

The studies of career changes have produced mixed results: Three suggest that incongruity of interests, personality, or abilities is associated with change in occupation or intention to change.

Wiener and Vaitenas (1977) studied only workers of the Enterprising type (management and sales occupations) who had intended to make a career change and compared this sample (N = 45) with a control sample (N = 66) of Enterprising types who had to show evidence that they intended to remain in the same occupation. Three personality inventories indicate that stayers and changers were significantly different. Changers were lower on ascendance, dominance, responsibility, endurance, and order. The results suggest that change is due in part to incongruity.

In a similar study, Vaitenas and Wiener (1977) compared young and old career changers with young and old controls (stable intentions) using the SCII and occupational codes and other measures. Career changers, both young and old, were lower on congruity of interests and occupation, and consistency of interests, and higher on emotional problems and fear of failure than controls.

The positive and relatively clear results in these investigations probably are the outcome of controlling for type, defining change in an explicit manner, and controlling for work experience. Other small-scale studies (Thomas and Robbins, 1979; Robbins, Thomas, Harvey, and Kandefer, 1978), which suggest that career change is not due to incongruity, may have failed because they did not control for type, confounded voluntary and involuntary change, and so on.

Several studies suggest that congruity is positively associated with job satisfaction. Mount and Muchinsky (1978a) administered the SDS and the Job Descriptive Index (Smith et al., 1969), which measures job satisfaction in five areas, to 362 workers. Congruence was defined as a person's high-point SDS code matching the first letter code of his or her current occupation. All other pairings of SDS and occupational code were defined as incongruent. The six dependent variables (job satisfaction scales) were analyzed by separate two-way analyses of variance. The results indicate that congruence of type and work environment is related to total job satisfaction ($P < .01$). Other analyses of percentage of variance accounted for by congruence are consistent with the magnitude of the findings in many other studies (correlations ranging from .25 to .35). In addition, the effects of congruence vary from one environment to the next. In another analysis of the same data, Mount and Muchinsky (1978b) found that 76 percent of this sample ($N = 362$) were working in environments that were congruent with their SDS codes.

A small-scale study (Wiggins, 1976) of job satisfaction among special education teachers ($N = 110$) indicates that job satisfaction is related to congruence of interests and occupation. Wiggins found that the job satisfaction of special education teachers (SAI) was correlated $-.54$ and .56 with the Realistic and Social scales of the VPI. In a closely related study, Wiggins and Moody (in press) discovered that the congruence of counselors' interests and clients' occupational codes had a strong positive association with supervisory (.62) and client (.68) ratings of a counselor's performance. These correlations are inflated by the omission of counselors with average ratings. Job satisfaction was also significantly correlated with congruence. In a similar investigation focused only on job satisfaction, Wiggins, Lederer, Salkowe, and Rys (1983) found that the job satisfaction of 247 high school teachers was correlated .57 with the congruence of three-letter VPI and occupational codes. A regression analysis showed that congruence was the best predictor of satisfaction followed next by differentiation (VPI). Background and training variables did not contribute to the regression equation.

Gottfredson (1981) performed an elaborate predictive study of job satisfaction and turnover for a sample of 310 newly hired bank tellers before and after a brief training program. Congruence of VPI and occupation (trainee had high-point code of C) was correlated .43 and .22 with satisfaction for males and females, but "expected" satisfaction had higher correlations with satisfaction for both sexes (.62 and .52).

Finally, three indirect investigations of the congruency hypothesis have been performed. They are indirect because researchers tested the congruency hypothesis with useful but divergent assessment devices and techniques. For example, Peiser and Meir (1978) administered the RA-

MAK Inventory (Meir, 1975), which assesses eight kinds of interests, and seven years later asked 100 males and 121 females to respond to a satisfaction with occupational choice item. Satisfaction with current occupational choice was positively correlated with congruence of interests measured seven years earlier and occupational field for both females and males.

Other studies of congruency have involved tests based on specific worker functions within a single occupation. Meir and Erez (1981) obtained relatively high correlations between three special interest measures and job satisfaction for a sample of 109 engineers. Similarly, Hener and Meir (1981) used an inventory of nine nursing functions to demonstrate that preference for a specific nursing area or role and working in the same area or role was positively related to job satisfaction.

Interpersonal Relations

The application of the theory to counselor-client, marital, and other social interactions has had some positive outcomes. And like the career studies, it is occasionally difficult to attribute failure to the theory or to bad research. The key assumption in these investigations is that identical or related types will be attracted to one another, will be more understanding of one another, and will enjoy one another, because similar types will act as reinforcing environments for one another. Ahammer (1973) has expressed a very similar formulation for comprehending adult personality development including marital interaction. Hogan, Hall, and Blank (1972) have also demonstrated in a simple experiment that the degree to which college students expect to like unknown persons and evaluate them positively is strongly related to the similarity of their interests.

Living arrangements. Several natural experiments support the hypothesis that congruency of types or type and immediate environment has an expected impact. Among these studies, one of the most convincing is a simple experiment by Williams (1967).

Williams examined a familiar problem in the present theoretical context—conflict between freshmen male roommates as a study of congruent or incongruent interactions. Because all entering freshmen were administered the VPI, Williams was able to locate 39 roommate pairs who were reported "in conflict" (according to housing staff) or who separated because of "conflict." Another 39 roommate pairs with no evidence of conflict were selected randomly from a population of 131 nonconflict pairs. All pairs in this study had been assigned to common double rooms. When the data is arranged in a two × two table, congruence of student codes is positively associated with lack of conflict ($P < .05$). And among the student pairs "in conflict," the most common pattern of VPI codes is Investigative-Enterprising (eight of 39). This simple study is difficult to fault since all available data were used, environments were standard (common double rooms), the criterion of conflict was overt enough to be assessed by outsiders, the assignment of roommates was random, and so on.

A less analytical experiment by Brown (1966) also suggests that different kinds of peers provide different kinds of reinforcement. In the Brown experiment, the proportions of peers with science or nonscience goals on a student's dorm floor clearly influenced a student's tendency to maintain or change goals. In this study, students in the minority fields (only 25 percent were in science) tended to move to majority fields (75 percent were in nonscience) when both groups lived on the same floor of a dormitory. The reverse situation also held. When nonscience students (25 percent) lived with science students (75 percent), nonscience students tended to switch to science fields. In theoretical terms, science majors equaled Realistic and Investigative types, and nonscience students equaled the remaining types. The results suggest how types in the majority manipulate types in the minority.

In a recent study, Meir and Hasson (1982) assumed that congruency of SDS code and the dominant type in three small settlements in Israel would predict the tendency to stay and the social acceptance of 71 couples. The correlation between congruence and the inclination to stay in the settlement was .44 (N = 142, p < .01). Congruence and social acceptance was not significant. This is a pioneering investigation that shows the way to a host of related experiments in natural settings.

Counselor-client relations. The first studies of counselor-client relations usually produced negative outcomes. Ingram's (1969) attempt to use the typology (VPI profiles) to forecast the outcomes of educational-vocational counseling, counselor-client interactions, and academic performance in college produced only negative findings. The sample of 304 "marginally-achieving" students may have represented too small a range of types and ability for the theory. A well-designed study by Whitney and Whittlesey (1972) in which counseling outcomes were predicted for different student types was also generally negative: "Exceptions were in the number of counseling interviews (where Investigative clients had the most sessions) and the degree of counselor's personal liking for client (counselors liked clients with moderately consistent profiles better than those with inconsistent profiles)." Both studies relied on student type and ignored counselor type.

A more successful experiment (Armstrong, 1976) assessed the similarity of high school counselors (N = 16) and their counselees (N = 204) by having both groups take the Whitehorn-Betz A-B Scale (1954), the SDS, and the EPPS. Similarity indices between each counselor and his or her counselees were calculated for each inventory. Each student also completed the Counseling Evaluation Inventory (CEI), which defines counseling success as a positive rating of the counseling relationship. Finally, student ratings (CEI) were correlated (rho) with the counselor-student similarity indices for each inventory. The results were as follows: SDS-CEI similarity indices correlated .21 (P < .001), or students whose interests resembled those of their counselor rated their counseling relationship positively. Correlations based on the A-B scale (.06) and the EPPS (.04) were not significant.

In a related experiment, Cox and Thoreson (1977) obtained mixed results when a small sample of college males and females listened to tapes characterizing three counseling types (Social, Investigative, and Conventional) and were then asked to select a counselor for themselves. There was a significant tendency for Artistic, Social, and Enterprising student types to select a counselor of the same type. On the other hand, Investigative students selected Social or dissimilar types, and Realistic and Conventional types made random selections.

Marital relations. Studies of marital relationships have often failed to produce positive results. Several studies are exceptions. Wiggins and Weslander (1979) assessed a small sample of couples (N = 23) who sought marital counseling with the VPI. The authors found a similar control group and compared couples in the treatment and control groups using an elaboration of the Zener-Schnuelle Index (Holland, 1979). The results indicate that couples "who were considering divorce" were more incongruent than the controls (P < .001). The partner who initiated counseling was most likely to be a Social type and least likely to be a Realistic type. This finding held for both sexes and is consistent with the characteristics attributed to those types. Wiggins and Weslander (1982) have also reported that women (N = 18) consistently chose second husbands who were more similar to themselves than were their first husbands. These studies are provocative, although they are experimentally fragile.

A more recent study (Wiggins, Moody, and Lederer, in press) is substantial (125 couples) and difficult to challenge. The investigators administered a Satisfaction with Spouse and Marriage (SWSM) blank, the VPI, and a background questionnaire. The couples' congruency (calculated from the couples' three-letter VPI codes) was the best predictor of reported marital satisfaction (r = .70). All other variables were weak predictors.

Bruch and Gilligan (1980) also used the VPI along with measures of marital and family interaction in applying the theory to social interaction. They used a sample of 81 volunteer college students and their partners. The results suggest that combinations of high degrees of person-environment congruence plus individual consistency and differentiation result in more satisfaction and adjustment in social interaction.

Other studies have produced only negative findings. In one instance (Mathis, 1977), failure may have been due to very homogeneous sampling. In another study (Dorset, 1977), no clear explanation of failure is obvious, although the definition of congruency by the hexagonal model is probably not as sensitive as the Zener-Schnuelle Index would have been. Likewise, the use of the separate-sex-normed SCII theme scales to assess types may have reduced the validity of the assessment.

CROSS-NATIONAL RESEARCH

Most of the main hypotheses in the theory have also been examined in one or more of the following foreign countries: Australia, New Zealand, Canada, the Netherlands, Switzerland, Italy, Israel, Nigeria, and Guyana. A few studies have been summarized in appropriate sections of this chapter, but it also appeared useful to summarize the remaining studies in a special section, for these investigations usually support the validity and usefulness of the theory, the assessment techniques, or the classification system.

Most studies have examined the validity of the VPI, SDS, or their foreign adaptations. Keeling and Tuck (1979) assessed high school students with an adapted SDS for New Zealand and found that the degree of agreement between aspiration and SDS code approximated the agreement found with the SDS in the United States. Aranya, Barak, and Amernic (1981) administered the SDS to samples of accountants and CPAs in California and Canada. The code of CES was obtained for both samples. Congruence, consistency, and differentiation usually had only trivial correlations with job satisfaction and organizational commitment. A Hebrew adaptation of the SDS (Feldman and Meir, 1976) administered to a sample of 167 working females yielded correlations between interest score for their occupation (R, I, A, S, E, C) and job satisfaction ranging from $-.09$ to $.59$ and averaging $.38$. Two other studies (Gesinde, 1973; Mercurius-Fraser, 1980) provide positive evidence for the validity of the SDS in Nigeria and Guyana. Taylor, Kelso, Pretty, and Power (1980) have compared Australian and American responses to the VPI and discovered that the patterns of relations among the interest scales differed between the sexes but not between countries. And N. Taylor (1980) reexamined the Identity Scale with an Australian sample—new item and factor analyses— and pronounced it sound except for one weak item. He also used the scale in a treatment experiment (Taylor, 1983) in which it proved to be related to a counselor's selection of career counseling techniques. Melamed (1976) discovered that the Occupations section of the SDS (the interest scales of the VPI) had more construct validity than the entire SDS. Of special importance, Melamed, using a sample of 240 male Australian workers, found that the category of a worker's first occupation predicted with marked efficiency his occupational category five and ten years later. Workers with consistent personality patterns (SDS) made fewer occupational changes than workers with inconsistent personality patterns. In addition, consistency and differentiation were not related to vocational satisfaction, but congruence was at a low level.

INTERPRETATIVE SUMMARY

The review of the evidence supports the main hypotheses of the theory. The types appear to grow up, perceive occupations, move among occupations, and behave according to theoretical expectations. The environmental models appear useful to characterize educational and occupational environments. Of special importance, the original environmental definitions, derived from environmental classifications based on a census of types, are related to aspects of environments measured in other ways: Structured job analysis information and information about working conditions can now be used to supplement the earlier definitions. And, to a limited degree, the interactive experiments suggest that types are influenced by environments as predicted. Finally, multiple studies imply that the hexagonal model is a useful if imperfect way to organize personal and occupational data. The ordering (RIASEC) of types or occupational categories is similar even when the data, sexes, and cultures vary. That the data are not always in accord with a perfect hexagon has been noticed by some researchers. At best, the hexagons resulting from real-world data are misshapen polygons, but this arrangement is superior to the use of unrelated or unordered occupational categories. The ordering of categories in the assessment devices and classification helps in the interpretation of a person's profiles and of the psychological distance between one occupation and another. Classifications with unordered categories provide little or no information about their relations so that the interpretation of profiles and occupational distances is more difficult. Like the personality types and environmental models, the hexagon is an ideal that provides an easily understood summary of major trends in the relations among types and occupations.

The virtues of the typology are easily summarized: (1) The typology is easily grasped; (2) it has many virtues of a useful theory—clear definitions, internally consistent structure, broad scope, and formalizations for dealing with both personal development and change; (3) its broad base of research support uses large samples of children, adolescents, college students, and adults as old as 88, and both men and women; and (4) the typology is easily applied to practical problems—the development of vocational-assessment devices, the classification and interpretation of personal and environmental data, and the conduct of vocational counseling.

The weaknesses of the typology appear to be as follows: (1) The hypotheses about the person-environment interactions have received support, but they also require more testing; (2) The formulations about personal development and change have received some support but they need a more comprehensive examination; (3) The classification of occupations may differ slightly for the different devices used to assess the types; and (4) Many important personal and environmental contingencies still lie outside the scope of the theory, although an attempt has been made to include the role of education, sex, intelligence, social class, and other major variables. Nevertheless, the distribution of influence and status within a person's social environment makes a difference, so researchers must control their experiments for social status, and practitioners must make some estimate of the role of social status in evaluating environments for their clients. The roles of social class, special advantage or disadvantage, intelligence, and special aptitudes are incorporated only indirectly in the typology, so these personal and environmental characteristics must also be weighed.

Last, this theoretical revision contains some promissory notes as well as some old unfinished business. The revisions of the environmental formulations, using environmental and occupational codes defined by the recent Dictionary of Holland Occupational Codes (Gottfredson et al., 1982), have never been tested. The incorporation of Staats' formulations about personality or behavioral repertoires has also not been tested in the context of the types. The addition of vocational identity shows promise, but the exploration of the usefulness of that variable has just begun. The need for more comprehensive studies of the environmental and interactive hypotheses remain. The importance of understanding stability and change in behavior cannot be overestimated. If we develop a good working knowledge of stability and change, a host of practical and potent applications become possible. They include how to design more effective guidance devices and systems, how to foster more satisfying vocational decisions, how to redesign jobs for greater personal fulfillment, and how to manipulate others for a variety of socially desirable purposes.

I have included "Some Research Suggestions for Students" as Appendix C to provide a convenient way to influence research and to help students.

CHAPTER 6
THE CLASSIFICATION SYSTEM

The theory's classification system is used to categorize people, occupations, or environments as types or subtypes. The classification includes six main categories corresponding to the types, and each main category contains five to sixteen subcategories such as Realistic-Investigative-Artistic, Realistic-Investigative-Social, and so on. Main categories and subcategories have also been characterized as *requiring* different levels of general educational development (GED) if the classification is applied to an occupation, or as *possessing* different levels of GED if the classification is applied to a person.

Because the classification system is an integral part of the theory, the act of classification makes it possible to use the theory to interpret or predict the behavior and activities of persons and the influence of occupations or environments assigned to a particular category. For example, a person categorized as an RIE should exhibit the characteristics of the Realistic type most, the Investigative type next, and so on. Occupations categorized as RIE should encourage Realistic activities, competencies, perceptions, and so on. In addition, the average GED level for RIE occupations indicates the level of GED required for satisfactory performance. Last, the arrangement of the classification according to the hexagonal model provides a method for estimating the psychological distance between successive jobs within a career, or between two or more vocational aspirations. In short, the *degree* of aspiration or career changing can be estimated so that it is not necessary to assume that little changes such as social worker to counselor equal large changes such as scientist to business executive.

The following sections summarize the development of the classification system and some tests of its usefulness or validity. Appendix A illustrates the current revision of the classification.

DEVELOPMENT

This section gives the history of the classification and its revisions from 1959 to 1982. In general, the goals of the following studies were usually to create a classification with desirable characteristics (comprehensiveness, independence of categories, classification by a single principle). The different stages in the development of the classification have been categorized as preliminary classifications, intermediate classifications, and the current classifications.

Preliminary classifications.   In 1959, an a priori classification of six categories was proposed (Holland, 1959):

1. Realistic (technical, skilled, and laboring occupations)
2. Intellectual (scientific occupations)
3. Social (educational and social welfare occupations)
4. Conventional (office and clerical occupations)
5. Enterprising (sales and managerial occupations)
6. Artistic (artistic, literary, and musical occupations)

From 1959 to 1965 this classification was used in several theoretical studies, but it was neither directly tested for its value as a classification system nor explicitly defined for clear and easy use.

Later, Holland (1966a, 1966b) defined the major categories of the classification—Realistic, Intellectual, Social, Conventional, Enterprising, and Artistic—in terms of the six Vocational Preference Inventory (VPI) scales having the same names. The VPI is a brief inventory of a person's interests consisting of 160 occupational titles (Holland, 1977). People take the inventory by indicating the occupations they "like" or "dislike." Each occupational title is assigned to a scale or category; for example, "bank teller" is assigned to the conventional category. Thus the VPI scales consist of six groups of occupations, one group for each scale or occupational class.

The assumption that each occupational title in the VPI can be classified into one of the six categories in the classification made it possible to reconstruct the classification scheme in an explicit manner. The VPI was administered to students planning to enter different professions. The mean number of occupations rated "like" was calculated for each scale

(Realistic, Intellectual, and so on) for all students planning to enter a given occupation. VPI profiles were then formed for each occupation by placing the highest scale mean first, the next highest mean second, and so on. The results defined an occupation's place in the classification. For example, the majority of students planning to be civil engineers obtained a profile of RIE; "civil engineer" was thus placed in the major category Realistic, and in the subcategory Realistic-Intellectual-Enterprising. This procedure was applied to the VPI data for 12,432 college freshmen in thirty-one institutions (Abe and Holland, 1965a), and produced separate occupational classifications for men and women.

As a next step, Holland, Whitney, Cole, and Richards (1969) added VPI data for a sample of two-year college students (12,345 men and 7,968 women in sixty-five colleges) to the data obtained in 1966 for four-year college students, along with some data for samples of employed adults. These additions made the classification more comprehensive and reliable. Occupations were assigned to classes exactly as before; that is, mean VPI scores of all students aspiring to an occupation indicated that occupation's place in the classification.

In earlier classifications, the ordering of major classes and the arrangement of subgroups within major classes had no special meaning. In this study, however, the major classes and subclasses were arranged according to the hexagonal model in Figure 3. The hexagonal model was discovered when it was noticed that the intercorrelational matrix for the VPI scales used in the classification can be approximated by the distances within a hexagon.

This geometric model arranges student occupational aspirations according to their psychological relatedness, thereby making the classification more useful for vocational guidance and research in careers. In the hexagonal model the main categories are arranged in the following order—Realistic, Investigative, Artistic, Social, Enterprising, and Conventional (proceeding around the hexagon in a clockwise direction)—so that adjacent categories are most closely related. In general, close relationships are represented by short distances on the hexagon.

Using Figure 3 as a model, we can apply the same principle of arrangement to the subclasses within a major category by observing the following rule: Within a major category, arrange the subclasses so that the second and third code letters follow in clockwise order starting from the major category's first code. Thus the order within the Realistic category is RI, RA, RS, RE, RC, and the order within the Realistic-Investigative subclass is RIA, RIS, RIE, and so on.

Intermediate classification.   The goals of this intermediate form of the classification were to extend the classification to all common occupations in the United States and to arrange each subclass of occupations in order of level of general educational development (GED). The assignment of

GED levels to occupations was, with few exceptions, a clerical task. Using the U.S. Department of Labor *Dictionary of Occupational Titles* (DOT, 1965), occupations were assigned GED levels (one through six) according to their six-digit DOT code.

The ideal way to increase the comprehensiveness of the classification could have been to administer the VPI to large representative samples of employed adults, calculate mean VPI profiles, and assign occupations to the classification according to profile patterns. Because this expensive data collection was not possible, other alternatives were sought. The following paragraphs describe how data from divergent sources were translated from other systems or scales into the six classes represented by the VPI.

Campbell (1971) created six simulated Vocational Preference Inventory scales for the Strong Vocational Interest Blank (SVIB). He accomplished this task by using the definitions of the personality types and lists of occupational titles given in Holland (1966b). Campbell's VPI lookalike scales provide an alternate form of the VPI. His brief scales, composed largely of occupational titles in the Strong, are similar to corresponding scales in the VPI. They contain many overlapping items, same or similar occupational titles, or related activity items. Campbell rescored some of the Strong criterion groups of employed adults with his alternate form of the VPI and produced simulated VPI profiles for samples of students and employed adults. (For a complete account, see Campbell and Holland, 1972, or Campbell, 1971.)

For a sample of 76 occupations, the simulated form of the VPI and the sixth revision of the VPI (Holland, 1965) agreed on the main classification of an occupation (one of the six categories) about 84 percent of the time. The next two letters in an occupational profile were rarely identical, but the majority of the occupations in question received some combination of three highest letters of VPI scales.

Parenthetically, the convergence of the SVIB simulated VPI profiles and the actual VPI profiles from other sources (Holland et al., 1969) is of marked value because *that convergence (84 percent) reveals that aspirants for particular occupations resemble the employed adults in the same occupations.*

The most sustained, scientific attempt to organize our knowledge of work activities is that of McCormick and his colleagues. Their contribution is not easily summarized because of its long time span, scope, and complexity. Their more recent work has been summarized by McCormick, Jeanneret, and Mecham (1969) and by McCormick, Jeanneret, and Mecham (1972). McCormick, Jeanneret, and Mecham (1969) developed the Position Analysis Questionnaire as a method for assessing jobs directly. This comprehensive questionnaire contains 189 job elements intended to characterize the human behavior required in different jobs.

Data based on the Position Analysis Questionnaire (McCormick, 1979) have been used (1) for deriving estimates of the human attributes (aptitudes, interests, physical capacities, and so on) that a job requires,

and (2) as the basis for identifying job dimensions. Mecham and McCormick (1969a) developed the attribute requirements (68) for the job elements (178) in the PAQ. In short, they used PAQ descriptions of individual jobs as data for deriving estimates of the human characteristics
needed to perform those jobs. To accomplish this task, 68 attributes were
selected as relevant to different kinds of work performance. Raters estimated the relevance of each attribute to the elements of the PAQ. Median
attribute ratings were derived and their reliabilities were estimated (most
of these were in the .80s and .90s). This estimation of the attribute requirements from the PAQ means that it may be possible to establish
useful job requirements using only job analysis data; that is, the usual
situational validation of predictors might be ignored. In a related study,
Mecham and McCormick (1969b) used the PAQ to estimate the attribute
requirements of jobs and validated these synthetic estimates against data
based on the General Aptitude Test Battery (GATB) (U.S. Dept. of Labor, 1967) of the U.S. Employment Service. The results clearly indicate
that the PAQ (a comprehensive job analysis) can be used to estimate the
aptitudes that jobs require.

Finally, Jeanneret and McCormick (1969) investigated the hypothesis that there is "some structure underlying the domain of human work."
Using 536 job analyses obtained by the PAQ, they performed principal
component analyses of PAQ items that resulted in five overall factors and
27 divisional job dimensions. The divisional dimensions resulted from
independent factor analyses of each of the major divisions of the PAQ.
They also performed factor analyses of the PAQ item attribute profiles
developed by Mecham and McCormick (1969a). The six independent
analyses produced 21 divisional dimensions. Generally, the job dimensions obtained from job analyses and from attribute profiles appear sensible and consistent with one another as well as with the related literature.

McCormick, Mecham, and Jeanneret provided the author with the
fruits of their work (called the Purdue data): 32 factor scores in standard
score form for a sample of 879 occupations, including five overall factor
scores and 27 factor scores resulting from factor analyses of the job elements within each of the six subdivisions of the PAQ (Jeanneret and
McCormick, 1969). The Purdue data were used for two purposes: (1) to
determine the relationship between the Holland classification and the
Purdue job factors, and (2) to extend the Holland classification to more
occupations.

The first task was accomplished in this way: The Purdue jobs (832 of
879) were classified into the Holland categories. Forty-seven jobs were not
classifiable, mainly because they had unusual occupational titles that could
not be located in the DOT. These were eliminated from further consideration. Independent classifications of the remaining 832 Purdue jobs by
two people resulted in 80 percent agreement; the other 20 percent were
resolved by discussion.

A simple analysis of variance across five Holland occupational classes was performed for each of the 32 Purdue factors (the Artistic class was omitted because the Purdue data contained only two Artistic jobs). The results of this analysis are shown in Table 11 (pp. 103–104), which gives the mean and standard deviation for each Purdue occupational dimension for the occupations classified as Realistic, Social, and so on.

The results in Table 11 are significant—all F tests are beyond the .001 level except two—and the implied relationships between Holland classes and Purdue factors are usually sensible and expected (see Jeanneret and McCormick, 1969, and Holland, 1966b, for complete explanations of the concepts in this table). The evidence in Table 11 demonstrates that the Holland classification, developed almost entirely from interest data, also encompasses more objective data about the human behavior performed in jobs.

The second task was to use the Purdue data to create simulated VPI profiles so that more occupations could be added to the classification. Using Table 11, five Purdue factors were selected to represent the corresponding VPI scales and their associated occupational classes. These factors are identified with asterisks in Table 11. To obtain five-variable VPI profiles for each of the 832 jobs, a computer was programmed to create a five-letter profile ranging from the highest to lowest standard score using the five Purdue factors. About 54 percent of the profiles had their peak or high point in agreement with their subjective classification obtained earlier. The errors of classification appeared plausible although large in number (46 percent); that is, if an occupation was misclassified, it was usually misclassified in an adjacent rather than distant category.

The final task was to integrate the data obtained from the Strong data, the data from the Purdue factors, and the data from the testing of employed adults or occupational aspirants with the VPI. The data for each occupation were put on a card that showed the profile, the number of subjects, the occupational title, and the source of data. Each occupation was represented by one to 42 cards, and the cards were collated by occupation.

To produce a single profile for an occupation, a variety of numerical, clerical, and artistic strategies were used. They included: (1) Counting the number of times a particular VPI letter or code occurred in the first, the second, or the third place in various profiles obtained from different sources and samples; (2) weighting subjectively the reliability and validity of one data source versus another; and (3) evaluating divergent profiles, particularly so that the data for men and women would be considered. In most cases, simple counting procedures were sufficient to arrive at a single profile. In general, divergences were not great, and resolutions of discrepancies were tied closely to the data.

Intermediate classification II.   This classification differs in minor ways from the intermediate classification I. An attempt was made to locate new VPI data for people in any occupation. These data were profiled for individual occupations and used to verify or revise the intermediate classification. A total of 21 changes were made. Of these, only five were changes in the first letter in an occupational code. In addition, occupations were added to clarify the meaning of small subcategories by adding a few related occupations and to make the classification more comprehensive. These additions were performed by using Viernstein's tables (1972) for extending the classification to all occupations in the Dictionary of Occupational Titles.

Current classifications.   At this time, there are two versions of the classification. The first version is contained in the Occupations Finder of the Self-Directed Search (Holland, 1978). The Occupations Finder, which contains 501 occupational titles—arranged according to the hexagonal model and by GED levels—is simply a minor revision of Intermediate classification II. As new SDS or VPI data were obtained a few minor code changes were made. The second and more comprehensive version of the classification is the *Dictionary of Holland Occupational Codes* (Gottfredson et al., 1982) in which the codes of 12,099 occupations are arranged according to the hexagonal model and GED level.

These classifications are very similar, although they were developed by very different methods. The development of the classification in the Occupations Finder was just reviewed. The Dictionary was developed by keying well-established codes in the Occupations Finder to occupational ratings for each of 12,099 occupations in the DOT; multiple discriminant analysis was used to develop classificatory functions based on DOT data (44 occupational ratings) to classify 189 occupational titles from the Occupations Finder into six occupational categories. The agreement between the first letter codes obtained from the Occupations Finder and the classificatory functions was 87.8 percent in the construction sample and 77.4 percent in the cross-validation sample. Gottfredson et al. (1982) summarize the development and validation of the codes in considerable detail and outline some applications to research and practice.

VALIDATION

There are several kinds of evidence for the usefulness of the classification and the validity of its categories: (1) The evidence for the validity of the types reviewed earlier is also evidence for the validity of the categories and subcategories in the classification, since the VPI scales have been used to define both types *and* occupational categories; (2) The efficiency with which the classification orders occupational aspirations, orders work histories, or identifies current status of an individual occupation is another index of usefulness; (3) Several studies show the convergence of the classification with data from other classification systems; and (4) The degree of fit between the hexagonal model and the data for a wide range of subjects assessed with diverse measures form another kind of evidence.

The purpose of the classificatory studies was to show that the classification organizes occupations or people into homogeneous groups. If the classification performs this task well, people in the same category should possess similar personal traits, competencies, and interests, and they should possess similar aspirational or work histories; that is, they should move among the same or closely related categories. The higher the predictive validity of the classification, the more the classification organizes changes or moves among occupational aspirations or jobs. The empirical tests of the classification are usually one of two kinds: comprehensive tests which examine the validity of all the main categories simultaneously, and individual tests of single categories. Comprehensive tests are valuable because they test the ability of the classification to order aspirations and work histories, but they yield little information about weaknesses of single categories. On the other hand, tests of single categories are valuable in identifying poorly defined categories, but they provide little information about the classification as a system of categories.

Comprehensive tests. The evidence for the predictive efficiency of the classification—its ability to order aspirational or work histories—is extensive and substantial. For example, Bartlett (1970) classified high school students' aspirations and found them moderately predictive of successive occupational choices (9th to 10th grade, 10th to 11th, and 11th to 12th). Holland and Whitney (1968) applied the classification to longitudinal data for college students and obtained efficient predictions over an 8- to 12-month interval. Elton and Rose (1970) found that the category of a college freshman's vocational choice predicted the category of his vocational choice as a senior with moderate to high efficiency (hits ranged from 49 to 87 percent in each category using a sampling of 530). Lucy (1976) performed a similar study, relating the category of major field at graduation to the category of current vocational interests (high-point code of VPI) and obtained substantial predictions. Contingency coefficients for 6×6 tables range from .64 for a 25-year interval to .74 for a 15-year interval. These are impressive findings, since Lucy's study spanned time intervals of ten to 35 years (803 alumni from the classes of 1935, 1940, 1945, 1950, 1955, and 1960).

Other studies demonstrate that successive vocational aspirations in adolescence and young adulthood have a lawful character when the classification is applied. L. Gottfredson (1979) has shown that the successive vocational aspirations (one-year interval) of young men (aged 16 to 28) in a nationally representative sample are closely related: 67.8 to 81.0 percent have successive aspirations that belong to the same category. Holland and Gottfredson (1975) have found that the retrospective vocational aspirations of high school and college students have coherence (tend to belong to the same category): The current aspiration obtained from the SDS Daydreams section is significantly related to most of the earlier aspirations when the classification is applied. Percentages of agreement range from 24 to 55 percent. An older retrospective survey (Holland, 1963) of high aptitude students produced a similar pattern of evidence: Current and retrospective aspirations tend to belong to the same category.

McLaughlin and Tiedeman (1974) applied the classification to the vocational aspirations of 12th graders in Project Talent and again to actual occupation held one, five, and 11 years after graduation. The results show that aspirations in high school are significantly related to actual occupation one, five, and 11 years later when aspirations and jobs are categorized. The efficiency of these predictions declines from 57.8 percent, one year after high school, to 38.6 percent, 11 years after high school. These and other analyses have demonstrated that aspirations have useful predictive validity and that aspirations obtained at older ages are more predictive than aspirations obtained at younger ages. Finally, the comparison of all three classification systems (Holland [1973], Roe [1956], and Flanagan [1973]) yielded similar results.

Noeth and Jepsen (1981) applied the classification to the aspirations of 11th graders (N = 1994) and their part-time or full-time jobs three years later. Expressed choices predicted the category of occupation for 38 percent and hit rates were higher for "very sure choosers"—43 percent.

When the classification has been applied to the work histories for large nationally representative samples, the results have also been positive and substantial. For example, Table 13 taken from Holland et al. (1973)— shows that 78.6 percent of the 5,812 transitions for 757 men (aged 30–39) are among the same major categories (R, I, A, S, E, or C). Other tests of the predictive validity of the subcategories within the Realistic category were also positive. The positive results of this study are consistent with similar studies. Parsons and Wigtil (1974) have shown that the application of the classification to the work histories of a representative national sample of older men (N = 5,000, aged 45 to 59) also produces moderately efficient predictions. In a study of a representative national sample of young men (N = 5,000, aged 14 to 24), Nafziger, Holland, Helms, and McPartland (1974) found that 69 percent of the white and 82 percent of the blacks remained in the same category over a two-year period. In another analysis, the authors report that the GED levels, used in the Holland classification, correlate .82 with the Duncan Socioeconomic Index (N = 4,035). Nafziger (1973) also attempted to increase the predictive efficiency of the classification by the use of Markov models, but discovered that the most efficient strategy was to predict that men would maintain the Holland category of their initial occupation.

L. Gottfredson and Becker (1981) have demonstrated how vocational aspirations are affected by the opportunity structure—"which both conditions aspirations to narrow ranges early in life and affects the direction of early career development." Their analyses provide useful explanations for the stability of work histories and suggest why aspirations are as

TABLE 13 The Application of the Classification to All Job Transitions

	RIS	RIE	RIC	RSI	RSE	RSC	REI	RES	RCI	RCS	RCE	I	A	S	E	C	OTHER	TOTAL
RIS	84	50	13		37	1	3	3	2	5	11	3		20	26	6	33	264
RIE	32	452	61	6	167	3	22	8	17	9	50	42	13	15	51	18	194	966
RIC	25	57	166	4	87		8	3	6	4	30	19		19	26	13	90	469
RSI		4		12	2		1		1					2	5	1	4	27
RSE	42	247	122	1	1029	10	20	17	26	27	107	16	6	46	80	54	300	1850
RSC	5	2	1		16	9		1		1		1		2	2	3	9	43
REI	5	15	3	1	10		17	3	2		3	3		1	10	4	12	77
RES	2	11	6		15	1	1	16	1	1	1	1		1	15	9	20	81
RCI	4	16	5	1	13		2	1	48	2	2	6	2	4	6	1	16	113
RCS	3	5	6		13	1	1		1	18	4	3	1		2	3	16	61
RCE	7	39	29		85		5	2	4	1	148	4	2	3	15	11	58	355
I	5	21	8		9				4	3	2	143	2	10	24	4	38	235
A	1	6	1		3						2	2	31	3	6		2	55
S	13	13	9	2	32	2	1	1	2		4	14	1	173	22	13	19	302
E	17	38	21	5	49	2	2	8	6		11	17	3	22	381	24	64	606
C	3	27	15	1	32		4	4	4	1	8	7	5	13	56	128	60	308
Other	43	221	129	5	244	11	23	20	11	16	58	38	6	23	80	69	241	997
Total	248	1003	466	35	1599	28	86	69	123	71	384	281	66	334	728	291		5812

Note: This table organizes the 5,812 job changes made by a sample of 757 men during their lifetime. For example, 84 job changes involved moving from an RIS job to another RIS job; 50 job changes involved moving from RIS to RIE jobs, etc. Note that most job changes involve moving between identical types or subtypes.

Source: Holland et al. (1973). © 1973 by the American Psychological Association and reproduced by permission.

predictive as they are. At the same time, they show that the opportunity structure may be more influential than a person's vocational aspiration in determining a person's future occupation.

The most impressive test of the classification is G. Gottfredson's (1977) reorganization of the 1970 census data. Using a one-in-1,000 sample of 21- to 70-year-old workers in the United States, Gottfredson demonstrated that career stability increased with age for both sexes, and older workers were more stable even when the analyses were restricted to occupational changers or socioeconomically mobile workers. In addition, as discussed earlier, people initially employed in "consistent" occupations were more stable than those initially employed in "inconsistent" occupations. Table 12 (p. 112) indicates the stability of workers' careers over five-year intervals.

The Gottfredson study, like other studies using nationally representative or large samples, is a test of the entire classification. If, for example, many occupations were misclassified (miscoded), such studies would not produce strong positive results.

Another group of studies also extends and supports the construct validity of the classification. Several investigators have analyzed the relation of the Holland classification to other classification systems. These studies are useful because they demonstrate that the Holland system has much in common with governmental and sociological systems. For example, L. Gottfredson (1980a) has explored the relation of the Holland classification to the census, Department of Labor, and prestige classifications and found that these diverse systems have substantial overlap or share considerable job content especially when the Holland classification is supplemented by a measure of prestige level. She reports that GED and prestige (Temme, 1975) correlate .95. This work provides the major justification for including GED levels as an integral part of the classification. Other comparisons by Viernstein (1972), Holland (1973), and by Rounds et al. (1978) provide more information. In general, these comparisons outline the construct validity of the Holland scheme and show the continuity with earlier systems. Finally, Nafziger and Helms (1974) applied McQuitty and Clark's (1968) iterative intercolumnar correlational analysis to the scales of the Strong Vocational Interest Blank (SVIB), the Minnesota Vocational Interest Inventory (MVII), and the Kuder Occupational Interest Survey (KOIS) for both men and women. The results of these entirely empirical analyses produced internally consistent clusters of occupations that usually agreed with the groups of occupations in the classification. The hierarchical structure of the clusters followed the hexagonal ordering, and the usefulness of all three letters in the classification was supported.

Individual categories. Along with these tests of the entire system, there have been numerous tests of individual occupational codes for workers in a particular occupation or for students training to enter a particular occupation. For example, Richards (1977) tested 74 students in the health assistant and associate programs at a private university. Their mean scores on the VPI resulted in the code ISA, which is the same as the code for physician. Other assessments with the SDS or the VPI were conducted by Spokane and Walsh (1978), Fabry (1976), Gaffey and Walsh (1974), Holland and Holland (1977a), Fishburne and Walsh (1976), Hollifield (1974), Horton and Walsh (1976), Johnson and Moore (1973), O'Brien and Walsh (1976), Wiggins (1976, 1982), Florence (1973), and Matthews and Walsh (1978). Additional studies are reported in the VPI and SDS manuals. Generally, these studies demonstrated that occupational codes were usually accurate or required only slight modification.

Other studies show that people or occupations belonging to the same category have similar characteristics. Holland (1968) found that people categorized as the same types have similar interests, self-ratings, life goals, competencies, personal traits, and attitudes. The relations between the Holland categories and the diverse occupational dimensions developed by McCormick et al. (1969) also suggest that occupations in the same category have similar characteristics.

Campbell's (1971) ranking of 202 occupations according to their mean score on the G.O.T. scales is vivid evidence that the scales defining the categories organize occupations in terms of their similarity (see Campbell, 1971, E10–E15, pages 464–69). For example, the ten highest occupations on the realistic scale are machinists, tool and die makers, vocational agriculture teachers, skilled tradespeople, highway patrolmen, electricians, farmers, carpenters, police officers, and foresters. The high-scoring occupations on the remaining five scales display similar homogeneity.

Categorical relations (hexagonal model).   The arrangement of the classification according to the hexagonal model receives strong support from the assessment of individuals (pp. 94–97) but mixed support from the assessment of occupations (pp. 104–105). In the aspirational and work histories reviewed in this chapter, most investigations demonstrate that job changes usually involve movement within the same major category (Gottfredson, 1977). At the same time, analyses of aspirational or job changes according to *degrees* of change, following the entire hexagonal model, have been only partially successful. Most changes should involve the same major category followed by less movement to adjacent, more distant, and remote categories. To illustrate, an R-person would be expected to remain in R-occupations, but if he or she leaves the R-category, movement should occur most frequently for moves to the I or C categories, followed by less frequent moves to E or A, and finally, moves to the S category will be least frequent.

Several studies typify how well or how poorly the hexagonal model fits the pattern of aspirational changes. Scott, Fenske, and Maxey (1974) have demonstrated that the pattern of changes in vocational aspiration over an 18-month period for a sample of college males (N = 903) fit the hexagonal model: The percentages of within-class changers (43.5), adjacent-class changers (28.4), distant-class changers (19.8), and across-hexagonal changers (8.3) are in the predicted descending order. The same analysis for females (N = 595) was less successful: The percentages for the same categories were 43.8, 23.3, 24.8, and 8.1. Other analyses by type and sex strongly suggest that the hexagonal model fits the pattern of changes observed for some types better than others. In contrast, Gottfredson's (1977) analyses of job changes for a sample of the entire labor force give only partial support.

In both of these studies, the influence of sex segregation and other constraints appears to distort the expected results. For example, Gottfredson found that those Realistic men who do move to another category in mid-career are more likely to enter Enterprising occupations rather than Investigative or Conventional occupations. These anomalies indicate the need to examine the influence of constraints such as age, sex, race, education, and other characteristics.

L. Gottfredson (1981) has provided an explicit account of how vocational aspirations are compromised by gender, social standing, and ability self-concepts. In addition, she outlines how people settle for satisfactory—not necessarily the optimal potential—choices, and how they "accommodate psychologically to the choices they make." These formulations provide the most plausible explanations for the systematic deviations from the hexagonal model when career shifts are examined.

SUMMARY

The evidence for the usefulness of the classification system is now extensive and typically positive. The application of the classification to the aspirations of adolescents and the work histories of adults demonstrates both the continuity in careers over the life span and the usefulness of the classification. The classification has been extended more precisely to the 12,099 occupations in the Dictionary of Occupational Titles than in the past, and the hexagonal arrangement of the classification has also received more support.

CHAPTER 7
PRACTICAL APPLICATIONS

The purpose of this chapter is to outline the chief practical applications of the theory to vocational assistance (vocational guidance and career development), education, social science, and other fields. The following applications are not exhaustive, but they illustrate the main theoretical ideas so that the reader can transfer the theoretical principles to old and new problems. The theory, the classification, the diagnostic scheme, and the assessment devices form a coordinated system for understanding and delivering vocational assistance. The application of the theory to problems in social science, education, and other fields has produced some provocative results, but applications to these more distant fields have been infrequent. This account of theoretical implications is not a manual for the practice of career assistance, although it is a beginning. And, the illustrations that follow need to be amended by the "Other Things Being Equal" cautions reviewed earlier (age, sex, social class, education, and so on).

CAREER ASSISTANCE

I have coined the term "career assistance" to span the wide range of activities developed to help people of all ages cope with vocational decisions and problems. It includes the goals and professional functions of vocational guidance, career development, career counseling, selection, placement ("in" and "out"), career courses and workshops, and portions of retirement planning and special programs for minorities and women. Within this diverse field, the theory provides some helpful tools for explaining common career problems, for improving career practices, for understanding the special problems of minorities, females, and other groups, and for providing career assistance in business and industry.

Explanation and Prediction

The theory and its classification can be used to explain and interpret vocational data and vocational behavior. Diagnostic activities can play a useful role in career assistance for both clients and practitioners. Students, parents, and workers want to know what tests mean, and what their personal values and competencies mean occupationally. They also want to make sense of their aspirations, work histories, and job satisfaction or dissatisfaction. They voice many other queries that call for valid assessments and reliable forecasts.

The theory, the classification, and the related assessment devices (VPI, SDS, MVS, DHOC) possess some explanatory possibilities for coping with common diagnostic problems in career practice. The typological formulations can be used to interpret interest inventories, to clarify the divergent occupational choices of people in conflict, to interpret work histories, to estimate the outcomes of proposed person-environment combinations, to explain the origins of interests, and to explain the occurrence of adaptive and maladaptive vocational development. And of equal or greater importance, the theory implies remedial actions or treatments for facilitating more adaptive vocational behavior. These ideas are elaborated in the next paragraphs.

Interest inventories closely modeled after the theory (the SDS, VPI, SCII, and some imitations) can make full use of the theory. Counselors can (1) interpret individual interest scores according to the formulations, (2) predict the categories of occupations that appear congruent for a person, (3) identify some probable sources of current job dissatisfaction by following the formulations about congruency of person and job (Table 5), (4) locate potentially compatible jobs for people facing unemployment using the DHOC and a person's educational level, and (5) identify clients whose characteristics imply more or less need for career assistance. Counselors can also amend their interpretations of interest profiles and congruent jobs by applying the concepts of differentiation, identity, and consistency, and by classifying expressed interests or aspirations.

All counselors perform most of these activities now. The contribution of the theory is to provide more explicit, comprehensive, and reliable rules for the diagnostic processes.

To illustrate, conflicting occupational options can be classified and examined for their special character and the psychological distance between them using the formulations for the types and the hexagonal model. Using the theory, a counselor can interpret a student's occupational conflict—a process that might aid both. For example, a boy trying to decide between mechanical engineering (RIE) and Farming (RIE) should experience little conflict. A discussion of their psychological similarities might simplify his decision and suggest that other factors—such as style of life, capital, and special aptitudes—may help resolve this difficulty. In contrast, a girl trying to decide between physician (ISA) and musician (ASI) might profit from a discussion of the relative importance of I and A in these codes, the life styles implied, her potentials for each, the specific roles she anticipated in each, her resources, and support for each goal.

A dissatisfied worker can use the congruence ideas to explore the sources of frustrations. For example, the entire interest profile can be compared with the full range of job duties starting with the three-letter code of the job and estimating the amount of time spent in all six areas of work. This simple comparison (six interest scores versus six areas of work) provides a structure for thinking about the congruence between a person's interests, competencies, values, and job duties. With the help of a counselor or an employer, it may be possible to imagine a more satisfying revision of job duties, to locate a more suitable job, or to find avocational activities for exercising interests or competencies that cannot be expressed at work.

The congruency principle is also useful for estimating the potential compatibility of a new job, or two or more job opportunities at any time in one's career. In each case, comparison of current interest and competencies with a similar profile of job requirements will often identify potential sources of achievement, satisfaction, and frustration. Again, everyone—workers, counselors, husbands, and wives—makes these estimates of compatibility, but the theory provides a studied structure for beginning this ambiguous and value-laden task.

The probable stability of a student's or worker's vocational aspiration can be estimated by using some unobtrusive signs. For example, people who would be expected to maintain their vocational goal or select a closely related goal (in the same main category) can be identified by the following signs: (a) The high-point interest inventory code and the code of the current aspiration belong to the same main category (one of six); (b) The two-letter interest code is at one of the two highest levels of consistency (see page 28); (c) The interest profile is well differentiated (see SDS Manual, Holland, 1979, pp. 65–66 for normative data); and (d) The listing of aspirations in the Daydreams section of the SDS has at least a moderate degree of agreement or coherence: Aspirations belong to the same or closely related categories. The latter estimate can be supplemented by a person's work history. If the person has taken the

Identity Scale in My Vocational Situation (Holland et al., 1981), high scores are also expected to contribute to stability of plans. The presence of all these characteristics implies a person whose aspirations or future work history will be very stable or predictable. In contrast, the absence of all signs implies a person whose aspirations and future work history will be unstable and unpredictable.

In this scheme, persons with many positive signs will be expected to need less assistance, if any, in choosing a career or changing jobs; whereas people with few positive signs will be expected to need much more assistance.

According to the theory, maladaptive career development equals the failure to develop a personality pattern that is consistent and differentiated or a clear sense of vocational identity, or a failure to establish a career in a congruent occupation. Maladaptive career development probably occurs in one or more of seven major ways:

1. A person has had *insufficient experience* to acquire well-defined interests, competencies, and self-perceptions.
2. A person has had *insufficient experience* to learn about the major kinds of occupational environments.
3. A person has had *ambiguous, conflicting, or deprecative experience* about his or her interests, competencies, and personal characteristics.
4. A person has acquired *ambiguous, conflicting, or deprecative information* about the major work environments.
5. These and other deficiencies make it difficult to translate personal characteristics into occupational opportunities. All four probably contribute to a diffuse sense of identity so that choosing an occupation or changing jobs within a career is more uncertain. In addition, many other variables make the translation task difficult or very time consuming. Some people simply have a slow rate of personal development and are slow in developing a well-defined profile of interests and competencies, or they may have a complex outlook so that decisions are made slowly. Still others may be so alienated that they are uninvolved with work or deny the need to choose. And for a few people, neuroticism and pathology make job choosing, changing, and holding precarious; for these tasks, like the other major problems of life, require effective interpersonal skills and some emotional stability.
6. Some persons lack the personal, educational, or financial resources to carry out their plans.
7. Some persons with consistent and differentiated profiles, and with a clear sense of identity, are unable to find congruent work due to economic or social barriers. The availability of work of different types is determined by the sociotechnical nature of the economy, cultural values, stages in the economic cycle, and traditional definitions of sexual or ethnic roles. And, hard times reduce both job opportunities and career assistance resources of all kinds.

When people are unable to resolve their own vocational decisions, a review of these seven possibilities can be undertaken with the person's active participation. At one extreme, many young people would be expected to be deficient in all seven ways. At the other extreme, many older people would be expected to possess all seven proficiencies and assets. In theoretical terms, psychological maturity and vocational maturity (Super, 1972; Crites, 1978) are similar concepts and are equivalent to freedom from many of the deficiencies outlined above.

In contrast, adaptive vocational behavior is the outcome of the following events:

1. A person has had sufficient experience to acquire well-defined interests and competencies.
2. A person has had sufficient experience to acquire a useful library of occupational stereotypes, especially in his or her area of interest.
3. A person has had sufficient self-clarifying experience so that the pictures of one's interests, competencies, and personal characteristics are accurate.
4. A person has had sufficient clarifying occupational experience so that his or her library of occupational information and stereotypes (generalizations) has a useful degree of validity and is free of major contradictions.
5. A person has acquired sufficient vocational identity, self-confidence, interpersonal competency, cultural involvement, and resources to make vocational decisions as the need occurs and to cope with other common job problems.
6. A person possesses the personal, educational, and financial resources to carry out his or her plans.
7. A person's plans are not deflected in major ways by cultural, economic, social, or technological influences.

We need to put substantial effort into creating conditions that lead to these outcomes and provide vocational assistance in more selective ways. For example, many people need only placement help because they have all the other prerequisites for employment. We also need to make occupational information more accessible. It should be available to young and old in easily comprehensible form without appointments and without professional supervision, and in many places beside employment centers or counseling offices. At the same time we need to make translation materials like interest inventories more accessible so that many people who require only superficial help can quickly receive what they need. Counseling resources can then be conserved for people with remedial or more complex requirements including a lack of educational or financial resources.

Career Interventions

The theory, the diagnostic formulations, and the classification system suggest some activities, methods, and ideas to facilitate vocational and personal development, to help people whose vocational development has gone awry, and to provide a structure for resolving career difficulties.

Using the diagnostic ideas. The diagnostic formulations and signs can be used to estimate a person's strengths and weaknesses and his or her need for minimal, moderate, or extensive assistance. To illustrate, persons with many positive signs (differentiated and consistent interest profile, congruent aspiration and interest profile, high identity score, and coherent set of aspirations and work history as assessed by the classification) should be able to get along with minimal assistance—usually just educational and occupational information. Persons with only a few positive signs probably require career counseling, a career course or workshop, and perhaps psychotherapy to resolve some gross misperceptions of self and the world. Between these two extremes, it is important to determine the specific kinds of information, experience, or clarification that a person needs.

The search for these informational gaps, needed skills (job finding, resumé writing, and so on), or needed clarifications can be performed with the active cooperation of the person by reviewing the meaning of the signs, the diagnostic formulations, or by having the person take the MVS. This activity can be performed in an interview, in a group, or at home. Both the MVS and the SDS can be used to generate a useful discussion of informational and skill needs (MVS) and of the origins of a person's interests (SDS). Filling out the MVS often elicits write-in "barriers" and "informational needs." And when people are asked to explain either their "Yes" or "No" responses for a few items of the SDS, they usually find it easy to relate how they came to reject some activities, why they failed to acquire some competencies, and why they rated themselves as they did on the self-ratings. This kind of inquiry is especially helpful in showing females and males how the culture has shaped them. The disliked occupations, activities, missing competencies, and low ratings can be helpful in planning for a change into a desired job, for these data often outline what must be learned or changed.

In general, the use of the diagnostic ideas can create self-understanding and stimulate more insightful and constructive planning that is also reassuring. This process is analogous to some of the work that takes place in many psychotherapeutic approaches, and in the life review work with older persons (Reedy and Birren, 1980; Lewis and Butler, 1974).

The diagnostic and correlated treatment ideas can be applied to groups of adolescents or workers in several ways. After taking the SDS and MVS, the total number of positive signs for each person can be determined and people can be assigned to one of two or three groups depending on the size of the group and the distribution of sign scores. This practice would enable counselors to identify and assist people in greatest need first and to assist the others with information, job search skills, or less expensive but appropriate forms of assistance.

Organizing information and interventions. The organization of information is a major problem in the practice of career assistance. Information about occupations comes in many forms that are difficult to integrate intellectually: brochures, rule-of-thumb classifications, lists of local occupations, complex and exhaustive classifications (DOT), single file drawers of material, whole filing cabinets of data, and even huge collections for which librarians are needed. In addition, the assessment of students or adults produces highly specific information that, if organized at all, is often organized in idiosyncratic and unexamined ways.

The present classification provides a simple method for organizing occupational information that is easily comprehensible by both clients and counselors, but that still allows for the complexity of occupations. The classification has undergone numerous positive tests, and its theoretical origin and construction ensure its continued revision and flexibility. The recent development of *The Dictionary of Holland Occupational Codes* (Gottfredson et al., 1982) makes the implementation of the classification for any purpose a simple clerical task. *The Canadian Classification and Dictionary of Occupations* (CCDO) has also been organized according to the Holland classification to facilitate the use of the CCDO (Employment and Immigration, 1973) in counseling and placement.

The organization of all occupational information in a single system would make the information more accessible and more easily understood and should reduce the number of personnel (such as special librarians or clerical workers) involved in maintaining such materials. Clients could use occupational materials almost as easily as counselors and would no longer have to be led through ad hoc occupational files and libraries. This change in role for client should encourage his or her independence and free counselors for more complex and appropriate activities. In recent years, many career centers in colleges and universities have used the classification to organize their occupational files and have discovered that this arrangement does facilitate student use of occupational information.

The organization of assessment data according to the classification should also be advantageous. Counselors can use the typological formulations to organize the data they obtain from interviews, records, and aptitude and interest devices. Clients can also use the typological formulations to understand their particular development. And because both client and counselor can share and use the concepts in the theory, their communication is probably increased, and the influence of the counselor may also be increased. This benefit stands in stark contrast to a client's ability to comprehend and use many other therapeutic systems.

The development of the Self-Directed Search (Holland, 1979) illustrates one way in which the classification and the theory have been used to organize the assessment of the person and the world of occupations within the same framework. The assessment booklet provides a simple way for the person to determine his or her resemblance to each of the six personality types, and the occupational classification booklet provides an "occupational file" in the same terms (six types of occupations) so that the person can search for occupations that correspond to his or her personality pattern. Without such a classification and its associated theory, it is not possible to organize both personal and occupational data and to explicitly integrate these divergent kinds of information. The development of multiple imitations of the SDS here and abroad provides similar evidence for the strength of the theory.

Seen another way, the SDS simulates in an explicit way what counselors, parents, psychologists, and personnel workers do in more intuitive and less precise ways. For example, career counselors usually obtain aptitude, interest, and personality data by diverse methods that often have poorly formulated and unrelated rationales. Using their best judgment, they attempt a formulation about a person (analogous to the summary code of the SDS). Then they attempt to determine what occupations go with the formulation. This task is especially hazardous for three reasons: (1) The formulation for the person usually lacks a clear and examined rationale; (2) The classification scheme usually lacks a clear and examined rationale; and (3) The translation from person to occupation or occupations is made even more difficult because the formulations do not share the same concepts and frequently no empirical tests have been made of the validity of the method of translation.

The classification can, in principle, be used to organize most of the components in an entire career program. For example:

1. The assessment of clients can be done with the Vocational Preference Inventory (Holland, 1977), The Self-Directed Search (Holland, 1979), or the Strong-Campbell Interest Inventory (Campbell and Hansen, 1981), which yield scores and profiles in terms of the personality types.

2. All data on client characteristics from interviews, tests, reports, and biographical questionnaires can be organized and stored with the framework of the theory's typology.

3. Career literature, employer announcements, and listings of vacant positions can all be organized and filed in a system that uses the classification. This would be more helpful and meaningful to clients than storing these items on the usual alphabetical or chronological basis, because it would immediately identify them in terms of related occupations, abilities required, and so on. It would also help counselors to locate and remedy any deficiencies that they may not have noticed when they were collecting these materials in the first place—for example, lack of information about Artistic or Social job opportunities would be apparent.

4. The theory should allow counselors to prepare occupational information programs that are reasonably representative of the world of work. The classification of occupations can be used to organize classroom projects, lectures by outside speakers, film programs, visits to places of employment, interviews with former students who have gone on to various types of work, and even trial job experiences. Hoppock (1968) has given details of the many ways in which occupational information can be presented, but the Holland theory can be used with any method of presentation to ensure that the content of programs is balanced. For example, if a program of visits is being planned, the person organizing it might arrange for students to make

at least one visit to observe a job in each of the six major categories of the occupational classification.

5. Information about college courses and vocational training opportunities can also be organized and filed on the basis of the Holland theory. In particular, colleges can be classified by using the Environmental Assessment Technique (EAT) (Astin and Holland, 1961) which employs the six Holland categories to characterize educational institutions.

6. Information about job opportunities within large industrial and governmental organizations might be more beneficial for both workers and human resource planners if jobs were classified by the present classification or some other studied system. Workers could more easily visualize career possibilities—promotions and transfer—and resource planners would have another tool for estimating and conceiving of future personnel requirements. For example, the structure of the classification implies how some job transfers would be more satisfying and economical (less training required) than others. The classification could be used to estimate where an organization might look for applicants for a new kind of position—namely, estimate the code for the new position and recruit people internally or externally who have the same or a related code.

7. The classification has been helpful in making computer-assisted information and career programs function more effectively by providing a system for organizing career data that is compatible with interest inventory data, current occupation, or work history (Katz and Shatkin, 1980). Some early computer-assisted or computer-interactive systems appear to have failed because they lacked a useful theoretical structure for manipulating vast amounts of personal and occupational data.

Creating more influential assistance. The application of the theory to the study of work histories and aspirations, to the experimental evaluation of the SDS and other inventories, and to the evaluations of career courses and other interventions now implies modest support for an educational-emotional rationale or a cognitive-emotional theory of career assistance (Winer, 1976). Chapter 6 summarizes the application of the classification to work histories and aspirations; the SDS manual (Holland, 1979) and a recent paper (Holland, 1983) summarize the experimental evaluations of the SDS and other interest inventories; and Spokane and Oliver (1983) evaluate the major forms of career intervention: vocational counseling, group or class interventions, self-administered inventories, and so on.

The chief findings from the aspirational and work history studies are that the average career shows continuity—a strong tendency to work in the same major area over the life time, that most moves are minor or related changes rather than moving among radically different kinds of work, and that there are many internal and external barriers to change: self-conceptions or a particular vocational identity, training, credentialing, biases of age, sex, and race, and financial and social resources. Consequently, major occupational changes are difficult to make unless the changer is given extensive support. It is not surprising that most people appear to maintain the same or a closely related goal before and after a vocational intervention.

The chief findings from the studies of the effects of different forms of career assistance are that almost any intervention helps, that group interventions may be more helpful than individual interventions, and that the search for special interventions for people with special problems has generally been fruitless.

Taken together, these outcomes have led to the following speculations about how career interventions work and how we can create more influential forms of assistance (Holland, Magoon, and Spokane, 1981). Some ideas are more directly related to the data than others.

Career courses, workshops, workbooks, interest inventories and counselors are helpful because they have some common denominators:

1. They provide organized, accessible occupational information.
2. They use assessment materials that clarify a person's self-picture and vocational potentials.
3. They stimulate the cognitive rehearsal of aspirations, work history, and plans. The oral or written rehearsal leads to perception of strengths and weaknesses, clarity or confusion in plans, need for information, and insight about self and work.
4. They provide reassurance or support from personal (peers, counselors, and groups) or impersonal sources (personality inventories, aptitude tests, exercises, and computers). The associated reduction in anxiety makes learning easier and increases self-esteem.
5. They usually provide cognitive structures (theories of career development) for comprehending and organizing information about self and occupational alternatives.

These career interventions are also helpful because the average person has little career knowledge, has at least a moderate degree of career identity, and needs to rationalize his or her decisions or situation. To elaborate:

1. The average person knows so little about careers that almost any career information is new and helpful.
2. The average person—especially an adult—has at least a moderate degree of vocational identity so that he or she can easily incorporate new information about his or her vocational potentials or work. Or, people already possess some relatively clear and accurate ideas about where they belong or fit in the occupational world.
3. The average person's occupational information and his or her private theories or understandings of careers—occupational stereotypes and the roads to success and failure—do not interfere with new learning because the person's occupational knowledge is either too limited to interfere with new learning on the same topic, or it is consistent with the structure of the present or other theories of career development. This situation—naive learning is consistent with scientific work in the same field—does not exist for mathematics and physics, where students' naive theories interfere with the learning of scientific knowledge (Resnick, 1983).
4. Vocational assistance may provide rationalizations for doing what one wants to do. For example, there is some evidence that people perceive rejected

occupations in complex ways and perceive desired occupations in simple ways—the opposite of what we would predict (Winer et al., 1980). A study of job-seeking behavior (Soelberg, 1967) "suggests that much of the effort that goes into decision-making is calculated to rationalize—rather than arrive at—a choice." In a world of uncertainty, rationalization should not always be deprecated; it can be reassuring and may be necessary to implement a vocational plan.

These interpretations imply that the most influential or helpful career assistance will entail self- and environmental explorations (interest and personality inventories, vocational exercises, values clarification, talking to employers, and discussing plans with a group or counselor), cognitive study (theories of career development, occupational classifications, and writing a case history), and emotional support and therapeutic assistance via the counselor and group. In short, more balanced or comprehensive assistance may be most useful. At present, career assistance tends to come in lopsided treatments: counselors who rely largely on their therapeutic skills and a few standardized inventories; career workers who use a diverse set of "helpful" exercises, a standard workbook, and group discussion; and career workers who rely entirely on do-it-yourself materials. All of these orientations probably have merit for some clients, although many of these materials have undergone no formal evaluation.

In contrast, balanced and comprehensive assistance would include comprehensive occupational information in an accessible form, individual *and* group sessions, an interest inventory (perhaps a personality inventory or aptitude tests for some people), employer encounters, lectures and reading assignments about career theory, and some structured and unstructured exercises including a report in which the person attempts to integrate all the treatment information and justify his or her vocational planning or current situation.

This assistance plan would not meet everyone's needs—too much for some and too little for others. Whatever the treatment, I am arguing for a more comprehensive use of current knowledge and materials. Until we can clearly demonstrate that a particular problem yields to a particular treatment, it appears wiser to create more comprehensive treatments and make greater use of the ideas included in self- and occupational exploration materials, cognitive research, and therapeutic techniques in the implementation of specific treatments.

Helping special groups. The theory and its assessment devices have some benefits for blacks, females, offenders, retirees, and physically handicapped groups. Some benefits have been demonstrated; others are potential applications that require evaluation. The SDS or its adapted forms have been given positive evaluations by groups of females (Galassi and Lemmon, 1978; Waters and Goodman, 1977), blacks (Zener and Schnuelle, 1976; Kimball, Sedlacek, and Brooks, 1973), and visually disabled college students (Reardon, White, Carlson, and Barker, 1978), and has been used successively by offenders (Bennight, 1975), retarded people (Beziat and Sellars, 1979), nonprofessional workers (Salomone and Slaney, 1978), and poorly prepared college students (Croft, 1976). The following paragraphs illustrate some actual and proposed applications.

The SDS and the theory can be used to understand female vocational aspirations and to plan for change in individuals or groups. For example, Hollinger (1983) found that the 12 self-estimates in the SDS (mechanical ability and manual skills, science and math abilities, artistic and musical abilities, and so on) discriminated talented high school girls aspiring to traditional math/science careers from girls aspiring to nontraditional math/science careers. These and other results specify some of the personal characteristics that require change, if women are to have more math/science careers.

The *individual* profiles of self-estimates could be used in conjunction with all other SDS and personal data to understand the trail of a particular woman's development and to plan for an expressed or more adventurous goal. The hexagonal model, the person's three-letter SDS code, and the *Dictionary of Holland Occupational Codes* can be used to find potential options and to estimate the relative congruency between current interests and competencies and each option. If a woman wants to make a change in the direction of her career—for example, from secretary to manager—these materials imply some of the needed changes in competencies or self-estimates that may be required and how the old skills and self-conceptions may or may not be advantageous in a particular managerial position.

The *average* SDS profiles of females for each section of the SDS can be used to plan environmental changes so that females leave grade school, high school, college, or other training with a more complete range of vocational alternatives. At any age, average SDS profiles, or distributions of vocational aspirations, could be used to identify the pattern of sex role socialization that is vividly displayed in the interests, competencies, self-perceptions, and aspirations of females and males. These educational-cultural forces can be slowed or interrupted by providing more females the opportunity and support to acquire the key experiences and competencies that lead to more divergent and higher level aspirations. The role of mathematics education in the selection of a scientific career is an outstanding illustration of how special experiences trigger careers. Fox (1981) has provided a succinct summary of this research; the theory implies the need for the identification of similar experiences for other major areas of work.

The applications of the theory to other groups—males or minorities—would follow the same principles outlined for females: (1) Use individual SDS materials to assess the current situation and to plan for a more desirable situation; (2) Use average profiles at any age but especially at younger ages to plan environmental changes for the encouragement of a full range of occupational opportunity; and (3) Evaluate the intervention using the same SDS materials to see whether or not beneficial change has occurred.

Bruch (1978) has spelled out some very specific implications of the theory for counseling men and has performed some related research on marital interaction (Bruch and Gilligan, 1980). Holland (1982) has outlined the applications of the theory to adult development and aging; and Mikelman (1980) has applied the theory to retirees and found that an adapted SDS produced some findings that were consistent with the formulations for the types—especially the Investigative and Conventional types.

SOCIAL SCIENCE

The typology and its tools lend themselves to applied and basic research in the social sciences. This section summarizes some positive results and suggests some potential applications.

Classification System

The use of the classification has become the most popular application, for it provides a relatively simple and tested tool for organizing occupational or personal data. The following paragraphs illustrate some of the ways that the classification can be or has been used to cope with some common problems.

The theory can be used in studies of work histories, occupational mobility, and census data. The reexamination of occupational data by classifying according to the theory appears to be one of its most promising applications. The classification will allow economists, psychologists, and sociologists to analyze occupational data in two major ways—according to personality pattern or kind of person and according to level of competence or talent. These differentiations are a simple way to avoid treating all people as interchangeable units, a common practice in economic and sociological research. For example, L. Gottfredson (1977, 1979; L. Gottfredson and Becker, 1981; L. Gottfredson and Brown, 1981) has used the occupational classification to extend sociological-attainment and mobility research beyond a single dimension—status or prestige. She demonstrates that income differences can be explained more efficiently with the use of the classification and finds that amount of education has different payoffs for various types of work.

L. Gottfredson and Brown (1978b) have provided Holland codes for the 297-category 1960 and the 440-category 1970 U.S. Census taxonomies of occupations. Two measures of occupational level—general educational development (GED) level and occupational prestige rating—are also provided for each census title. These codes provide a tool for relating studies employing census data (job opportunities, employment barriers, and other labor market conditions) to studies employing personal data (abilities, interests, values, and personality traits).

The flexibility of the classification makes it possible to cope with both representative and unrepresentative populations. To illustrate, when the number of people or occupations in a main category is large, all three-letter subcategories of a main category can be used to analyze the data; when the number is small, only the main categories or the two-letter categories can be used. Studies by Holland et al. (1973) and Nafziger et al. (1972) illustrate how the classification can be contracted or expanded to deal with a skewed distribution of occupational data. Because a national representative sample of youth had a skewed distribution of types (R = 82 percent, I = 5 percent, A = 2 percent, S = 2 percent, E = 6 percent, and C = 4 percent), Nafziger et al. (1972) used all the three-letter Realistic categories for the Realistic data, but used only single categories for the remaining data. In contrast, distributions of the occupational aspirations of college students will usually contain few Realistic occupations but many Social and Investigative occupations, and so on. Accordingly, the Realistic categories can be contracted and the Social and Investigative categories expanded to deal with this nonrepresentative sample.

The classification can be used to form groups and subgroups to interpret the results of experiments or surveys or to simplify the individual-differences treatment problem. For instance, Owens (1968), in modifying Cronbach's proposal (1957) for a single scientific discipline of psychology, stresses the need to group people according to their patterns of prior experience so that we can develop laws for different types and subtypes rather than going to either extreme—to studies of individuals or whole populations. The present typology is a practical method for this purpose.

The classification can be used to equate experimental and control groups according to personality patterns when true experiments are not possible. Depending upon the data and sample size, the social scientist can compare experimentals and controls of the same type only, compare experimentals and controls whose distributions of types are identical or not significantly different, or compare only experimentals and controls who have identical personality patterns—RSEs versus RSEs, and so on.

The classification can be applied in the experimental study of educational, social, and work groups. These might include studies of various typological combinations and their outcomes: group productivity, satisfaction, learning, creative performance, and personal development. For example, the typology provides a simple technique for creating groups ranging from extreme homogeneity (SEAs only) to extreme heterogeneity (equal numbers of each type).

Finally, the application of the classification to census data has indicated where blacks and women are under- and over-represented as well as the proportions of the total working population engaged in the six kinds of work. Gottfredson (1978a; 1978b) uses these data to suggest job seeking strategies for blacks and females. In an earlier analysis, Gottfredson, Holland, and Gottfredson (1975) have shown that the distribution of young men's and women's aspirations (high school and college students) resemble the distribution of actual employment with some notable exceptions, and Gottfredson and Daiger (1977) used 1960 and 1970 census data to show how the distribution of work for the two sexes changes over time and with age. Later, L. Gottfredson (1979), using a nationally representative sample of young men, has demonstrated how the congruency of aspiration and job increases with age. Taken together, these studies imply some more effective job seeking strategies for females and blacks as well as some new directions for research. For example, these studies imply the need for early interventions to modify the aspirations of blacks, females, and other groups so that they could reach higher levels of occupational achievement and satisfaction.

Interpersonal Relations

The theory appears helpful for explaining the outcomes of selected interpersonal relations (see pp. 115–118): living arrangements, counselor-client relations, and marital relations. In all of these investigations, similarity between types appears to make for better or more satisfying relationships.

Bruch and Skovholt (1982) have used the typology to explain why adult males use mental health services at a lower rate than females. Females, who are more likely to have social dispositions, find the social or therapeutic encounter more congenial than males. In contrast, males, who are more likely to have realistic dispositions, find the social environment of the therapeutic encounter to be especially difficult and unrewarding. These reactions are predictable from the theory—Realistic types are described as uninsightful and asocial.

This interpretation is also supported by the relations between vocational interest and developmental measures. Empirically, vocational interests are related to vocational maturity (Crites, 1978), conceptual systems (Chase, 1980), and Erikson's construct of identity (Holland et al., 1980). In all three instances, realistic interests represent the lowest level of development, and social interests usually represent the highest level of development.

The differences between Realistic and Social types also appear to explain the lack of involvement of foster fathers in the foster care process. Wiehe's (1982) assessment of foster parents (N = 218) with the VPI shows that foster fathers are more likely to be Realistic types and that foster mothers are more likely to be Social types. He uses these findings to suggest a training program for foster fathers that is more in keeping with the formulation for the Realistic type.

These studies imply that it might be useful to explore the application of the theory to a wider range of interpersonal situations: salespersons and customers, students and teachers, supervisors and workers, and so on. Informal attempts to pair people or to form work groups have always taken place. The theory provides some methods for studying these interactions in a simple but more explicit way.

Cultural Change and Comparisons

The cross-national comparisons summarized earlier (p. 118) were used to support the validity of the theory. However, the same or similar studies can be cited as illustrations of the value of theory for understanding different cultures and nations. For example, Richards (1971) has shown that the application of the classification to Japanese universities yields results that closely resemble the results obtained from American universities. And Nafziger et al. (1974) have shown that the typology is helpful for understanding the differences between two subcultures (blacks and whites) in the United States. They show that the distributions of types in national representative samples of men and women are different for blacks and whites; larger proportions of blacks are Realistic types. Turner and Horn (1975), using the Kuder Occupational Interest Survey (Kuder and Diamond, 1979) and the Guilford-Zimmerman Temperament Survey (Guilford and Zimmerman, 1949) found support for the formulations for the types in a sample of Mexican-American males. In another study, Gottfredson and Daiger (1977) used the classification with the 1960 and 1970 census data to describe differences in employment patterns.

In short, because occupational titles are found everywhere in the world, it is a relatively easy task to apply the theory and make comparisons and generate potential explanations. It may even be possible to estimate the rigidity of a culture or nation by developing an index of the continuity of careers for females and males. For example, the present classification appears to produce stronger results—career changes or transitions are more predictable—in some countries than others.

EDUCATION

The applications cited for career assistance also apply to education. The diagnostic and treatment ideas can be applied at all levels of education. In addition, the theory implies that it would be beneficial to match teaching styles to student types.

Elementary and Secondary Education

The distributions of student vocational aspirations or SDS profiles could be used to organize and distribute a school's counseling resources. In this approach, the idea is to provide information and experience that will foster the development of adaptive vocational behavior. Presumably, normal or adaptive personal development leads to a differentiated, consistent personality pattern or a clear sense of vocational identity. In general, the theory suggests the following strategies:

1. Provide students with relevant school and nonschool experiences. This means giving them the opportunity to experience the six curricula *and* the six kinds of nonschool experiences. This orientation implies that unless schools, parents, or other agencies provide a full range of experiences, they lessen students' abilities to understand themselves and their future possibilities.
2. Provide students with accurate and accessible information about themselves and jobs over a long time span rather than at a few critical decision points.
3. Provide students with translations of personal characteristics and jobs that are readily accessible and easily comprehended. The typical use of tests violates this principle. Test information is usually inaccessible, not clearly translated, incomplete, and unintegrated with other data.

By establishing a coherent and integrated set of experiences and informative methods, schools should be able to reach most students. These preliminary diagnostic and treatment plans could be elaborated so that a number of special treatments would be available and effective for students who are at different stages of development or who have different requirements.

In addition, schools should create special programs or adopt only portions of standard programs to meet the typical needs of their student populations. Because student needs for vocational assistance will vary according to distributions of student types and family economic background, standard programs in which everyone gets everything can be wasteful and ineffective.

In elementary education, the emphasis would be on strategies 1 and 2, for without a full range of experiences, boys and girls and rich and poor acquire aspirations that are limited largely to the ghettos of sex and income that narrow the range of acceptable interests, competencies, and goals. In secondary education, strategy 3 becomes more important.

The theory also suggests that teaching might be more effective if students and teachers were paired according to type, or if teachers could adapt teaching styles to student types. Teachers do this now, but again the theoretical formulations provide more explicit guidelines. The typology also provides a practical tool for implementing some of the matching ideas proposed by Hunt (1975) that usually require elaborate student assessments. Amernic and Enns (1979) suggest that the conceptual systems ideas (Hunt, 1975) could be used in conjunction with the present typology.

Career and Vocational Education

The classification implies six "curricular clusters" in secondary and technical schools or institutes, and the subcategories imply some ways to structure single clusters. Such clusters would demand consonant competencies and interests and make teaching a more manageable and effective experience for both students and teachers. The classification links fields of training to occupational possibilities. In vocational education or "career education," the theory could be used to organize an entire school program: curricular clusters, vocational guidance and placement services, occupational exploration programs, and evaluations of programs and services. The clarity and content of the vocational education or career education missions make them especially amenable to the user of the theory. In career education, the SDS is especially useful as a vocational assessment for theoretical studies and as an outcome measure in career education. For example, Wirtenberg (1979) used the SDS to assess effects of a sex-desegregated practical arts course for seventh graders.

Higher Education

The classification implies a clustering or reorganization of curricula in two- and four-year colleges. Whitney and Holland (1969) have proposed such a reorganization for colleges and outlined its advantages for students, faculty, and administrators. The authors believe that their six-cluster scheme would increase the similarity between teacher and student interests, encourage vocational exploration, and improve student learning and development. Independently, Conary (1969) has used the classification as a rationale for organizing a new two-year college into four institutes: (1) Institute of Applied Humanities (Artistic types), (2) Institute of Business and Management (Social-Conventional and Social-Enterprising types), (3) Institute of Human Affairs (Social-Investigative and Social-Artistic types), and (4) Institute of Natural and Applied Sciences (Realistic and Investigative types). This particular plan appears to be working well. What we need now are some comprehensive evaluations of its virtues and deficiencies and a few adventurous colleges to try out the proposal or some variation of it. More recently, Illinois Valley Community College (Andrews, 1980) has used the classification system to code curricula so that students could use SCII or SDS scores in career decision making. The college catalogue underwent a radical revision in which curricular codes and occupational information play a prominent and useful role for prospective students. These revisions have received positive evaluations from high school counselors.

BUSINESS AND INDUSTRY

The classification may be particularly useful in two situations. First, in large organizations, in which problems of staff development, transfer, promotion, and personnel planning have to be solved by moving personnel from one function to another. For example, the classification can be used to organize and locate similar jobs for people who must be transferred; the classification can be used in human resource planning to compare the distribution of types needed in the future with the distribution of types currently employed. The relations among types and subtypes can be used to estimate the degree of flexibility in the workforce, or the degree to which shifts in jobs could be accomplished with minimal training and dissatisfaction to meet future work requirements. Second, in rapidly changing organizations where technological developments and altered objectives necessitate the creation of totally new jobs, the classification has clear practical implications for recruitment and selection procedures, training programs, analysis and redesign of jobs, improvement of communication and cooperation within and between work groups, and for the formulation of personnel policies and practices. For instance, a person's interest profile, in conjunction with other data, could be used to design a more satisfying job that would maximize his or her interests and competencies and minimize his or her aversions and deficiencies. Congenial work groups with more effective matching of supervisors and employees might be obtained by taking advantage of individual personality patterns.

At a higher level, the classification provides a theoretical system for assessing the effects of national workforce recruiting and training policies. For instance, the occupation-industry data could be converted to the present classification and studied longitudinally for the effects of economic, recruiting, and training policies of business and government. The problems of retraining Realistic types, who form the main group and who are now being displaced by new technology and special educational requirements, could be examined in terms of the classification and the formulations for the Realistic type. *The Dictionary of Holland Occupational Codes* provides a tool for searching for related realistic jobs.

The theory is also useful in the more popular career development services within large corporations: retirement planning, job separation counseling, career exploration, and career ladders. In these functions, the SDS, VPI, and classification have been used with and without modification. The diagnostic and treatment ideas reviewed earlier are applicable.

SUMMARY

The theory has implications for organizing information; explaining common career, educational and industrial problems; facilitating career development; and remedying career problems. It has been applied in broad areas in career assistance, social science research, education, and business and industry. Because the theory's origins were in career assistance, its applicability is best understood in that area. The organizational functions, as opposed to the explanatory and facilitative functions, are more firmly grounded in research and are applied most often. The practical applications of the theory should be extended and studied in a greater variety of settings—clinical, educational, and industrial.

REFERENCES

ABE, C., & HOLLAND, J. L. A description of college freshmen: I. Students with different choices of major field. ACT Research Report No. 3. Iowa City, Iowa: The American College Testing Program, 1965(a).

ABE, C., & HOLLAND, J. L. A description of college freshmen: II. Students with different vocational choices. ACT Research Report No. 4. Iowa City, Iowa: The American College Testing Program, 1965(b).

ADERINTO, K. M. Predicting initial academic achievement of college freshmen using Holland's constructs in an urban private four year liberal arts college. Unpublished doctoral dissertation, Fordham University, 1974.

ADLER, A. *Social interest.* New York: Putnam's, 1939.

AHAMMER, I. M. Social-learning theory as a framework for the study of adult personality development. Chapter 11 in *Life-span development psychology: personality and socialization.* P. B. Baltes and K. W. Schaie, eds., New York: Academic Press, 1973.

AIKEN, J., & JOHNSTON, J. A. Promoting career information seeking behaviors in college students. *Journal of Vocational Behavior,* 1973, *3*, 81–87.

ALDERFER, C. P. *Existence, relatedness, and growth: Human needs in organizational settings.* New York: The Free Press, 1972.

ALSTON, H. L., WAKEFIELD, J. A., JR., DOUGHTIE, E. B., & BOBELE, R. M. Correspondence of constructs in Holland's theory for male and female college students. *Journal of Vocational Behavior,* 1976, *8*, 85–88.

AMERNIC, J. H., & ENNS, R. J. Levels of cognitive complexity and the design of accounting curriculum. *The Accounting Review,* 1979, *54*, 133–46.

ANDREWS, H. A. Personality patterns and vocational choice: A test of Holland's theory with adult part-time community college students. *Journal of Counseling Psychology,* 1973, *20,* 482–83.

ANDREWS, H. A. Beyond the high-point code in testing Holland's theory. *Journal of Vocational Behavior,* 1975, *6,* 101–108.

ANDREWS, H. A. The community college catalogue and career decision-making. *Community College Frontiers,* 1980, *9,* 11–17.

APOSTAL, R. A. Personality type and preferred college subculture. *Journal of College Student Personnel,* 1970, *11,* 206–209.

APOSTAL, R. A. & HARPER, P. Basic interests in personality. *Journal of Counseling Psychology,* 1972, *19,* 167–168.

ARANYA, N., BARAK, A., & AMERNIC, J. A test of Holland's theory in a population of accountants. *Journal of Vocational Behavior,* 1981, *19,* 15–24.

ARMSTRONG, P. J. The relationship of counselor-counselee background experiences to high school students' evaluations of counseling. Unpublished doctoral dissertation, Catholic University, Washington, D.C., 1976.

ASHBY, J. D., WALL, H. W., & OSIPOW, S. H. Vocational certainty and indecision in college freshmen. *Personnel and Guidance Journal,* 1966, *44,* 1037–1041.

ASTIN, A. W. Further validation of the environmental assessment technique. *Journal of Educational Psychology,* 1963, *54,* 217–226. (a)

ASTIN, A. W. Undergraduate institutions and the production of scientists. *Science,* 1963, *141,* 334–38. (b)

ASTIN, A. W. Distribution of students among higher educational institutions. *Journal of Educational Psychology,* 1964, *55,* 276–87.

ASTIN, A. W. *Who goes where to college?* Chicago: Science Research Associates, 1965. (a)

ASTIN, A. W. Effects of different college environments on the vocational choices of high aptitude students. *Journal of Counseling Psychology,* 1965, *12,* 28–34. (b)

ASTIN, A. W. Classroom environment in different fields of study. *Journal of Educational Psychology,* 1965, *56,* 275–82. (c)

ASTIN, A. W. *The college environment.* Washington, D.C.: American Council on Education, 1968.

ASTIN, A. W. & HOLLAND, J. L. The environmental assessment technique: A way to measure college environments. *Journal of Educational Psychology,* 1961, *52,* 308–316.

ASTIN, A. W., & NICHOLS, R. C. Life goals and vocational choice. *Journal of Applied Psychology,* 1964, *48,* 50–58.

ASTIN, A. W., & PANOS, R. J. *The educational and vocational development of American college students.* Washington, D.C.: American Council on Education, 1969.

ATTARIAN, P. J. Early recollections: predictors of vocational preference. Unpublished doctoral dissertation, University of Arizona, 1973.

AUL, J. C. A new index of differentiation for Holland's theory of careers. Unpublished doctoral dissertation, Case Western Reserve University, Cleveland, 1979.

AVALLONE, V. L. A comparative study of the effects of two vocational guidance systems: The Self-Directed Search and a traditional vocational guidance model. Doctoral dissertation, University of Northern Colorado, 1974. *Dissertation Abstracts International,* 1974, *35,* 2670A–2671A. (University Microfilms No. 74–24, 472.

BACHTOLD, L. M. Personality characteristics of women of distinction. *Psychology of Women Quarterly,* 1976, *1,* 70–78.

BAILEY, R. L. Testing Holland's theory. *Measurement and Evaluation in Guidance,* 1971, *4,* 107–114.

BAIRD, L. L. The relation of vocational interests to life goals, self-ratings of ability, and personality traits, and potential for achievement. *Journal of Educational Measurement,* 1970, *7,* 233–39.

BAIRD, L. L. *Using self-reports to predict student performance.* Research Monograph No. 7, College Entrance Examination Board, New York, 1976.

BAIRD, L. L. The role of academic ability in high-level accomplishment and general success. College Board Report No. 82–6. New York: College Entrance Examination Board, 1982.

BANDUCCI, R. Accuracy of stereotypic perceptions of types and levels of occupations in relation to background and personal characteristics of high school senior boys. Unpublished doctoral dissertation, University of Iowa, 1968.

BARAK, A., & RABBI, B. Predicting persistence, stability, and achievement in college by major choice consistency: A test of Holland's consistency hypothesis. *Journal of Vocational Behavior,* 1981, *20,* 235–43.

BARCLAY, J. R. Approach to the measurement of teacher "press" in the secondary curriculum. Monograph, *Journal of Counseling Psychology,* 1967, *14,* 552–67.

BARCLAY, J. R. *Barclay classroom assessment system (BCAS).* Los Angeles: Western Psychological Services. 1983.

BARCLAY, J. R., STILLWELL, W. E., & BARCLAY, L. K. The influence of paternal occupation on social interaction measures in elementary school children. *Journal of Vocational Behavior,* 1972, *2,* 433–446.

BARKER, R. G. *Ecological psychology.* Stanford: Stanford University Press, 1968.

BARRY, W. A., & BORDIN, E. S. Personality development and the vocational choice of the ministry. *Journal of Counseling Psychology,* 1967, *14,* 395–403.

BARTLETT, W. E. Vocational choice stability matrix: Development, application, and implications. *Indiana Personnel and Guidance Journal,* Spring 1970, 71–77.

BARTLING, H. C., & HOOD, A. B. An 11-year follow-up of measured interest and vocational choice. *Journal of Counseling Psychology,* 1981, *28,* 27–35.

BATEMAN, T., & ROE, A. College seniors' plans and their implementation. Center for research in careers, Harvard University, Harvard Studies in Career Development, 1966, No. 47.

BATES, G. L., PARKER, H. J., & McCOY, J. F. Vocational rehabilitants' personality and work adjustment: A test of Holland's theory of vocational choice. *Psychological Reports,* 1970, *26,* 511–16.

BELL, R. Q. A reinterpretation of the direction of effects in studies of socialization. *Psychological Review,* 1968, *75,* 81–95.

BELL, R. Q., & HARPER, L. V. *Child or adult: Who's likely to change?* Hillsdale, N.J.: Erlbaum, 1977.

BENNIGHT, K. C. A model program for counseling and placement of offenders. *Journal of Employment Counseling,* 1975, *12,* 168–173.

BENNINGER, W. B., & WALSH, W. B. Holland's theory and non-college-degreed working men and women. *Journal of Vocational Behavior,* 1980, *17,* 81–88.

BESYNER, J. K., BODDEN, J. L., & WINER, J. L. Differentiation of Holland's personality types by means of psychological need variables. *Measurement and Evaluation in Guidance,* 1978, *10,* 237–40.

BEZIAT, R. E., & SELLARS, S. G. Adaptation of Holland's SDS for the retarded. Final Report. Office of Career Education, Project No. 554AH80103. Department of Industrial Education, University of Maryland, 1979.

BIHM, E. M., & WINER, J. L. The distortion of memory for careers: The influence of the thematic organization of occupational information. *Journal of Vocational Behavior,* 1983, *23,* 356–66.

BINGHAM, R. P. Concurrent validity of Holland's theory for college-degreed black women. *Journal of Vocational Behavior,* 1978, *13,* 242–50.

BLAKENEY, R. N., MATTESON, M. T., & HOLLAND, T. A. A research note on the new SVIB Holland scales. *Journal of Vocational Behavior*, 1972, *2*, 239–43.

BLAU, P. M., & DUNCAN, O. D. *The American occupational structure*. New York: John Wiley, 1967.

BLOCK, J. Advancing the science of personality: Paradigmatic shift or improving the quality of research. In D. Magnusson and N. S. Endler (eds.), *Psychology at the Crossroads: Current issues in interactional psychology*. Hillsdale, N.J.: Erlbaum (John Wiley), 1977.

BOBELE, R. M., ALSTON, H. L., WAKEFIELD, J. A., JR., & DOUGHTIE, E. B. A comparison of Holland's model using constructs measured by two different methods. *Journal of Vocational Behavior*, 1976, *9*, 245–50.

BOBELE, R. M., ALSTON, H. L., WAKEFIELD, J. A., JR., & SCHNITZEN, J. P. Relationships among Holland's personality types measured by an adjective checklist. *Journal of Vocational Behavior*, 1975, *7*, 201–206.

BODDEN, J. L., & KLEIN, A. J. Cognitive differentiation and affective stimulus value in affective judgments. *Journal of Vocational Behavior*, 1973, *3*, 75–79.

BOHN, M. J., JR. Psychological needs related to personality types. *Journal of Counseling Psychology*, 1966, *13*, 306–309.

BOLLES, R. C. Whatever happened to motivation? *Educational Psychologist*, 1978, *13*, 1–13.

BORDIN, E. S. A theory of interests as dynamic phenomena. *Educational and Psychological Measurement*, 1943, *3*, 49–66.

BORGEN, F. H., & SELING, M. J. Expressed and inventoried interests revisited: Perspicacity in the person. *Journal of Counseling Psychology*, 1978, *25*, 536–43.

BOYD, V. S. Neutralizing sexist titles in Holland's Self-Directed Search: What difference does it make? *Journal of Vocational Behavior*, 1976, *9*, 191–99.

BRAUNSTEIN, D. N., HAINES, G. H., JR., LEIDY, T. R., & STARRY, A. *Student stereotypes of business*. College of Business Administration, University of Rochester, Rochester, N.Y., November 1970.

BROUSSEAU, K. R., & PRINCE, J. B. Job-person dynamics: an extension of longitudinal research. *Journal of Applied Psychology*, 1981, *66*, 59–62.

BROWN, R. D. Peer group influence in a college residence hall. Unpublished doctoral dissertation, University of Iowa, 1966.

BROWN, S. H. Long-term validity of a personal history item scoring procedure. *Journal of Applied Psychology*, 1978, *63*, 673–76.

BRUCH, M. A. Holland's typology applied to client-counselor interaction: Implications for counseling with men. *Counseling Psychologist*, 1978, *7*, 26–32.

BRUCH, M. A., & GILLIGAN, J. F. Extension of Holland's theory to assessment of marital and family interaction. *American Mental Health Counselors Association Journal*, 1980, *2*, 71–82.

BRUCH, M. A., & KRIESHOK, T. S. Investigative versus realistic types and adjustment in theoretical engineering majors. *Journal of Vocational Behavior*, 1981, *18*, 162–173.

BRUCH, M. A., & SKOVHOLT, T. M. Counseling services and men in need: a problem in person-environment matching. *American Mental Health Counselors Association*, July 1982, 89–96.

BRUE, E. J. Characteristics of transfer and occupational students in community colleges: A comparative study. Unpublished doctoral dissertation, University of Iowa, 1969.

CAMPBELL, D. P. The stability of vocational interests within occupations over long time spans. *Personnel and Guidance Journal*, 1966, *44*, 1012–1019. (a)

CAMPBELL, D. P. *Handbook for the Strong vocational interest blank*. Stanford, Calif.: Stanford University Press, 1971.

CAMPBELL, D. P. *Manual for the Strong-Campbell Interest Inventory T325 (Merged form).* Stanford, Calif.: Stanford University Press, 1974.

CAMPBELL, D. P. Stability of interests within an occupation over thirty years. *Journal of Applied Psychology,* 1966, *50,* 51–56. (b)

CAMPBELL, D. P., & HANSEN, J. C. *Manual for the SVIB-SCII.* Stanford, Calif.: Stanford University Press, 1981.

CAMPBELL, D. P. & HOLLAND, J. L. A merger in vocational interest research: Applying Holland's theory to Strong's data. *Journal of Vocational Behavior,* 1972, *2,* 353–76.

CAMPBELL, D. P., & ROSSMAN, J. E. Liberalism-conservatism, men and women, and occupations. Paper presented at American Psychological Association Convention, 1972.

CAMPBELL, R. E., & CELLINI, J. V. A diagnostic taxonomy of adult career problems. *Journal of Vocational Behavior,* 1981, *19,* 175–90.

CAPEHART, J. L., JR. The relationship of vocational maturity to Holland's theory of vocational choice. Unpublished doctoral dissertation, University of North Carolina, Chapel Hill, 1973.

CARMODY, J. F. A descriptive analysis of students expressing a proposed future vocation in an area of education and a test of the suitability of Holland's personality model to describe future educators (Doctoral dissertation, University of Iowa, 1971). *Dissertation Abstracts International,* 1972, *32,* 2477A–2478A. (University microfilms No. 71–30, 411.)

CARTWRIGHT, R. A., & POWER, P. G. The effect of teaching practice on the differentiation scores of current and end-on student teachers. Unpublished ms., Melbourne State College, 1982.

CATTELL, R. B., EBER, H. W., & TATSUOKA, M. M. *Handbook for the Sixteen Personality Factor Questionnaire* (16PF). Champaign, Ill.: Institute for Personality and Ability Testing, 1970.

CHANEY, F. B., & OWENS, W. A. Life history antecedents of sales, research, and general engineering interests. *Journal of Applied Psychology,* 1964, *48,* 101–105.

CHAPMAN, D. W., & HUTCHESON, S. M. Attrition from teaching careers: A discriminant analysis. *American Educational Research Journal,* 1982, *19,* 93–105.

CHASE, J. A. A study of three sets of personological variables and vocational choice. Unpublished doctoral dissertation, University of Colorado, Boulder, 1980.

CHRISTENSEN, K. C., & SEDLACEK, W. E. Diagnostic use of Holland's Self-Directed Search. *Vocational Guidance Quarterly,* 1974, *22,* 214–17.

CLEVELAND, C. E. The relationships among field dependence, Holland's personality types and perceived traditionality of occupational choice. Unpublished doctoral dissertation, Howard University, Washington, D.C., 1979.

COCKRIEL, I. W. Some data concerning the Vocational Preference Inventory and the Strong Vocational Interest Blank. *Journal of Vocational Behavior,* 1972, *2,* 251–254.

COLE, J. A study of person-environment interactions in a school system. Unpublished master's thesis. University of Melbourne, 1975.

COLE, N. S. On measuring the vocational interests of women. *Journal of Counseling Psychology,* 1973, *20,* 105–112.

COLE, N. S., & COLE, J. W. An analysis of spatial configuration and its application to research in higher education. ACT Research Report No. 35. Iowa City, Iowa: The American College Testing Program, 1970.

COLE, N. S., & HANSON, G. R. An analysis of the structure of vocational interests. ACT Research Report No. 40. Iowa City, Iowa: American College Testing Program, 1971.

COLE, N. S., WHITNEY, D. R., & HOLLAND, J. L. A spatial configuration of occupations. *Journal of Vocational Behavior*, 1971, *1*, 1–9.

CONARY, F. M. An alternate approach to clustering. Research Advisory No. 5, Brookdale Community College, Lincroft, N.J., 1969.

COOK, M. A., & ALEXANDER, K. L. Preparing for work: Manifest interests and adolescent vocational development. Final Report, Grant No. NIE–G–76–0078. National Institute of Education, September 1979.

COSTA, P. T., JR., FOZARD, J. L., & McCRAE, R. R. Personological interpretation of factors from the Strong Vocational Interest Blank scales. *Journal of Vocational Behavior*, 1977, *10*, 231–43.

COSTA, P. T., JR., & MC CRAE, R. R. Age differences in personality structure: A cluster analytic approach. *Journal of Gerontology*, 1976, *31*, 564–70.

COSTA, P. T., JR., & McCRAE, R. R. Still stable after all these years: Personality as a key to some issues in adulthood and old age. Pp. 65–102 in *Life-span Development and Behavior*, volume 3. P. Baltes and O. Brim, eds., Academic Press, New York, 1980.

COSTA, P. T., JR., McCRAE, R. R., & HOLLAND, J. L. Personality and vocational interests in adulthood. *Journal of Applied Psychology*, 1984, *69*, 390-400.

COX, J. G., & THORESON, R. W. Client-counselor matching: A test of the Holland model. *Journal of Counseling Psychology*, 1977, *24*, 158–61.

CRABTREE, P. D., & HALES, L. W. Holland's hexagonal model applied to rural youth. *Vocational Guidance Quarterly*, 1974, *22*, 218–23.

CRITES, J. O. *Career maturity inventory*. Monterey, Calif.: McGraw-Hill, 1978.

CROFT, D. B. Predictors of success in college for low prior educational attainment multicultural students. (Grant No. OEG–0–74–1712.) Educational Research Center, Las Cruces: New Mexico State University, 1976.

CRONBACH, L. J. The two disciplines of scientific psychology. *American Psychologist*, 1957, *12*, 671–84.

CRUTCHFIELD, R. S., WOODWORTH, D. G., & ALBRECHT, R. E. Perceptual performance and the effective person. Personnel Laboratory, U.S. Air Force, ASTIA Document No. AD 151 039. Lackland Air Force Base, Texas, 1958.

CSIKSZENTMIHALYI, M. *Beyond boredom and anxiety*. San Francisco, Calif.: Jossey-Bass, 1975.

CUNNINGHAM, C. H., ALSTON, H. L., DOUGHTIE, E. B., & WAKEFIELD, J. A., JR. Use of Holland's vocational theory with potential high school dropouts. *Journal of Vocational Behavior*, 1977, *10*, 35–38.

CURETON, L. W. Early identification of behavior problems. National Institute of Mental Health Grant No. MH–07274, Final Report. Washington, D.C.: American Institutes for Research, 1970.

DANEK, T. A. A test of predictions based on the consistency and homogeneity dimensions of Holland's personality theory. (Doctoral dissertation, University of North Carolina at Chapel Hill, 1971.) *Dissertation Abstracts International*, 1971, *32*, 2414A. (University Microfilms No. 71–30, 551.)

DARLEY, J. G. A preliminary study of relations between attitude, adjustment, and vocational interest tests. *Journal of Educational Psychology*, 1938, *29*, 467–73.

DARLEY, J. G., & HAGENAH, T. *Vocational interest measurement*. Minneapolis: University of Minnesota Press, 1955.

DAVIES, K. F. A comparative and normative study of Holland's Self-Directed Search modified for elementary school students. Unpublished paper required for master's degree, University of Maryland, 1971.

DAYTON, C. M., & UHL, N. P. Relationship between Holland Vocational Preference Inventory scores and performance measures of high school students. Cooperative Project Research No. 5–0581–2–12–1. College Park, Md.: Research and Demonstration Center, University of Maryland, 1966.

DeVoge, S. D. A test of the validity of Holland's personality theory of vocational choice. Doctoral dissertation, University of North Carolina at Chapel Hill, 1973.

DeWinne, R. F., Overton, T. D., & Schneider, L. J. Types produce types—especially fathers. *Journal of Vocational Behavior*, 1978, *12*, 140–144.

Dolliver, R. H. Strong Vocational Interest Blank versus expressed vocational interests: a review. *Psychological Bulletin*, 1969, *72*, 95–107.

Dolliver, R. H., & Mixon, R. J. Classifying occupations with ego states. *Transactional Analysis Journal*, 1977, *7*, 170–75.

Dorset, B. M. Vocational interest similarity and marital satisfaction. Unpublished doctoral dissertation, University of Minnesota, Minneapolis, 1977.

Doughtie, E. B., Chang, W. C., Alston, H. L., Wakefield, J. A., Jr., & Yom, B. L. Black-white differences on the Vocational Preference Inventory. *Journal of Vocational Behavior*, 1976, *8*, 41–44.

Eberhardt, B. J., & Muchinsky, P. M. Biodata determinants of vocational typology: An integration of two paradigms. *Journal of Applied Psychology*, 1982, *67*, 714–27.

Eberhardt, B. J., & Muchinsky, P. M. Structural validation of Holland's hexagonal model: Vocational classification through the use of biodata. *Journal of Applied Psychology*, 1984, *69*, 174–181.

Edwards, A. L. *Manual for the Edwards Personal Preference Schedule.* New York: Psychological Corporation, 1959.

Edwards, K. J., Nafziger, D. H., & Holland, J. L. Differentiation of occupational perceptions among different age groups. *Journal of Vocational Behavior*, 1974, *4*, 311–18.

Edwards, K. J., & Whitney, D. R. A structural analysis of Holland's personality types using factor and configural analysis. *Journal of Counseling Psychology*, 1972, *19*, 136–45.

Eggenberger, J., & Herman, A. The Strong Inventory and Holland's theory. *Journal of Vocational Behavior*, 1972, *2*, 447–56.

Elton, C. F. The interaction of environment and personality: A test of Holland's theory. *Journal of Applied Psychology*, 1971, *55*, 114–18.

Elton, C. F. Male career role and vocational choice: Their prediction with personality and aptitude variables. *Journal of Counseling Psychology*, 1967, *14*, 99–105.

Elton, C. F., & Rose, H. A. Male occupational constancy and change: Its prediction according to Holland's theory. *Journal of Counseling Psychology*, 1970, *17*, Part 2, No. 6.

Elton, C. F., & Rose, H. A. The relation of congruence, differentiation and consistency to interest and aptitude scores in men with stable and unstable vocational choices. Unpublished manuscript, Department of Higher Education, University of Kentucky, Lexington, 1982.

Employment and Immigration. *Holland codes for C.C.D.O.* Occupational and career analysis and development, Employment and Immigration, Canada, 1973.

Endler, N. S., & Magnusson, D. Toward an interactional psychology of personality. *Psychological Bulletin*, 1976, *83*, 956–74.

Epstein, W. The stability of behavior: I. On predicting most of the people much of the time. *Journal of Personality and Social Psychology*, 1979, *37*, 1097–1126.

Erwin, T. D. The predictive validity of Holland's construct of consistency. *Journal of Vocational Behavior*, 1982, *20*, 180–92.

Fabry, J. J. An investigation of Holland's vocational theory across and within selected occupational groups. *Journal of Vocational Behavior*, 1976, *9*, 73–76.

Feldman, S., & Meir, E. I. Measuring women's interests using Holland's vocational classification. *Journal of Vocational Behavior*, 1976, *9*, 345–53.

FISHBURNE, F. J., JR., & WALSH, W. B. Concurrent validity of Holland's theory for non-college-degreed workers. *Journal of Vocational Behavior*, 1976, *8*, 77–84.

FLANAGAN, J. C., TIEDEMAN, D. V., WILLIS, M. B., & McLAUGHLIN, D. H. *The Career Data Book*. American Institutes for Research: Palo Alto, Calif., 1973.

FLORENCE, J. W. An investigation of Holland's theory of vocational psychology. Doctoral dissertation, University of Tulsa, 1973. *Dissertation Abstracts International*, 1973, *34*, 1076A. (University Microfilms No. 73–19, 752.)

FOLSOM, C. H., JR. An investigation of Holland's theory of vocational choice. *Journal of Counseling Psychology*, 1969, *16*, 260–66.

FORER, B. R. A diagnostic interest blank. *Rorschach Research Exchange and Journal of Projective Techniques*, 1948, *12*, 1–11.

FORER, B. R. Personality dynamics and occupational choice. Paper presented at the American Psychological Association meetings, Chicago, 1951.

FORTNER, M. L. Vocational choices of high school girls: Can they be predicted? *Vocational Guidance Quarterly*, 1970, *19*, 203–206.

FOSTER, J., & GADE, E. Locus of control, consistency of vocational interest patterns, and academic achievement. *Journal of Counseling Psychology*, 1973, *20*, 290–92.

FOX, L. H. The problem of women and mathematics. Report to the Ford Foundation, New York 10017, August 1981.

FRANTZ, T. T. Backgrounds of student personnel workers. *Journal of College Student Personnel*, 1969, *10*, 193–203.

FRANTZ, T. T., & WALSH, E. P. Exploration of Holland's theory of vocational choice in graduate school environments. *Journal of Vocational Behavior*, 1972, *2*, 223–32.

FROMM, E. *Man for himself*. New York: Holt, Rinehart and Winston, 1947.

GAFFEY, R. L., & WALSH, W. B. Concurrent validity and Holland's theory. *Journal of Vocational Behavior*, 1974, *5*, 41–51.

GALASSI, M. D., & LEMMON, S. M. Life direction seminars: facilitating human development at a women's college. *Personnel and Guidance Journal*, 1978, *57*, 172–175.

GALE, E. M., & SOLIAH, D. Vocational preference inventory high-point codes versus expressed choices as predictors of college major and career entry. *Journal of Counseling Psychology*, 1975, *22*, 117–21.

GECHT, J. R. A study of personality patterns and occupational aspirations of male college undergraduates and alumni using Holland's typology. Unpublished doctoral dissertation, Florida State University, Tallahassee, 1978.

GENDRE, F. Etude des relations entre l'Inventaire Personnel de J. L. Holland et l'Adjective Check-list de H. Gough. *Le Travail Humain*, 1975, *38*, 265–78.

GENDRE, F., DUPONT, J. B., FATIO, P., & RUSSO, H. Analyse discriminate de l'inventaire personnel de J. L. Holland. *Le Travail Humain*, 1974, *37*, 117–26.

GENTRY, J. M., WINER, J. L., SIGELMAN, C. K., & PHILLIPS, F. L. Adlerian lifestyle and vocational preference. *Journal of Individual Psychology*, 1980, *36*, 80–86.

GESINDE, S. A. Congruence of basic personal orientation with vocational training: Its relationship to conditions of choice and to performance and satisfaction in selected vocational training programs in Nigeria. Unpublished doctoral dissertation, Teachers College, Columbia University, New York, 1973.

GORDON, L. V. *The measurement of interpersonal values*. Chicago: Science Research Associates, 1975.

GOTTFREDSON, D. C. Personality and persistence in education: a longitudinal study. *Journal of Personality and Social Psychology*, 1982, *43*, 532–45.

GOTTFREDSON, G. D. An assessment of a mobility-based occupational classification for placement and counseling. *Journal of Vocational Behavior*, 1982, *21*, 71–98.

GOTTFREDSON, G. D. A note on sexist wording in interest measurement. *Measurement and Evaluation in Guidance,* 1976, *8,* 221–23.

GOTTFREDSON, G. D. Career stability and redirection in adulthood. *Journal of Applied Psychology,* 1977, *62,* 436–45.

GOTTFREDSON, G. D. Why don't interests predict job satisfaction better than they do? Paper presented at American Psychological Association Convention, August 24, 1981, Los Angeles.

GOTTFREDSON, G. D., & DAIGER, D. C. Using a classification of occupations to describe age, sex, and time differences in employment patterns. *Journal of Vocational Behavior,* 1977, *10,* 121–28.

GOTTFREDSON, G. D., & HOLLAND, J. L. Some normative self-report data on activities, competencies, occupational preferences, and ability ratings for high school and college students, and employed men and women. *JSAS Catalog of Selected Documents in Psychology,* 1975, *5,* 192. (Ms. No. 859) (a)

GOTTFREDSON, G. D., & HOLLAND, J. L. Vocational choices of men and women: A comparison of predictors from the Self-Directed Search. *Journal of Counseling Psychology,* 1975, *22,* 28–34. (b)

GOTTFREDSON, G. D., HOLLAND, J. L., & GOTTFREDSON, L. S. The relation of vocational aspirations and assessments to employment reality. *Journal of Vocational Behavior,* 1975, *7,* 135–148.

GOTTFREDSON, G. D., HOLLAND, J. L., & HOLLAND, J. E. The seventh revision of the Vocational Preference Inventory. *Psychological Documents,* 1978, *8,* 98. (Ms. 1783).

GOTTFREDSON, G. D., HOLLAND, J. L., & OGAWA, D. K. *Dictionary of Holland occupational codes.* Palo Alto, Calif.: Consulting Psychologists Press, 1982.

GOTTFREDSON, G. D., & LIPSTEIN, D. J. Using personal characteristics to predict parolee and probationer employment stability. *Journal of Applied Psychology,* 1975, *60,* 644–48.

GOTTFREDSON, L. S. A multiple labor market model of occupational achievement. Research Report No. 225. Center for Social Organization of Schools, Johns Hopkins University, Baltimore, Md., 1977.

GOTTFREDSON, L. S. Providing black youth more access to enterprising work. *Vocational Guidance Quarterly,* 1978, *27,* 114–23. (a)

GOTTFREDSON, L. S. An analytical description of employment according to race, sex, prestige and Holland type of work. *Journal of Vocational Behavior,* 1978, *13,* 210–21. (b)

GOTTFREDSON, L. S. Aspiration-job match: age trends in a large, nationally representative sample of young white men. *Journal of Counseling Psychology,* 1979, *26,* 319–28.

GOTTFREDSON, L. S. Construct validity of Holland's occupational typology in terms of prestige, census, department of labor, and other classification systems. *Journal of Applied Psychology,* 1980, *65,* 697–714.

GOTTFREDSON, L. S. Circumscription and compromise: A developmental theory of occupational aspirations. *Journal of Counseling Psychology Monograph,* 1981, *28,* 545–79.

GOTTFREDSON, L. S., & BECKER, H. J. A challenge to vocational psychology: How important are aspirations in determining male career development? *Journal of Vocational Behavior,* 1981, *18,* 121–37.

GOTTFREDSON, L. S., & BROWN, V. C. Holland codes for the 1960 and 1970 Census Detailed Occupational Titles. *Psychological Documents,* 1978, *8,* 22. (Ms. No. 1660)

GOTTFREDSON, L. S., & BROWN, V. C. Occupational differentiation among white men in the first decade after high school. *Journal of Vocational Behavior,* 1981, *19,* 251–89.

GOTTFREDSON, L. S., GOTTFREDSON, G. D., & HOLLAND, J. L. A complementary perspective on occupational structure. Unpublished manuscript, Johns Hopkins University, Center for Social Organization of Schools, 1975.

GOUGH, H. G. *Manual for the California Psychological Inventory.* Palo Alto, Calif.: Consulting Psychologists Press, 1957.

GOUGH, H. G., & HEILBRUN, A. B., JR. *Manual for the Adjective Check List.* Palo Alto, Calif.: Consulting Psychologists Press, 1965.

GRANDY, T. G., & STAHMANN, R. F. Family influence on college students' vocational choice: Predicting Holland's personality types. *Journal of College Student Personnel,* 1974, *15,* 404–409. (a)

GRANDY, T. G., & STAHMANN, R. F. Types produce types: An examination of personality development using Holland's theory. *Journal of Vocational Behavior,* 1974, *5,* 231–39. (b)

GREENBERGER, E., JOSSELSON, R., KNERR, C., & KNERR, B. The measurement and structure of psychosocial maturity. *Journal of Youth and Adolescence,* 1975, *4,* 127–43.

GREENBERGER, E., & SORENSEN, A. B. Toward a concept of psychosocial maturity. *Journal of Youth and Adolescence,* 1974, *3,* 329–58.

GROSS, L. J., & FARR, S. D. A multidimensional scaling of Holland's vocational personality stereotypes. Paper presented at Annual Meeting of the American Educational Research Association, New York City, 1977.

GROSS, L. J., & GAIER, E. L. College major and career choice: A retest of Holland's theory. *Journal of Vocational Behavior,* 1974, *5,* 209–213.

GROTEVANT, H. D. Environmental influences on vocational interest development in adolescents from adoptive and biological families. *Child Development,* 1979, *50,* 854–60.

GROTEVANT, H. D., SCARR, S., & WEINBERG, R. A. Patterns of interest similarity in adoptive and biological families. *Journal of Personality and Social Psychology,* 1977, *35,* 667–76.

GROTEVANT, H. D., & THORBECKE, W. L. Sex differences in styles of occupational identity formation. *Developmental Psychology,* 1982, *18,* 396–405.

GRUNES, W. F. Looking at occupations. *Journal of Abnormal and Social Psychology,* 1957, *54,* 86–92.

GUILFORD, J. P., CHRISTENSEN, P. R., BOND, N. A., JR. & SUTTON, M. A. A factor analysis study of human interests. *Psychological Monographs,* 1954, *68* (4, Whole No. 375).

GUILFORD, J. P., & ZIMMERMAN, W. S. *Guilford-Zimmerman Temperament Survey.* Beverly Hills,Calif.: Sheridan Supply, 1949.

GUILFORD, J. S. Isolation and description of occupational stereotypes. *Occupational Psychology,* 1967, *41,* 57–64.

GUPTA, W. B. A factor analytic validation of vocational trait structure with ninth grade boys and girls. Unpublished doctoral dissertation, University of California, Los Angeles, 1977.

HAASE, R. F. A canonical analysis of the Vocational Preference Inventory and the Strong Vocational Interest Blank. *Journal of Counseling Psychology,* 1971, *18,* 182–83.

HAASE, R. F., REED, C. F., WINER, J. L., & BODDEN, J. L. Effect of positive, negative, and mixed occupational information on cognitive and affective complexity. *Journal of Vocational Behavior,* 1979, *15,* 294–302.

HALL, D. T., & HALL, F. S. The relationship between goals, performance, success, self-image, and involvement under different organizational climates. *Journal of Vocational Behavior,* 1976, *9,* 267–78.

HANSEN, J. C., & JOHANSSON, C. B. The application of Holland's vocational model to the Strong Vocational Interest Blank for women. *Journal of Vocational Behavior,* 1972, *2,* 479–93.

HARREN, V. A., & BISCARDI, D. L. Sex roles and cognitive styles as predictors of Holland typologies. *Journal of Vocational Behavior,* 1980, *17,* 231–41.

HARVEY, D. W., & WHINFIELD, R. W. Extending Holland's theory to adult women. *Journal of Vocational Behavior,* 1973, *3,* 115–27.

HAUSELMAN, A. J. Personality and the choice of undergraduate major: A test of Holland's theory. Doctoral dissertation, University of Kentucky, 1971. *Dissertation Abstracts International,* 1972, *32,* 4948A. (University Microfilms No. 72–9397, 167.)

HAZANOVITZ-JORDAN, S. Occupational choice and early family relationships: A study of sexual symbolism. *Genetic Psychology Monographs,* 1982, *105,* 309–62.

HEALY, C. C., & MOURTON, D. L. Derivatives of the Self-Directed Search: Potential clinical and evaluative uses. *Journal of Vocational Behavior,* 1983, *23,* 318–28.

HEARN, J. C., & MOOS, R. H. Social climate and major choice: A test of Holland's theory in university student living groups. *Journal of Vocational Behavior,* 1976, *8,* 293–305.

HEARN, J. C., & MOOS, R. H. Subject matter and classroom climate: A test of Holland's environmental propositions. *American Educational Research Journal,* 1978, *15,* 111–24.

HEIST, P., & YONGE, G. *Manual for the Omnibus Personality Inventory, Form F.* New York: The Psychological Corporation, 1968.

HELMS, S. T. Practical applications of the Holland occupational classification in counseling. *Communique,* 1973, *2,* 69–71.

HELMS, S. T., & WILLIAMS, G. D. An experimental study of the reactions of high school students to simulated jobs (Research Report No. 161). Baltimore, Md.: Center for Social Organization of Schools, Johns Hopkins University, 1973. (ERIC Document Reproduction Service No. ED 087 882.)

HENER, T., & MEIR, E. I. Congruency, consistency, and differentiation as predictors of job satisfaction within the nursing occupation. *Journal of Vocational Behavior,* 1981, *18,* 304–309.

HENKELS, M. T., SPOKANE, A. R., & HOFFMAN, M. A. Vocational identity, personality, and preferred mode of interest inventory feedback. *Measurement and Evaluation in Guidance,* 1981, *14,* 71–76.

HENRY, J. A. A multidimensional evaluation structure analysis of Holland's occupational typology. Doctoral dissertation, University of North Dakota, 1975.

HESSELDENZ, J. S. Personality-based faculty workload analysis. *Research in Higher Education,* 1976, *5,* 321–34.

HOGAN, R., HALL, R., & BLANK, E. An extension of the similarity-attraction hypothesis to the study of vocational behavior. *Journal of Counseling Psychology,* 1972, *19,* 238–46.

HOLLAND, J. L. A personality inventory employing occupational titles. *Journal of Applied Psychology,* 1958, *42,* 336–42.

HOLLAND, J. L. A theory of vocational choice. *Journal of Counseling Psychology,* 1959, *6,* 35–45.

HOLLAND, J. L. The relation of the Vocational Preference Inventory to the Sixteen Personality Factor Questionnaire. *Journal of Applied Psychology,* 1960, *44,* 291–96.

HOLLAND, J. L. Some explorations of a theory of vocational choice: I. One-and two-year longitudinal studies. *Psychological Monographs,* 1962, *76,* No. 26 (Whole No. 545).

HOLLAND, J. L. Explorations of a theory of vocational choice and achievement: II. A four-year prediction study. *Psychological Reports,* 1963, *12,* 537–94.

HOLLAND, J. L. Explorations of a theory of vocational choice: IV. Vocational preferences and their relation to occupational images, daydreams and personality. *Vocational Guidance Quarterly*, published in four parts in Summer, Autumn, and Winter issues, 1963–64.

HOLLAND, J. L. *Explorations of a theory of vocational choice: V. A one year prediction study.* Moravia, N.Y.: Chronical Guidance Professional Services, 1964.

HOLLAND, J. L. A psychological classification scheme for vocations and major fields. *Journal of Counseling Psychology*, 1966, *13*, 278–88. (a)

HOLLAND, J. L. *The psychology of vocational choice.* Waltham, Mass.: Blaisdell, 1966. (b)

HOLLAND, J. L. Explorations of a theory of vocational choice: VI. A longitudinal study using a sample of typical college students. Monograph Supplement, *Journal of Applied Psychology*, February 1968, *52*, No. 1, Part 2.

HOLLAND, J. L. *Making vocational choices.* Englewood Cliffs, N.J.: Prentice-Hall, 1973.

HOLLAND, J. L. Some practical remedies for providing vocational guidance for everyone. *Educational Researcher*, 1974, *3*, 9–15.

HOLLAND, J. L. *Manual for the Vocational Preference Inventory.* Palo Alto, Calif.: Consulting Psychologists Press, 1977.

HOLLAND, J. L. *The Occupations Finder.* Palo Alto, Calif.: Consulting Psychologists Press, 1978.

HOLLAND, J. L. *Professional manual for the Self-Directed Search.* Palo Alto, Calif.: Consulting Psychologists Press, 1979.

HOLLAND, J. L. Some implications of career theory for adult development. Invited address, American Psychological Convention, Washington, D.C., August 15, 1982.

HOLLAND, J. L. New directions for interest testing. In B. Blake & J. C. Witt (eds.), *The Future of Testing.* Hillsdale, N.J.: Erlbaum, in press.

HOLLAND, J. L., DAIGER, D. C., & POWER, P. G. Some diagnostic scales for research in decision-making and personality: Identity, information and barriers. *Journal of Personality and Social Psychology*, 1980, *39*, 1191–1200.

HOLLAND, J. L., & GOTTFREDSON, G. D. Predictive value and psychological meaning of vocational aspirations. *Journal of Vocational Behavior*, 1975, *6*, 349–63.

HOLLAND, J. L., & GOTTFREDSON, G. D. Sex differences, item revisions, validity, and the Self-Directed Search. *Measurement and Evaluation in Guidance*, 1976, *8*, 224–28. (a)

HOLLAND, J. L., & GOTTFREDSON, G. D. Using a typology of persons and environments to explain careers: some extensions and clarifications. *The Counseling Psychologist*, 1976, *6*, 20–29. (b)

HOLLAND, J. L., GOTTFREDSON, G. D., & NAFZIGER, D. H. Testing the validity of some theoretical signs of vocational decision-making ability. *Journal of Counseling Psychology*, 1975, *22*, 411–22.

HOLLAND, J. L., & HOLLAND, J. E. Distributions of personalities within occupations and fields of study. *Vocational Guidance Quarterly*, 1977, *25*, 226–31. (a)

HOLLAND, J. L., & HOLLAND, J. E. Vocational indecision: more evidence and speculation. *Journal of Counseling Psychology*, 1977, *24*, 404–414. (b)

HOLLAND, J. L., & LUTZ, S. W. The predictive value of a student's choice of vocation. *Personnel and Guidance Journal*, 1968, *46*, 428–36.

HOLLAND, J. L., MAGOON, T. M., & SPOKANE, A. R. Counseling psychology: career interventions, research, and theory. *Annual Review of Psychology*, 1981, *32*, 279–305.

HOLLAND, J. L., & NAFZIGER, D. H. A note about the validity of the Self-Directed Search. *Measurement and Evaluation in Guidance*, 1975, *4*, 259–62.

HOLLAND, J. L., & NICHOLS, R. C. Explorations of a theory of vocational choice: III. A longitudinal study of change in major field of study. *Personnel and Guidance Journal*, 1964, *43*, 235–42.

HOLLAND, J. L., SORENSEN, A. B., CLARK, J. P., NAFZIGER, D. H., & BLUM, Z. D. Applying an occupational classification to a representative sample of work histories. *Journal of Applied Psychology*, 1973, *58*, 34–41.

HOLLAND, J. L., VIERNSTEIN, M. C., KUO, H., KARWEIT, N. L., & BLUM, Z. D. A psychological classification of occupations. *Journal Supplement Abstract Service*, 1972, *2*, 84.

HOLLAND, J. L., & WHITNEY, D. R. Changes in the vocational plans of college students: orderly or random? ACT Research Report No. 25. American College Testing Program, Iowa City, Iowa, 1968.

HOLLAND, J. L., WHITNEY, D. R., COLE, N. S., & RICHARDS, J. M., JR. An empirical occupational classification derived from a theory of personality and intended for practice and research. ACT Research Report No. 29. Iowa City, Iowa: The American College Testing Program, 1969.

HOLLANDER, M. A., & PARKER, H. J. Occupational stereotypes and needs: Their relationship to vocational choice. *Vocational Guidance Quarterly*, 1969, *18*, 91–98.

HOLLANDER, M. A., & PARKER, H. J. Occupational stereotypes and self-descriptions: Their relationship to vocational choice. *Journal of Vocational Behavior*, 1972, *2*, 57–65.

HOLLIFIELD, J. H. An examination of the validity of the Self-Directed Search for writers. *Measurement and Evaluation in Guidance*, 1974, *6*, 247.

HOLLINGER, C. L. Self-perception and the career aspirations of mathematically talented female adolescents. *Journal of Vocational Behavior*, 1983, *22*, 49–62.

HOPPOCK, R. *Occupational information*. New York: McGraw-Hill, 1968.

HORTON, J. A., & WALSH, W. B. Concurrent validity of Holland's theory for college-degreed working women. *Journal of Vocational Behavior*, 1976, *9*, 201–208.

HOUNTRAS, P. T., LEE, D. L., & HEDAHL, B. M. Relationships between SVIB nonoccupational scales and achievement for six Holland personality types. *Journal of Vocational Behavior*, 1973, *3*, 195–208.

HUGHES, H. M., JR. Vocational choice, level, and consistency: An investigation of Holland's theory in an employed sample. *Journal of Vocational Behavior*, 1972, *2*, 377–88.

HUNT, D. Person-environment interaction: A challenge found wanting before it was tried. *Review of Educational Research*, 1975, *45*, 209–230.

HUSEN, T. Talent, opportunity, and career: A twenty-six year follow-up. *The School Review*, 1968, *76*, 190–209.

IACHON, R. A measure of agreement for use with the Holland classification system. *Journal of Vocational Behavior*, 1984, *24*, 133–141.

IACHON, R. A. Family of differentiation indices. *Psychometrika*, 1984, *49*, 217-222.

IMADA, A. S., FLETCHER, C., & DALESSIO, A. Individual correlates of an occupational stereotype: A reexamination of the stereotype of accountants. *Journal of Applied Psychology*, 1980, *65*, 436–39.

INGRAM, R. T. Holland's typology of personality in the prediction of certain counseling outcomes. Unpublished doctoral dissertation, University of Maryland, College Park, 1969.

JACKSON, D. N. *Personality Research Form*. Goshen, N.Y.: Research Psychologists Press, 1967.

JACKSON, D. N., PEACOCK, A. C., & SMITH, J. P. Impressions of personality in the employment interview. *Journal of Personality and Social Psychology*, 1980, *39*, 294–307.

JEANNERET, P. R., & McCORMICK, E. J. The job dimensions of "worker-oriented" job variables and their attribute profiles as based on data from the Position Analysis Questionnaire. Office of Naval Research Contract Nonr-1100(28), Report No. 2, Lafayette, Ind.: Occupational Research Center, Purdue University, 1969.

JOHANSSON, C. B., & CAMPBELL, D. P. Stability of the Strong Vocational Interest Blank for men. *Journal of Applied Psychology*, 1971, *55*, 34–36.

JOHNSON, D. M., & MOORE, J. C. An investigation of Holland's theory of vocational psychology. *Measurement and Evaluation in Guidance*, 1973, *5*, 488–95.

JONES, L. K., & CHENERY, M. F. Multiple subtypes among vocationally undecided college students: A model and assessment instrument. *Journal of Counseling Psychology*, 1980, *27*, 469–77.

JUNG, C. G. *Psychological types.* New York: Harcourt Brace Jovanovich, Inc., 1933.

KAHN, R. L. *Work and health.* New York: John Wiley, 1981.

KATZ, W. J. Person-job interactions: A test of Holland's theory for an employed sample. Paper for Final Honours in Department of Psychology, University of Melbourne, September, 1974.

KATZ, M. R., & SHATKIN, L. Computer-assisted guidance: Concepts and practices. Research Report 80–1. Princeton, N.J.: Educational Testing Service, 1980.

KEELING, B., & TUCK, B. F. The validity of Holland's occupational typology with male and female New Zealand secondary school students. *New Zealand Journal of Educational Studies*, 1979, *14*, 50–57.

KELSO, G. I. Explorations of the developmental antecedents of Holland's occupational types. (Doctoral dissertation, Johns Hopkins University, 1976.) *Dissertation Abstracts International*, 1976, *37* (1-B), 440.

KELSO, G. I., HOLLAND, J. L., & GOTTFREDSON, G. D. The relation of self-reported competencies to aptitude test scores. *Journal of Vocational Behavior*, 1977, *10*, 99–103.

KELSO, G. I., & TAYLOR, K. F. Psychologists as judges: A consensual validation of a personality typology. *Australian Journal of Psychology*, 1980, *32*, 135–39.

KERLIN, B. D. A study of John Holland's theory of careers as it applies to employed adults. Unpublished doctoral dissertation, University of Maryland, College Park, 1975.

KERNEN, P. J. An investigation of personality characteristics of counselees and non-counselees as related to Holland's theory. Unpublished doctoral dissertation, University of North Carolina, 1971.

KIMBALL, R. L., SEDLACEK, W. E., & BROOKS, G. C., JR. Black and white vocational interests in Holland's Self-Directed Search (SDS). *Journal of Negro Education*, 1973, *42*, 1–4.

KIPNIS, D., LANE, G., & BERGER, L. Character structure, vocational interest, and achievement. *Journal of Counseling Psychology*, 1967, *16*, 335–41.

KOESTLER, A. *The act of creation.* New York: Macmillan, 1964.

KRISTJANSON, R. W. Personality types and their hypothesized attributes: An application of Holland's vocational choice theory. Unpublished master's thesis, University of North Dakota, 1969.

KRIVATSY, S. E., & MAGOON, T. M. Differential effects of three vocational counseling treatments. *Journal of Counseling Psychology*, 1976, *43*, 112–18.

KRULEE, G. K., O'KEEFE, R., & GOLDBERG, M. *Influence of identity processes on student behavior and occupational choice.* Cooperative Research Project No. 5–0809. Evanston, Ill.: Northwestern University, 1966.

KRUMBOLTZ, J. D. A social learning theory of career decision-making. In A. M. Mitchell, G. B. Jones, and J. D. Krumboltz (eds.), *Social learning and career decision-making* (pp.19–49). Cranston, R.I.: Carrol, 1979.

KRUSE, M. A. Ordinal position and the occurrence of Holland's personality types among talented adolescent females. Unpublished doctoral dissertation, Case Western Reserve University, Cleveland, 1979.

KUDER, F., & DIAMOND, E. E. General manual for the Kuder DD Occupational Interest Survey. Chicago: Science Research Associates, 1979.

KUDER, G. F. Administrator's manual: Kuder Preference Record, Vocational, Form C. Chicago: Science Research Associates, 1960.

Kuhlberg, G. E., & OWENS, W. A. Some life history antecedents of engineering interests. *Journal of Educational Psychology*, 1960, *51*, 26–31.

KUNCE, J. T., DECKER, G. L., & ECKELMAN, C. C. Strong Vocational Interest Blank basic interest clusters and occupational satisfaction. *Journal of Vocational Behavior*, 1976, *9*, 355–62.

KUNCE, J. T., & KAPPES, B. M. The Vocational Preference Inventory scores and environmental preferences. *Journal of Vocational Behavior*, 1976, *9*, 363–66.

LACEY, D. Holland's vocational models: a study of work groups and need satisfaction. *Journal of Vocational Behavior*, 1971, *1*, 105–122.

LAUDEMAN, K. A., & GRIFFETH, P. Holland's theory of vocational choice and postulated value dimensions. *Educational and Psychological Measurement*, 1978, *38*, 1165–1175.

LAUFER, W. S. Vocational interests of criminal offenders: A typological and demographic investigation. *Journal of Vocational Behavior*, 1980, *46*, 315–24.

LAURENT, H., JR. A study of the developmental backgrounds of men to determine by means of the biographical information blank the relationship between factors in their early backgrounds and their choice of professions. Unpublished doctoral dissertation, Western Reserve University, 1951.

LEE, D. L. Selected interest factors related to academic achievement at the University of North Dakota. Unpublished doctoral dissertation, University of North Dakota, 1970.

LEE, D. L., & HEDAHL, B. Holland's personality types applied to the SVIB Basic Interest Scales. *Journal of Vocational Behavior*, 1973, *3*, 61–68.

LEWIS, A. H., & SEDLACEK, W. E. Socioeconomic level differences on Holland's Self-Directed Search (SDS). *Proceedings, 80th Annual Convention of the American Psychological Association*, 1972, 587–88.

LEWIS, M. I., & BUTLER, R. N. Life review therapy: Putting memories to work in individual and group psychotherapy. *Geriatrics*, 1974, *29*, 165–73.

LINTON, R. *The cultural background of personality.* New York: Century, 1945.

LIVENT, G. R. Holland's theory of vocational choice and ego identity. Doctoral dissertation, State University of New York at Buffalo, 1971. *Dissertation Abstracts International*, 1971, *32*, 1277A. (University Microfilms No. 71–22,578.)

LORR, M., & STEFIC, E. An orientation and motivation inventory. *Psychological Reports*, 1978, *42*, 911–14.

LOUGHMILLER, G. C., ELLISON, R. L., TAYLOR, C. W., & PRICE, P. B. Predicting career performance of physicians using the biographical inventory approach. *Journal of Vocational Behavior*, 1973, *3*, 269–78.

LOWMAN, R. L., & SCHURMAN, S. J. Psychometric characteristics of a vocational preference inventory short form. *Educational and Psychological Measurement*, 1982, *42*, 601–613.

LUCY, W. T. An adult population reflects the stability of Holland's personality types over time. *Journal of College Student Personnel*, 1976, *17*, 76–79.

LUNNEBORG, C. E., & LUNNEBORG, P. W. Factor structure of the vocational interest models of Roe and Holland. *Journal of Vocational Behavior*, 1975, *7*, 313–16.

LUNNEBORG, P. W. Interest differentiation in high school and vocational indecision in college. *Journal of Vocational Behavior*, 1975, *7*, 297–303.

LUNNEBORG, P. W. *Manual for the Vocational Interest Inventory.* Seattle: University of Washington, Educational Assessment Center, 1975.

MARKS, E., & WEBB, S. C. Vocational choice and professional experience as factors in occupational image. *Journal of Applied Psychology,* 1969, *53,* 292–300.

MARTIN, J. W. Job satisfaction differences among mental health workers, using Holland's theory of person-environment congruence. Unpublished doctoral dissertation, Florida State University, Tallahassee, 1980.

MARTINS, J. R., & PULVINO, C. J. Differences in vocational adjustment of consistent and inconsistent superior students. *Vocational Guidance Quarterly,* 1975, *23,* 238–41.

MATHIS, L. A. Marital satisfaction as a function of congruence on Holland's types in seminary couples. Unpublished doctoral dissertation, Rosemead Graduate School of Psychology, Rosemead, Calif., 1977.

MATTHEWS, D. F., & WALSH, W. B. Concurrent validity of Holland's theory for non-college-degreed working women. *Journal of Vocational Behavior,* 1978, *12,* 317–79.

McCORMICK, E. J. *Job analysis: Methods and applications.* AMACOM, American Management Association, 1979.

McCORMICK, E. J., JEANNERET, P. R., & MECHAM, R. C. The development and background of the position analysis questionnaire, Office of Naval Research Contract Nonr-1100(28), Report No. 5. Lafayette, Ind.: Occupational Research Center, Purdue University, 1969.

McCORMICK, E. J., JEANNERET, P. R., & MECHAM, R. C. A study of the job characteristics and job dimensions as based on the Position Analysis Questionnaire. *Journal of Applied Psychology Monograph,* 1972, *56,* No. 4, 347–68.

McGOWAN, A. S. Vocational maturity and anxiety among vocationally undecided and indecisive students. *Journal of Vocational Behavior,* 1977, *10,* 196–204.

McGOWAN, A. S. The predictive efficiency of Holland's SDS summary codes in terms of career choice: A four-year follow-up. *Journal of Vocational Behavior,* 1982, *20,* 294–303.

McLAUGHLIN, D. H., & TIEDEMAN, D. V. Eleven-year career stability and change as reflected in project talent data through the Flanagan, Holland, and Roe occupational classification systems. *Journal of Vocational Behavior,* 1974, *5,* 177–96.

McMULLIN, J. D. Differences analyzed on EPPS variables for samples selected on SVIB criteria: A test of Holland's theory. Unpublished doctoral dissertation, Boston College, 1973.

McQUITTY, L. L., & CLARK, J. A. Clusters from iterative, intercolumnar correlational analysis. *Educational and Psychological Measurement,* 1968, *28,* 211–38.

MECHAM, R. C., & McCORMICK, E. J. The rated attribute requirements of job elements in the Position Analysis Questionnaire. Office of Naval Research Contract Nonr-1100 (28), Report No. 1. Lafayette, Ind.: Occupational Research Center, Purdue University, 1969. (a)

MECHAM, R. C., & McCORMICK, E. J. The use of data based on the Position Analysis Questionnaire in developing synthetically-derived attribute requirements of jobs. Office of Naval Research Contract Nonr-1100 (28), Report No. 4. Lafayette, Ind.: Occupational Research Center, Purdue University, 1969. (b)

MEDVENE, A. M. Occupational choice of graduate students in psychology as a function of early parent-child interactions. *Journal of Counseling Psychology,* 1969, *16,* 385–89.

MEIR, E. I. Manual for the Ramak and Courses interest inventories. Tel-Aviv University, Department of Psychology, 1975.

MEIR, E. I., & BEN-YEHUDA, A. Inventories based on Roe and Holland yield similar results. *Journal of Vocational Behavior*, 1976, *8*, 269–74.

MEIR, E. I., & EREZ, M. Fostering a career in engineering. *Journal of Vocational Behavior*, 1981, *18*, 115–20.

MEIR, E. I., & HASSON, R. Congruence between personality type and environment type as a predictor of stay in an environment. *Journal of Vocational Behavior*, 1982, *21*, 309–17.

MELAMED, S. Vocational and avocational choices and satisfaction: A test of Holland's theory. Unpublished doctoral dissertation. Department of Psychology, University of Sydney, Australia, 1976.

MELAMED, S., & MEIR, E. I. The relationship between interests-job incongruity and selection of avocational activity. *Journal of Vocational Behavior*, 1981, *14*, 310–25.

MERCURIUS-FRASER, E. P. Personality types and vocational choice. Doctoral dissertation, Catholic University of America, Washington, D.C., 1980.

MIKELMAN, S. L. The application of Holland's theory of personality to senior adults and the process of retirement planning. Unpublished doctoral dissertation in education, University of California at Los Angeles, 1980.

MILLER, M. F. Interest pattern structure and personality characteristics of clients who seek career information. *Vocational Guidance Quarterly*, 1982, *31*, 28–42.

MOHR, L. B. *Explaining organizational behavior.* San Francisco, Calif.: Jossey-Bass, 1982.

MOLLA, B. The relationship of the components of the SDS and theoretically related stereotypes to Holland's types. Unpublished doctoral dissertation. University of Maryland, College Park, 1978.

MORRISON, R. F., & ARNOLD, S. J. A suggested revision in the classification of nonprofessional occupations in Holland's theory. *Journal of Counseling Psychology*, 1974, *21*, 485–88.

MORROW, J. M., JR. A test of Holland's theory. *Journal of Counseling Psychology*, 1971, *18*, 422–25.

MORSTAIN, B. R., & SMART, J. C. Educational orientations of faculty: Assessing a personality model of the academic professions. *Psychological Reports*, 1976, *39*, 1191–1211.

MOUNT, M. K., & MUCHINSKY, P. M. Person-environment congruence and employee job satisfaction: A test of Holland's theory. *Journal of Vocational Behavior*, 1978, *13*, 84–100. (a)

MOUNT, M. K., & MUCHINSKY, P. M. Concurrent validation of Holland's hexagonal model with occupational workers. *Journal of Vocational Behavior*, 1978, *13*, 348–54. (b)

MUMFORD, M. D., & OWENS, W. A. Life history and vocational interests. *Journal of Vocational Behavior*, 1982, *21*, 330–48.

MURRAY, H. A. *Explorations in personality.* New York: Oxford, 1938.

NACHMANN, B. Childhood experience and vocational choice in law, dentistry, and social work. *Journal of Counseling Psychology*, 1960, *7*, 243–50.

NAFZIGER, D. H. A Markov chain analysis of the movement of young men using the Holland occupational classification (Report No. 148). Johns Hopkins University, Center for Social Organization of Schools, 1973. (ERIC Document Reproduction Service No. ED 074 283.)

NAFZIGER, D. H., & HELMS, S. T. Cluster analysis of interest inventory scales as tests of Holland's occupational classification. *Journal of Applied Psychology*, 1974, *59*, 344–53.

NAFZIGER, D. H., HOLLAND, J. L., & GOTTFREDSON, G. D. Student-college congruency as a predictor of satisfaction. *Journal of Counseling Psychology*, 1975, *22*, 132–39.

Nafziger, D. H., Holland, J. L., Helms, S. T., & McPartland, J. M. Applying an occupational classification to a national representative sample of work histories of young men and women. Report No. 132. Center for Social Organization of Schools, Johns Hopkins University, Baltimore, June 1972.

Nafziger, D. H., Holland, J. L., Helms, S. T., & McPartland, J. M. Applying an occupational classification to the work histories of young men and women. *Journal of Vocational Behavior,* 1974, *5,* 331–45.

Nichols, R. C., & Holland, J. L. Prediction of the first year college performance of high aptitude students. *Psychological Monographs,* 1963, *77,* No. 7 (Whole No. 570).

Nichols, W. R. Relationship between Holland's personality types and consistent-inconsistent personality patterns and educational decisions. Unpublished doctoral dissertation, University of Virginia, 1971. *Dissertation Abstracts International,* 1971, *32,* 4356A.

Noeth, R. J., & Jepsen, D. A. Predicting field of job entry from expressed vocational choice and certainty level. *Journal of Counseling Psychology,* 1981, *28,* 22–26.

Nolan, J. J. The effectiveness of the Self-Directed Search compared with group counseling in promoting information-seeking behavior and realism of vocational choice. (Doctoral dissertation, University of Maryland, College Park, 1974.) *Dissertation Abstracts International,* 1974, *35,* 195A. (University microfilms No. 74–16, 569.)

Noland, E. W., & Bakke, E. W. *Workers wanted: A study of employers' hiring policies, preferences, and practices in New Haven and Charlotte.* New York: Harper & Row, 1949.

Nord, C. Personality types of undecided students. Unpublished doctoral dissertation, Florida State University, 1976.

Norman, R. D., & Bessemer, D. W. Job preferences and preference shifts as functions of job information, familiarity, and prestige level. *Journal of Applied Psychology,* 1968, *52,* 280–85.

O'Brien, W. F., & Walsh, W. B. Concurrent validity of Holland's theory for non-college-degreed black working men. *Journal of Vocational Behavior,* 1976, *8,* 239–46.

O'Dowd, D. D., & Beardslee, D. C. College student images of a selected group of professions and occupations. USOE, Cooperative Research No. 562 (8142). Wesleyan University, Middletown, Conn., 1960.

O'Dowd, D. D., & Beardslee, D. C. Development and consistency of student images of occupations. USOE, Cooperative Research Project No. 5–0858, Oakland University, 1967.

Olson, S. K. Validity of My Vocational Situation for homemakers and displaced homemakers. *Measurement and Evaluation in Guidance,* in press.

O'Neil, J. M. Holland's theoretical signs of consistency and differentiation and their relationship to academic potential and achievement. *Journal of Vocational Behavior,* 1977, *11,* 166–73.

O'Neil, J. M., & Magoon, T. M. The predictive power of Holland's investigative personality type and consistency levels using the Self-Directed Search. *Journal of Vocational Behavior,* 1977, *10,* 39–46.

O'Neil, J. M., Magoon, T. M., & Tracey, T. J. Status of Holland's investigative personality types and their consistency levels seven years later. *Journal of Counseling Psychology,* 1978, *25,* 530–35.

Osborne, R. T. *Twins: Black and White.* Foundation for Human Understanding: Athens, Ga., 1980.

OSIPOW, S. H. Cognitive styles and educational-vocational preferences and selection. *Journal of Counseling Psychology*, 1969, *16*, 534–46.

OSIPOW, S. H. The interaction between occupational environments and personality types. Paper presented at conference on the development of religious vocations, Notre Dame University, South Bend, Ind., 1970.

OSIPOW, S. H., & ASHBY, J. D. Vocational preference inventory high point codes and educational preferences. *Personnel and Guidance Journal*, 1968, *47*, 126–29.

OSIPOW, S. H., ASHBY, J. D., & WALL, H. W. Personality types and vocational choice: A test of Holland's theory. *Personnel and Guidance Journal*, 1966, *45*, 37–42.

OWENS, W. A. Toward one discipline of scientific psychology. *American Psychologist*, 1968, *23*, 782–785.

OWENS, W. A., & SCHOENFELDT, L. F. Toward a classification of persons. *Journal of Applied Psychology*, 1979, *53*, 570–607.

PACE, C. R. College and University Environment Scales. Princeton, N.J.: Educational Testing Service, 1963.

PALLAS, A. M., DAHMANN, J. S., GUCER, P. W., & HOLLAND, J. L. Test-taker evaluations of the Self-Directed Search and other psychological tests. *Psychological Documents*, 1983, *13*, 11, Ms. No. 2550.

PARSONS, G. E., & WIGTIL, J. V. Occupational mobility as measured by Holland's theory of career selection. *Journal of Vocational Behavior*, 1974, *5*, 321–30.

PATTERSON, T. W., MARRON, J. P., & PATTERSON, N. B. A partial validation of Holland's theory of vocational choice. Paper presented at Rocky Mountain Psychological Convention, Denver Colo., May 1971.

PEISER, C., & MEIR, E. I. Congruency, consistency, and differentiation of vocational interests as predictors of vocational satisfaction and preference stability. *Journal of Vocational Behavior*, 1978, *12*, 270–78.

PETERSON, R. E. Technical manual, College Student Questionnaires. Princeton: Educational Testing Service, 1965.

POLACEK, K., & BORGIA, M. Verifica sulla consistenza e differenziazione delle preferenze professionali regli allievi della scuola secondaria superiore. *Orientamenti Pedagogici*, 1981, *28*, 990–1005.

POSTHUMA, A. B., & NAVRAN, L. Relation of congruence in student-faculty interests to achievement in college. *Journal of Counseling Psychology*, 1970, *17*, 352–56.

POWER, P. G. Aspects of the transition from education student to beginning teacher. *Australian Journal of Education*, 1981, *25*, 288–96.

PREDIGER, D. J. Dimensions underlying Holland's hexagon: Missing link between interests and occupations? *Journal of Vocational Behavior*, 1982, *21*, 259–87.

PRIVATEER, G. J. The effect of a college environment upon an incoming freshman class. Unpublished doctoral dissertation, State University of New York at Buffalo, 1971.

RACHMAN, D., AMERNIC, J., & ARANYA, N. A factor-analytic study of the construct validity of Holland's Self-Directed Search test. *Educational and Psychological Measurement*, 1981, *41*, 425–37.

RAYMAN, J. R., & BERNARD, C. B. Strong and weak vocational identities: A post mortem of a career course. Unpublished manuscript, 1982.

RAYMAN, J. R., BERNARD, C. B., HOLLAND, J. L., & BARNETT, D. C. The effects of a career course and some other popular treatments. *Journal of Vocational Behavior*, 1983, *23*, 346–55.

REARDON, R. C., & DOMKOWSKI, D. Building instruction into a career information center. *Vocational Guidance Quarterly*, 1977, *25*, 274–78.

REARDON, R. C., & MINOR, C. W. Revitalizing the career information service. *Personnel and Guidance Journal,* 1975, *54,* 169–71.

REARDON, R., WHITE, P., CARLSON, A., & BARKER, S. A self-directed career planning program for the visually disabled. Final Report, September 15, 1978, Florida State University, Tallahassee, Fla.

REEDY, M. N., & BIRREN, J. E. Life review through guided autobiography. Paper presented at American Psychological Association Convention, Montreal, September 3, 1980.

RESNICK, L. B. Mathematics and science learning: A new conception. *Science,* 1983, *220,* 477–78.

REZLER, A. G. Characteristics of high school girls choosing traditional or pioneer vocations. *Personnel and Guidance Journal,* 1967, *4,* 659–65.

RICHARDS, J. M., JR. A diagonal factor analysis of the Vocational Preference Inventory. In the ACT Guidance Profile Manual. Iowa City, Iowa: The American College Testing Program, 1968.

RICHARDS, J. M., JR. A study of the "environments" of Japanese universities. Paper presented at Western Psychological Association Meeting, San Francisco, Calif., 1971.

RICHARDS, J. M., JR. "Environments" of British Commonwealth universities. *Journal of Educational Psychology,* 1974, *66,* 572–79. (a)

RICHARDS, J. M., JR. Personality type and characteristics of nations in international higher education exchange with the United States. *Research in Higher Education,* 1974, *2,* 189–94. (b)

RICHARDS, J. M., JR. Personality type for physicians' assistants and associates based on the Vocational Preference Inventory. *Psychological Reports,* 1977, *41,* 397–98.

RICHARDS, J. M., JR., BULKELEY, E. M., & RICHARDS, B. M. Faculty and curriculum as measures of two-year college environments. Paper presented at the American Educational Research Association Convention, New York, 1971.

RICHARDS, J. M., JR., RAND, L. P., & RAND, L. M. Description of junior colleges. *Journal of Educational Psychology,* 1966, *57,* 207–14.

RICHARDS, J. M., JR., & SELIGMAN, R. Measurement of graduate school environments. Paper presented at American Educational Research Association Meeting, Los Angeles, 1969.

RICHARDS, J. M., JR., SELIGMAN, R., & JONES, P. K. Faculty and curriculum as measures of college environment. *Journal of Educational Psychology,* 1970, *61,* 324–32.

RICHARDS, J. M., JR., WILLIAMS, G. D., & Holland, J. L. An Evaluation of the 1977 Minority Introduction of Engineering Summer Program. Report No. 270. Social Organization of Schools, Johns Hopkins University, Baltimore, Md., 1978.

RIDGEWAY, C. L. Affective interaction as a determinant of musical involvement. *Sociological Quarterly,* 1976, *17,* 414–28.

RITCHIE, R. J., & BOEHM, V. R. Biographical data as a predictor of women's and men's management potential. *Journal of Vocational Behavior,* 1977, *11,* 363–68.

ROBBINS, P. I., THOMAS, L. E., HARVEY, D. W., & KANDEFER, C. Career change and congruence of personality type: An examination of DOT-derived work environment designations. *Journal of Vocational Behavior,* 1978, *13,* 15–25.

ROBERTS, C. A., & JOHANSSON, C. B. The inheritance of cognitive interest styles among twins. *Journal of Vocational Behavior,* 1974, *4,* 237–43.

ROE, A. *The psychology of occupations.* New York: John Wiley, 1956.

ROE, A., & SIEGELMAN, M. *The origin of interests.* Washington, D.C.: American Personnel and Guidance Association, 1964.

ROKEACH, M. *The nature of human values.* New York: The Free Press, 1973.

ROSE, H. A., & ELTON, C. F. Relation of congruence, differentiation, and consistency to interest and aptitude scores in women with stable and unstable career choices. *Journal of Vocational Behavior,* 1982, *20,* 162–74.

ROSE, R. G. The use of conditional probabilities in applications of Holland's theory. *Journal of Vocational Behavior,* 1984, *25,* 284-289.

ROSEN, G. A., & BAGGALEY, A. R. The Milwaukee Academic Interest Inventory as related to Holland's personality types. *Educational and Psychological Measurement,* 1982, *42,* 615–23.

ROTHKOPF, E. Z. What are we trying to understand and improve? Educational research as leerlaufreaktion. *Educational Psychologist,* 1973, *10,* 58–66.

ROUNDS, J. B., JR., DAVISON, M. L., & DAWIS, R. V. The fit between Strong-Campbell Interest Inventory Themes and Holland's hexagonal model. *Journal of Vocational Behavior,* 1979, *15,* 303–15.

ROUNDS, J. B., JR., SHUBSACHS, A. P., DAWIS, R. V., & LOFQUIST, L. H. A test of Holland's environmental formulations. *Journal of Applied Psychology,* 1978, *63,* 609–16.

SALOMONE, P. R., & SLANEY, R. B. The applicability of Holland's theory to nonprofessional workers. *Journal of Vocational Behavior,* 1978, *13,* 63–74.

SCHAEFER, B. E. Holland's SDS: Is its effectiveness contingent upon selected variables? *Journal of Vocational Behavior,* 1976, *8,* 113–23.

SCHAEFFER, E. S., & BELL, R. Q. Development of a parental attitude research instrument. *Child Development,* 1958, *29,* 339–61.

SCHLOSSBERG, N. K., & GOODMAN, J. A. Women's place: children's sex stereotyping of occupations. *Vocational Guidance Quarterly,* 1972, *20,* 266–70.

SCHMITT, N., & WHITE, J. K. Relationships between job motivation variables and interest measures. *Journal of Vocational Behavior,* 1978, *12,* 333–41.

SCHNEIDER, L. J., DEWINNE, R. F., & OVERTON, T. D. Influence of congruity between personality types on offspring's personality development. *Journal of Counseling Psychology,* 1980, *27,* 40–43.

SCHNEIDER, L. R., & STEVENS, N. D. Personality characteristics associated with job-seeking behavior patterns. *Vocational Guidance Quarterly,* 1971, *19,* 194–200.

SCHUTZ, R. A., & BLOCHER, D. H. Self-concepts and stereotypes of vocational preferences. *Vocational Guidance Quarterly,* 1960, *8,* 241–44.

SCHUTZ, R. A., & BLOCKER, D. H. Self-satisfaction and level of occupational choice. *Personnel and Guidance Journal,* 1961, *39,* 595–98.

SCOTT, C. S., FENSKE, R. H., & MAXEY, E. J. Vocational choice change patterns of a national sample of community-junior college students. Research Report No. 64. American College Testing Program, Iowa City, Iowa, 1974.

SCOTT, N. A., & SEDLACEK, W. E. Personality differentiation and prediction of persistence in physical science and engineering. *Journal of Vocational Behavior,* 1975, *6,* 205–216.

SEEMAN, J. *Personality integration.* New York: Human Sciences, 1983.

SEWELL, W., HALLER, A., & PORTES, A. The educational and early occupational attainment process. *American Sociological Review,* 1969, *34,* 82–92.

SHELDON, W. H. *Atlas of men: A guide for somatotyping the adult male at all ages.* New York: Harper & Row, 1954.

SHINAR, E. H. Sexual stereotypes of occupations. *Journal of Vocational Behavior,* 1975, *7,* 99–111.

SHUBSACHS, A. P., & DAVISON, M. L. Individual differences in perceptions of occupations and occupational reinforcers. *Journal of Occupational Psychology,* 1979, *52,* 299–310.

SLANEY, R. B. Expressed vocational choice and vocational indecision.. *Journal of Counseling Psychology*, 1980, *27*, 122–29.

SLANEY, R. B., PALKO-NOVEMAKER, D., & ALEXANDER, R. An investigation of two measures of career indecision. *Journal of Vocational Behavior*, 1981, *18*, 92–103.

SLANEY, R. B., & RUSSELL, J. E. An investigation of different levels of agreement between expressed and inventoried vocational interests among college women. *Journal of Counseling Psychology*, 1981, *28*, 221–28.

SLANEY, R. B., & SALOMONE, P. R. Selection of vocational counselors by non-professional workers: An applied aspect of Holland's theory. *Vocational Guidance Quarterly*, 1978, *26*, 222–28.

SLAUGHTER, E. A. Family environment, personality and vocational behavior: A test of Holland's theory. Unpublished doctoral dissertation, University of Massachusetts, 1978.

SMART, J. C. Environments as reinforcer systems in the study of job satisfaction. *Journal of Vocational Behavior*, 1975, *6*, 337–47.

SMART, J. C. Distinctive career orientations of Holland's personality types. *Journal of Vocational Behavior*, 1976, *8*, 313–19. (a)

SMART, J. C. Duties performed by department chairmen in Holland's model environments. *Journal of Educational Psychology*, 1976, *68*, 1944–204. (b)

SMART, J. C., & McLAUGHLIN, G. W. Variations in goal priorities of academic departments: A test of Holland's theory. *Research in Higher Education*, 1974, *2*, 377–90.

SMITH, P. C., KENDALL, L. M., & HULIN, C. L. *The measurement of satisfaction in work and retirement.* Skokie, Ill.: Rand McNally, 1969.

SMITH, P. J. Comparison of counselees and noncounselees with reference to Holland's theory. *Journal of Counseling Psychology*, 1977, *24*, 244–46.

SMITH, T. A. Dental practice and the psychology of vocational choice. *Journal of American Dental Association*, 1979, *98*, 538–44.

SOELBERG, P. O. Unprogrammed decision-making. *Industrial Management Review*, 1967, *8*, 19–29.

SOUTHWORTH, J. A., & MORNINGSTAR, M. E. Persistence of occupational choice and personality congruence. *Journal of Counseling Psychology*, 1970, *17*, 409–412.

SPOKANE, A. R. Validity of the Holland categories for college women and men. *Journal of College Student Personnel*, 1979, *20*, 335–40.

SPOKANE, A. R., & DERBY, D. P. Congruence, personality pattern, and satisfaction in college women. *Journal of Vocational Behavior*, 1979, *15*, 36–42.

SPOKANE, A. R., & GOTTFREDSON, G. D. *The Holland Reader: A theory of careers—origins, influence, and interventions.* Dubuque, Iowa: Kendall Hunt, in press.

SPOKANE, A. R., MALETT, S. D., & VANCE, F. L. Consistent curricular choice and congruence of subsequent choices. *Journal of Vocational Behavior*, 1978, *13*, 45–53.

SPOKANE, A. R., & OLIVER, L. W. The outcomes of vocational intervention. In S. Osipow and W. Walsh (eds.), *Handbook of Vocational Psychology.* Hillsdale, N.J.: Erlbaum, 1983.

SPOKANE, A. R., & WALSH, W. B. Occupational level and Holland's theory for employed men and women. *Journal of Vocational Behavior*, 1978, *12*, 145–54.

SPRANGER, E. *Types of men.* Halle: Max Niemeyer Verlag, 1928.

STAATS, A. W. *Social behaviorism.* Homewood, Ill.: Dorsey, 1975.

STAATS, A. W. Paradigmatic behaviorism, unified theory, unified theory construction methods, and the zeitgeist of separatism. *American Psychologist*, 1981, *36*, 239–56.

STAATS, A. W., GROSS, M. C., GUAY, P. F., & CARLSON, C. C. Personality and social systems and attitude-reinforcer-discriminative theory: Interest (attitude) formation, function, and measurement. *Journal of Personality and Social Psychology*, 1973, *26*, 251–61.

STEVENS, N. D. Job-seeking behavior: A segment of vocational development. *Journal of Vocational Behavior*, 1973, *3*, 209–219.

STOCKIN, B. C. A test of Holland's occupational level formulation. *Personnel and Guidance Journal*, 1964, *54*, 599–602.

STRONG, E. K., JR. *Vocational interests of men and women*. Stanford, Calif.: Stanford University Press, 1943.

SUPER, D. E. *Manual: Work values inventory*. Boston: Houghton Mifflin, 1968.

SUPER, D. E. Vocational development theory: Persons, positions, processes. In J. M. Whiteley & A. Resnikoff (eds.), *Perspectives on Vocational Development*. Washington, D.C.: American Personnel and Guidance Association, 1972, pp. 13–33.

SUPER, D. E., & CRITES, J. O. *Appraising vocational fitness* (rev. ed.). New York: Harper & Row, 1962.

SWATKO, M. K. Personality characteristics and job performance as a function of traditional and non-traditional values in women. Master's thesis. Loyola College, Baltimore, Md., 1979.

SWEET, R. The occupational choices of sixth form students in relation to aptitudes, vocational interests, and work values. (Research report.) Division of Vocational Guidance Services, New South Wales: Department of Labour and Industry, 1975.

SWEET, R. Work values and Holland typologies—some side excursions. Research Workshop, Australian Council for Educational Research, Melbourne, Australia, February 1982.

TAYLOR, K. F., & KELSO, G. I. Course of study and personality: An Australian test of Holland's theory. *Australian Journal of Psychology*, 1973, *25*, 199–209.

TAYLOR, K. F., KELSO, G. I., COX, G. N., ALLOWAY, W. J., & MATTHEWS, J. P. Applying Holland's vocational categories to leisure activities. *Journal of Occupational Psychology*, 1979, *52*, 199–207.

TAYLOR, K. F., KELSO, G. I., LONGTHORP, N. E., & PATTISON, P. E. Differentiation as a construct in vocational theory and a diagnostic sign in practice. *Melbourne Psychology Reports*, No. 68, 1980 ISBN 0–86839–362–2.

TAYLOR, K. F., KELSO, G. I., PRETTY, H. I., & POWER, P. G. Some cultural and sex differences in response to the VPI: An Australian-American comparison. *Melbourne Psychology Reports*, No. 65, 1980, Dept. of Psychology, University of Melbourne, Melbourne, Australia.

TAYLOR, K. F., & LOKAN, J. L. (eds.). *Holland in Australia: A vocational choice theory in research and practice*. Victoria, Australia: Australian Council for Educational Research, in press.

TAYLOR, N. B. Decidedness, vocational identity, and brief career counseling. Master of Arts thesis, School of Behavioural Sciences, Macquarie University, Australia, 1983.

TAYLOR, N. B. Vocational identity, information needs and barriers: A diagnostic framework examined. New South Wales Department of Technical Education, Student Counseling Service ISBN 7240–3646–6, 1980. (a)

TAYLOR, N. B. The relationship between vocational identity and decidedness. New South Wales Department of Technical Education, Student Counseling Service ISBN 7240–3662–8, 1980. (b)

TEMME, L. V. Occupation: Meanings and measures. Washington, D.C.: Bureau of Social Science Research, 1975.

THOMAS, A., CHESS, S., & BIRCH, H. G. The origin of personality. *Scientific American*, 1970, *223*, 102–109.

THOMAS, L. E., & ROBBINS, P. I. Personality and work congruence of mid-life career changers. *Journal of Occupational Psychology*, 1979, *52*, 177–83.

TOENJES, C. M., & BORGEN, F. H. Validity generalization of Holland's hexagonal model. *Measurement and Evaluation in Guidance*, 1974, *7*, 79–85.

TONESK, X., SUZIEDELIS, A., & LORR, M. Vocational interest types of men-in-general. *Measurement and Evaluation in Guidance*, 1974, *7*, 74–78.

TOUCHTON, J. G., & MAGOON, T. M. Occupational daydreams as predictors of vocational plans of college women. *Journal of Vocational Behavior*, 1977, *10*, 156–66.

TURNER, C. J. Selected bibliography on the career development of women. *Psychological Documents*, 1983, *13* (1), 15. Ms. 2560.

TURNER, R. G., & HORN, J. M. Personality correlates of Holland's occupational types: A cross-cultural study. *Journal of Vocational Behavior*, 1976, *6*, 379–89.

TURNER, R. G., & HORN, J. M. Personality, husband-wife similarity, and Holland's occupational types. *Journal of Vocational Behavior*, 1977, *10*, 111–20.

TYLER, L. E. The development of "vocational interests": I. The organization of likes and dislikes in ten-year-old children. *Journal of Genetic Psychology*, 1955, *86*, 33–44.

U.S. DEPARTMENT OF LABOR. *Dictionary of occupational titles* (Fourth ed.). Washington, D.C.: U.S. Government Printing Office, 1977.

U.S. DEPARTMENT OF LABOR. Manual for the General Aptitude Test Battery. Washington, D.C.: U.S. Government Printing Office, 1967.

U.S. DEPARTMENT OF LABOR, Manpower Administration. *Dictionary of occupational titles. Vol. II Occupational classification.* Washington, D.C.: U.S. Government Printing Office, 1965.

UTZ, P., & HARTMAN, B. An analysis of the discriminatory power of Holland's types for business majors in three concentration areas. *Measurement and Evaluation in Guidance*, 1978, *11*, 175–82.

UTZ, P., & KORBEN, D. The construct validity of the occupational themes on the Strong-Campbell Interest Inventory. *Journal of Vocational Behavior*, 1976, *9*, 31–42.

VAITENAS, R., & WIENER, Y. Developmental, emotional, and interest factors in voluntary mid-career change. *Journal of Vocational Behavior*, 1977, *11*, 291–304.

VARCA, P. E., & SCHAFFER, G. S. Holland's theory: Stability of vocational interests. *Journal of Vocational Behavior*, 1982, *21*, 288–98.

VIERNSTEIN, M. C. The extension of Holland's occupational classification to all occupations in the Dictionary of Occupational Titles. *Journal of Vocational Behavior*, 1972, *2*, 107–21.

VIERNSTEIN, M. C., & HOGAN, R. Parental personality factors and achievement motivation in talented adolescents. *Journal of Youth and Adolescence*, 1975, *4*, 183–90.

VILLWOCK, J. D., SCHNITZEN, J. P., & CARBONARI, J. P. Holland's personality constructs as predictors of stability of choice. *Journal of Vocational Behavior*, 1976, *9*, 77–85.

WACHTEL, P. L. Psychodynamics, behavior therapy, and the implacable experimenter: An inquiry into the consistency of personality. *Journal of Abnormal Psychology*, 1973, *82*, 324–34.

WAKEFIELD, J. A., JR., ALSTON, H. L., YOM, B. L., & DOUGHTIE, E. B. Personality types and traits in the Vocational Preference Inventory. *Journal of Vocational Behavior*, 1975, *6*, 19–26.

WAKEFIELD, J. A., JR., & CUNNINGHAM, C. H. Relationships between the Vocational Preference Inventory and the Edwards Personal Preference Schedule. *Journal of Vocational Behavior*, 1975, *6*, 373–77.

WAKEFIELD, J. A., JR., & DOUGHTIE, E. B. The geometric relationship between Holland's personality typology and the Vocational Preference Inventory. *Journal of Counseling Psychology*, 1973, *20*, 513–18.

WAKEFIELD, J. A., JR., YOM, B. L., DOUGHTIE, E. B., CHANG, W. C., & ALSTON, H. L. The geometric relationship between Holland's personality typology and the vocational preference inventory for Blacks. *Journal of Counseling Psychology*, 1975, *22*, 58–60.

WALL, H. W., OSIPOW, S. H., & ASHBY, J. D. SVIB scores, occupational choices, and Holland's personality types. *Personnel and Guidance Journal*, 1967, *15*, 201–205.

WALL, R. E. Engineering freshmen responses to the Holland Vocational Preference Inventory and persistence in the University of Maryland College of Engineering. Unpublished doctoral dissertation, University of Maryland, College Park, Md., 1969.

WALSH, W. B., & BARROW, C. A. Consistent and inconsistent career preferences and personality. *Journal of Vocational Behavior*, 1971, *1*, 271–77.

WALSH, W. B., & HANLE, N. A. Consistent occupational preferences, vocational maturity, and academic achievement. *Journal of Vocational Behavior*, 1975, *7*, 89–97.

WALSH, W. B., HILDEBRAND, J. O., WARD, C. M., & MATTHEWS, D. F. Holland's theory and non-college-degreed working black and white women. *Journal of Vocational Behavior*, 1983, *22*, 182–90.

WALSH, W. B., HORTON, J. A., & GAFFEY, R. L. Holland's theory and college-degreed working men and women. *Journal of Vocational Behavior*, 1977, *10*, 180–86.

WALSH, W. B., & LACEY, D. W. Perceived change and Holland's theory. *Journal of Counseling Psychology*, 1969, *16*, 348–52.

WALSH, W. B., & LACEY, D. W. Further exploration of perceived change and Holland's theory. *Journal of Counseling Psychology*, 1970, *17*, 189–90.

WALSH, W. B., & LEWIS, R. O. Consistent, inconsistent, and undecided career preferences and personality. *Journal of Vocational Behavior*, 1972, *2*, 309–316.

WALSH, W. B., & RUSSELL, J. H. College major choice and personal adjustment. *Personnel and Guidance Journal*, 1969, *47*, 685–88.

WALSH, W. B., SPOKANE, A. R., & MITCHELL, E. Consistent occupational preferences and academic adjustment. *Research in Higher Education*, 1976, *4*, 123–29.

WALSH, W. B., VAUDRIN, D. M., & HUMMEL, R. A. The accentuation effect and Holland's theory. *Journal of Vocational Behavior*, 1972, *2*, 77–85.

WARD, C. M., & WALSH, W. B. Concurrent validity of Holland's theory for non-college-degreed black women. *Journal of Vocational Behavior*, 1981, *18*, 356–61.

WARD, G. R., CUNNINGHAM, C. H., & WAKEFIELD, J. A., JR. Relationships between Holland's VPI and Cattell's 16 PF. *Journal of Vocational Behavior*, 1976, *8*, 307–312.

WARREN, G. D., WINER, J. L., & DAILEY, K. C. Extending Holland's theory to the later years. *Journal of Vocational Behavior*, 1981, *18*, 104–114.

WARSHAW, P. Differential treatment of career clients according to Holland code. Unpublished doctoral dissertation, University of Utah, 1976.

WASSERMAN, D. Personality and vocational choice of adolescent girls. Unpublished master's thesis, University of Calgary, Alberta, Canada, 1974.

WATERS, E., & GOODMAN, J. Career counseling for adults: Why, when, where, how. *Vocational Guidance Quarterly*, 1977, *25*, 337–43.

WEIL, P. A., & SCHLEITER, M. K. National study of internal medicine manpower: VI. Factors predicting preferences of residents for careers in primary care or subspeciality care and clinical practice or academic medicine. *Annals of Internal Medicine,* 1981, *94,* 691–703.

WEIL, P. A., SCHLEITER, M. K., & TARLOV, A. R. National study of internal medicine manpower: V. Comparison of residents in internal medicine—future generalists and subspecialists. *Annals of Internal Medicine,* 1981, *94,* 678–90.

WELSH, G. S. *Creativity and intelligence.* Chapel Hill, N.C.: Institute for Research in Social Science, University of North Carolina, 1975.

WERNER, J. E. A study of Holland's theory as it applies to selected working women. Unpublished doctoral dissertation, State University of New York at Buffalo, 1969.

WERNER, W. E. Effect of role choice on vocational high school students. *Journal of Vocational Behavior,* 1974, *4,* 77–84.

WERTS, C. E., & WATLEY, D. J. Paternal influence on talent development. *Journal of Counseling Psychology,* 1972, *19,* 367–73.

WESLANDER, D. L., & WIGGINS, J. D. A test of the predictive validity of Holland's vocational theory for teacher performance. Unpublished manuscript, 1982. Department of Evaluation and Research, Des Moines Public Schools, Des Moines, Iowa.

WESTBROOK, F. D., & MOLLA, B. Unique stereotypes for Holland's personality types, testing the traits attributed to men and women in Holland's typology. *Journal of Vocational Behavior,* 1976, *9,* 21–30.

WHITEHORN, J. C., & BETZ, B. A study of the psychotherapeutic relationships between physicians and schizophrenic patients. *American Journal of Psychiatry,* 1954, *111,* 321–31.

WHITNEY, D. R. Predicting from expressed vocational choice: A review. *Personnel and Guidance Journal,* 1969, *48,* 279–86.

WHITNEY, D. R. Predicting vocational interests of high ability students. Unpublished paper, 1970.

WHITNEY, D. R., & HOLLAND, J. L. Clustering student personalities to facilitate learning, guidance, and educational administration. Unpublished manuscript, 1969.

WHITNEY, D. R., & WHITTLESEY, R. R. Two hypotheses about Holland's personality types and counseling outcomes. *Journal of Counseling Psychology,* 1972, *19,* 323–27.

WICKER, A. W. Ecological psychology: Some recent and prospective developments. *American Psychologist,* 1979, *34,* 755–65.

WIEHE, V. R. Differential personality types of foster parents. *Social Work Research and Abstracts,* 1982, *18,* 16–20.

WIEHE, V. R. Foster mothers: Are they unique? *Psychological Reports,* 1983, *53,* 1215–1218.

WIENER, Y., & VAITENAS, R. Personality correlates of voluntary midcareer change in Enterprising occupations. *Journal of Applied Psychology,* 1977, *62,* 706–712.

WIGGINS, J. D. Holland's theory and retired teachers. *Vocational Guidance Quarterly,* 1982, *30,* 236–42.

WIGGINS, J. D. The relation of job satisfaction to vocational preferences among teachers of the educable mentally retarded. *Journal of Vocational Behavior,* 1976, *8,* 13–18.

WIGGINS, J. D., LEDERER, D. A., SALKOWE, A., & RYS, G. S. Job satisfaction related to tested congruence and differentiation. *Journal of Vocational Behavior,* 1983, *23,* 112–21.

WIGGINS, J. D., & MOODY, A. D. A field-based comparison of four career-exploration approaches. *Vocational Guidance Quarterly,* 1981, *30,* 15–20.

WIGGINS, J. D., & MOODY, A. D. Identifying effective counselors through client-supervisor ratings and personality-environmental variables. *Vocational Guidance Quarterly,* in press.

WIGGINS, J. D., MOODY, A. D., & LEDERER, A. D. Personality typologies related to marital satisfaction. Unpublished manuscript, 1983.

WIGGINS, J. D., & WESLANDER, D. L. Expressed vocational choices and later employment compared with Vocational Preference Inventory and Kuder Preference Record-Vocational scores. *Journal of Vocational Behavior,* 1977, *11,* 158–65.

WIGGINS, J. D., & WESLANDER, D. L. Personality characteristics of counselors rated as effective or ineffective. *Journal of Vocational Behavior,* 1979, *15,* 175–85.

WIGGINS, J. D., & WESLANDER, D. L. Tested compatibility in first and second marriages. *American Mental Health Counselors Association Journal,* January 1982, 25–29.

WIGINGTON, J. H. The applicability of Holland's typology to clients. *Journal of Vocational Behavior,* 1983, *23,* 286–93.

WIGINGTON, J. H., & APOSTAL, R. A. Personality differences among men in selected Air Force specialties. *Journal of Counseling Psychology,* 1973, *20,* 454–58.

WILEY, M. O., & MAGOON, T. M. Holland high-point social types: Is consistency related to persistence and achievement? *Journal of Vocational Behavior,* 1982, *20,* 14–21.

WILKINSON, L. V. The ability of students to predict their personality types as measured by Holland's Self-Directed Search. Doctoral dissertation, East Texas State University, 1977.

WILLEMS, E. P. Sense of obligation to high school activities as related to school size and marginality of student. *Child Development,* 1967, *38,* 1247–1260.

WILLIAMS, C. M. Occupational choice of male graduate students as related to values and personality: A test of Holland's theory. *Journal of Vocational Behavior,* 1972, *2,* 39–46.

WILLIAMS, G. D. Student perceptions of occupational congruency (Report No. 156). Baltimore, Md.: Johns Hopkins University, Center for Social Organization of Schools, 1973.

WILLIAMS, J. E. Conflict between freshmen male roommates. Research Report No. 10–67, Counseling Center, University of Maryland, College Park, 1967.

WINCHELL, A. E. Conceptual systems and Holland's theory of vocational choice. *Journal of Personality and Social Psychology,* 1984, *46,* 376–383.

WINER, J. L. Cognitive and cognitive-plus-affective curricula and the facilitation of career and general development. (Doctoral dissertation, Ohio State University, 1976.) *Dissertation Abstracts International,* 1976, *36,* No. 76–3594.

WINER, J. L., HAASE, R. F., GLENN, C. M., CESARI, J., & BODDEN, J. L. Cognitive complexity and vocational preference among college students. Paper presented at Southwestern Psychological Association, San Antonio, Texas, April 1979.

WINER, J. L., WARREN, G. D., DAILEY, K. C., & HIESBERGER, J. Complexity of judgment of occupational titles among Holland types. *Vocational Guidance Quarterly,* 1980, *28,* 12–24.

WIRTENBERG, J. T. The impact of the sex-desegregated practical arts course on maximization of occupational potential in seventh grade girls. Unpublished doctoral dissertation, University of California at Los Angeles, 1979.

WITKIN, H. A. *Cognitive styles in personal and cultural adaptation.* Heinz Werner Lecture Series, Vol. 11, 1977. Worcester, Massachusetts: Clark University Press, 1978.

WONG, K. K. An investigation of Holland's personality types and engineering specialties. Master's thesis, Education, University of Alberta, Alberta, Canada, 1981.

YOM, B. L., DOUGHTIE, E. B., CHANG, W. C., ALSTON, H. L., & WAKEFIELD, J. A., JR. The factor structure of the Vocational Preference Inventory for black and white college students. *Journal of Vocational Behavior,* 1975, *6,* 15–18.

YONGE, G. D., & REGAN, M. C. A longitudinal study of personality and change of major. *Journal of Vocational Behavior,* 1975, *7,* 41–65.

YOUNG, F. W., & TORGERSON, W. S. TORSCA, a Fortran IV program for Shepard-Kruskel multidimensional scaling analysis. *Behavioral Science,* 1967, *12,* 498.

ZENER, T. B., & SCHNUELLE, L. Effects of the Self-Directed Search on high school students. *Journal of Counseling Psychology,* 1976, *23,* 353–59.

APPENDIX A
THE OCCUPATIONAL
CLASSIFICATION

THE OCCUPATIONS FINDER

The 500 occupations in this classification include all of the most common occupations in the United States. They are arranged in a system that uses the code letters (R, I, A, S, E, C).

Realistic occupations (R) include skilled trades, technical and some service occupations.
Investigative occupations (I) include scientific and some technical occupations.
Artistic occupations (A) include artistic, musical, and literary occupations.
Social occupations (S) include educational and social welfare occupations.
Enterprising occupations (E) include managerial and sales occupations.
Conventional occupations (C) include office and clerical occupations.

The three-letter codes provide descriptions of occupations. For example, the code of ESC for sales manager means that sales managers resemble people in Enterprising occupations most of all, that they resemble people in Social occupations somewhat less, and people in Conventional occupations still less. In this way, the codes provide a brief summary of what an occupation is like by showing its degrees of resemblance to three occupational groups.

There are a few combinations of the code letters which do not occur at all, or which occur infrequently. In such cases a person may use a two-letter rather than a three-letter code and study the nature of all the occupations with that code.

The single digit indicates the level of general educational development an occupation demands. Levels 5 and 6 mean college training is necessary. Levels 3 and 4 mean high school and some college, technical, or business training is needed. Levels 1 and 2 mean that an occupation requires only elementary school training or no special training at all. In general, these levels are only estimates and should not be regarded as precise requirements.

The six-digit number is from the *Dictionary of Occupational Titles* (DOT), which can be found in most libraries and employment and counseling offices. The DOT contains descriptions of occupations and estimates of interests and aptitudes associated with each occupation.

Using the six-digit code and the DOT, it is possible to extend one's understanding of any occupation listed and this process is an important part of *The Self-Directed Search.* Unless you are well-informed about the world of work, there will be many occupations in The Occupations Finder that you have never heard of, that sound humorous, that you are sure you would never enjoy, although you know little about what the occupation is like. Don't reject occupations until you know what they are about.

Additional useful information about occupations can be obtained from the *Occupational Outlook Handbook,* U.S. Department of Labor, Bureau of Labor Statistics, which is published every two years. (See your counselor or library, or write.Superintendent of Documents, U.S. Government Printing Office, Washington, D.C., 20402, and enclose a check for $8.00.) This handbook provides a wide range of information about occupations, income, training, and employment trends.

REALISTIC OCCUPATIONS

CODE: RIA	ED
Landscape Architect (001.061-018)	5
Architectural Drafter (001.261-010)	4
Dental Technician (712.381-018)	4
Reproduction Technician (976.361-010)	4

CODE: RIS	ED
Range Manager (040.061-046)	6
Commercial Engineer (003.187-014)	5
Forester (040.061-034)	5
Industrial Arts Teacher (091.221-010)	5
Electrician (824.261-010)	4
Glazier (Glass Setter) (865.381-010)	4
Jeweler (700.281-010)	4
Loom Fixer (683.260-018)	4
Miller Supervisor (521.130-010)	4
Powerhouse Mechanic (631.261-014)	4
Power-Plant Operator (952.382-018)	4
Tool and Die Maker (601.280-046)	4
Baker (526.381-010)	3
Cook (315.361-010)	3
Filling Station Attendant (915.467-010)	3
Heat Treater (504.682-018)	3
Optician (716.280-014)	3
Welder (819.384-010)	3
Offset-Press Operator (651.685-018)	2

CODE: RIE	ED
Automotive Engineer (007.061-010)	6
Mechanical Engineer (007.061-014)	6
Petroleum Engineer (010.061-018)	6
Airline Radio Operator (193.262-010)	5
Building Inspector (168.267-010)	5
Industrial Engineer Technician (012.267-010)	5
Mechanical-Engineering Technician (007.161-026)	5
Mining Engineer (010.061-014)	5
Air Conditioning Mechanic (637.261-014)	4
Air Traffic Controller (193.162-018)	4
Aircraft Mechanic (862.381-010)	4
Automobile Mechanic (620.261-010)	4
Automobile-Repair-Service Estimator (620.261-018)	4
Boilermaker (805.261-014)	4
Diesel Mechanic (625.281-010)	4
Drafter, Detail (017.261-030)	4
Electronic Technician (726.281-014)	4
Electroplater (500.380-010)	4
Farm Equipment Mechanic (624.281-010)	4
Farmer (421.161-010)	4
Field Engineer (828.261-014)	4
Flight Engineer (621.261-018)	4
Garage Supervisor (620.131-014)	4
Line Installer-Repairer (822.381-014)	4
Loom Changer (683.360-010)	4
Machinist (600.280-042)	4
Machine Repairer (600.280-042)	4
Mechanic/Repair Worker*	4
Millwright (638.281-018)	4
Plumber (862.381-030)	4
Radio Repairer (720.281-010)	4
Sheet Metal Worker (804.281-010)	4
Shipfitter (806.381-046)	4

CODE: RIE (cont.)	ED
Watch Repairer (715.281-010)	4
Automobile-Body Repairer (807.381-010)	3
Compressor-House Operator (953.382-010)	3
Engraver, Machine (704.682-010)	3
Forging-Press Operator (611.685-010)	3
Furniture Upholsterer (780.381-018)	3
Heavy Equipment Operator (859.683-010)	3
Roofer (866.381-010)	3
Logger (454.684-018)	2
Machine Operator (616.360-018)	2
Tool Crib Attendant (222.367-062)	2

CODE: RIC	ED
Automatic-Equipment Technician (822.281-010)	4
Automotive Parts Clerk (279.357-062)	4
Elevator Mechanic (825.281-030)	4
Load Checker (952.367-010)	4
Locksmith (709.281-010)	4
Nuclear Reactor Operator (015.362-026)	4
Nursery Manager (180.167-042)	4
Piano Tuner (730.361-010)	4
Refinery Operator (549.260-010)	4
Stone Cutter (771.381-014)	4
Tree Surgeon (408.181-010)	4
Turret Lathe Operator (604.685-026)	4
Assembler (780.684.062)	3
Drill Press Operator (606.682-014)	3.
Dry Cleaner (362.382-014)	3
Hardness Inspector (504.387-010)	3
Printer (651.380-010)	3
Roller (613.682-018)	3
Rotary Driller (petro. prod.) (930.382-026)	3
Shipping and Receiving Clerk (222.387-050)	3
Shoe Repairer (365.361-014)	3
Structural Steel Worker (801.361-014)	3
Tire Builder (750.684-022)	3
Groundskeeper (406.687-010)	2
Teamster (919.664-010)	2
Laundry Worker (361.684-014)	2

CODE: RAI	ED
Compositor (Typesetter) (973.381-010)	4
Bookbinder (977.381-010)	3

CODE: RSE	ED
Blacksmith (610.381-010)	4
Experimental Molder (518.361-010)	4
Locomotive Firer (910.363-010)	4
Pipefitter (862.381-018)	4
Railroad Conductor (198.167-010)	4
Taxi Driver (913.463-018)	3
Butcher (316.684-022)	3
Coal Equipment Operator (921.683-022)	3
Chauffeur (913.663-010)	3
Fire Fighter (373.364-010)	3
Streetcar Operator (913.463-014)	3

(continued)

*May carry other D.O.T. numbers when a more detailed job title is given.

REALISTIC OCCUPATIONS (CONTINUED)

CODE: RSE (cont.)	ED
Waiter/Waitress (311.677-010)	3
Parking-Lot Attendant (915.473-010)	2
Soda Clerk (319.474-010)	2
Warehouse Worker (922.687-058)	1

CODE: RSC	ED
Exterminator (389.684-010)	3
Elevator Operator (388.663-010)	2
Stock Clerk (222.387-058)	2
Kitchen Helper (318.687-010)	1

CODE: RSI	ED
Vocational Agriculture Teacher (091.227-010)	5
Appliance Repairer (637.261-018)	4
Weaver (683.682-038)	3
Knitter (685.665-014)	2

CODE: REC	ED
Supervisor, Natural-Gas Plant (542.130-010)	4

CODE: REI	ED
Ship Pilot (197.133-026)	4
Shop Supervisor (638.131-026)	4
Supervisor, Paper Machine (539.132-010)	4

CODE: RES	ED
Fish and Game Warden (379.167-010)	5
Cattle Rancher (410.161-018)	4
Locomotive Engineer (910.363-014)	4
Crater (920.484-010)	3
Braker, Passenger Train (910.364-010)	3
Construction Worker (869.664-014)	3
Fisher (442.684-010)	2
Track Layer (869.687-026)	2

CODE: RCI	ED
Surveyor, Geodetic (018.167-038)	5
Carpenter (860.381-022)	4

CODE: RCI (cont.)	ED
Instrument Mechanic (710.281-026)	4
Motion-Picture Projectionist (960.362-010)	4
Office-Machine Servicer (633.281-018)	4
Signal-Tower Operator (Railroad Trans) (910.362-010)	4
Supervisor, Painting (840.131-010)	3
Surveyor Helper (869.567-010)	3

CODE: RCS	ED
Furrier (783.261-010)	4
Tailor (785.261-010)	4
Telephone Repairer (822.281-022)	4
Bus Driver (913.463-010)	3
Sewage-Plant Operator (955.362-010)	3
Blaster (859.261-010)	3
Bricklayer (861.381-018)	3
Cement Mason (844.364-010)	3
Dressmaker (785.361-010)	3
Furnace Installer (862.361-010)	3
Garment Cutter (781.584-014)	3
Mail Carrier (230.367-010)	3
Meter Reader (209.567-010)	3
Miner (939.281-010)	3
Paperhanger (841.381-010)	3
Plasterer (842.361-018)	3
Sailor (911.687-030)	3
Tile Setter (861.381-054)	3
Industrial-Truck Operator (921.683-050)	2
Spinner (682.685-010)	2

CODE: RCE	ED
Crane Operator (921.663-010)	3
Lumber Inspector (669.587-010)	3
Tractor Operator (929.683-014)	3
Tractor-Trailer-Truck Driver (904.383-010)	3
Truck Driver, Light (906.683-022)	3
Fork-Lift Truck Operator (921.683-050)	2

INVESTIGATIVE OCCUPATIONS

CODE: IAS	ED
Economist (050.067-010)	6
Mathematician/Statistician (020.067-014)	6
Market-Research Analyst (050.067-014)	5

CODE: IAR	ED
Anthropologist (055.067-010)	6
Astronomer (021.067-010)	6
Chemist (022.061-010)	6
Pathologist (070.061-010)	6
Physicist (023.061-014)	6

CODE: ISC	ED
Mathematics Teacher (091.227-010)	5
Production Planner (012.167-050)	5
Medical-Laboratory Assistant (078.381-010)	4
Television-and-Radio Repairer (720.281-018)	4

CODE: ISR	ED
Biologist (041.061-030)	6
Dentist (072.101-010)	6
Osteopathic Physician (071.101-010)	6
Sanitarian (079.117-018)	6
Chiropractor (079.101-010)	5
Natural Science Teacher (091.227-010)	5
Optometrist (079.101-018)	5

CODE: ISA	ED
Experimental Psychologist (045.061-018)	6
Physician* (070.101-022)	6
Psychiatrist (070.107-014)	6
Medical Technologist (078.361-014)	5
Nurse, Practitioner (075.264-010)	5
Physician Assistant (079.364-018)	5

*May carry other D.O.T. numbers when a more detailed job title is given.

INVESTIGATIVE OCCUPATIONS (CONTINUED)

CODE: IES	ED
Bacteriologist (041.061-058)	6
Physiologist (041.061-078)	6
Pharmacist (074.161-010)	5

CODE: IEC	ED
Actuary (020.167-010)	5

CODE: ICR	ED
Quality Control Technician (012.261-014)	5
Computer Operator (213.362-010)	4
Radiation Monitor (199.167-010)	4
Research Assistant (199.364-014)	4

CODE: IRA	ED
Geologist (024.061-018)	6
Surgeon (070.101-094)	6
Urban Planner (199.167-014)	6
Meteorologist (025.062-010)	5
Weather Observer (025.267-014)	5

CODE: IRS	ED
Agronomist (040.061-010)	6
Animal Scientist (040.061-014)	6
Biochemist (041.061-026)	6
Botanist (041.061-038)	6
Dairy Technologist (040.061-022)	6
Environmental Analyst (029.081-010)	6
Geneticist (041.061-050)	6
Horticulturist (040.061-038)	6
Oceanographer (024.061-018)	6
Soil Conservationist (040.061-054)	6
Zoologist (041.061-090)	6

CODE: IRS (cont.)	ED
Geographer (029.067-010)	5
Heat-Transfer Technician (007.181-010)	5
Veterinarian (073.101-010)	5
EKG Technician (078.362-018)	4
X-Ray Technician (199.361-010)	4

CODE: IRE	ED
Administrator, Engineer*	6
Aeronautical Engineer (002.061-014)	6
Chemical Engineer (008.061-018)	6
Civil Engineer (005.061-014)	6
Electrical Engineer (003.061-010)	6
Engineer*	6
Metallurgist, Physical (011.061-022)	6
Chemical-Laboratory Technician (022.261-010)	5
Metallurgical-Laboratory Assistant (011.261-010)	4

CODE: IRC	ED
Airplane Navigator (196.167-014)	5
Airplane Pilot (196.263-014)	5
Computer Programmer (020.187-010)	5
Engineering Technician (007.161-026)	5
Model Maker (777.261-010)	5
Tool Designer (007.061-026)	5
Instrument Repairer (710.261-010)	4
Laboratory Tester (029.261-010)	4
Tester, Electrical Accessories (729.381-010)	4

ARTISTIC OCCUPATIONS

CODE: ASE	ED
Actor/Actress (150.047-010)	5
Dancing Teacher (151.027-014)	5
Dramatic Coach (150.027-010)	5
Drama Teacher (150.027-010)	5
English Teacher (091.227-010)	5
Foreign Language Interpreter (137.267-010)	5
Reporter (131.267-018)	5

CODE: ASI	ED
Philosopher (090.227-010)	6
Writer (131.067-046)	6
Advertising Copy Writer (131.067-014)	5
Artist (144.061-010)	5
Art Teacher (149.021-010)	5
Commercial Artist (141.061-022)	5
Literature Teacher (091.227-010)	5
Musician (152.041-010)	5
Music Teacher (152.021-010)	5
Orchestra Conductor (152.047-014)	5
Technical Writer (131.267-026)	5

CODE: AES	ED
Account Executive (164.167-010)	5
Advertising Manager (164.117-010)	5

CODE: AES (cont.)	ED
Entertainer (Dancer, Singer)*	5
Public-Relations Representative (165.067-010)	5
Fashion Model (297.667-014)	3

CODE: AIS	ED
Dramatist (131.067-038)	6
Editor (132.037-014)	6
Critic (Reviewer) (131.067-018)	5
Fashion Artist (141.061-014)	5
Furniture Designer (142.061-022)	5
Interior Decorator (142.051-014)	5
Package Designer (142.081-018)	5
Set Designer (142.061-050)	5
Clothes Designer (142.061-018)	4

CODE: AIE	ED
Decorator (298.381-010)	4

CODE: AIR	ED
Architect (001.061-010)	6
Photographer (143.457-010)	4
Photolithographer (972.382-014)	4
Sign Writer (970.281-022)	4
Photograph Retoucher (970.281-018)	3

*May carry other D.O.T. numbers when a more detailed job title is given.

SOCIAL OCCUPATIONS

CODE: SEC	ED
Director Social Service (195.117-010)	6
Business Representative, Labor Union (187.167-018)	5
Chamber of Commerce Executive (187.117-030)	5
Dormitory Supervisor (045.107-038)	5
Employment Interviewer (166.267-010)	5
Funeral Director (187.167-030)	5
Hotel Manager (187.117-038)	5
Job Analyst (166.267-018)	5
YMCA Physical Director (195.167-026)	5
YMCA Secretary (195.117-010)	5
Camp Director (195.167-018)	4
Food-Service Supervisor (319.137-010)	4
Manager, Benefits (166.167-018)	4
Bartender (312.474-010)	3
Host/Hostess (Hotel & Rest.) (310.137-010)	3
Manager, Fast Food Services (185.137-010)	3

CODE: SER	ED
Claim Adjuster (241.217-010)	5

CODE: SEI	ED
Hospital Administrator (187.117-010)	6
President, Educational Institution (090.117-034)	6
Historian (052.067-022)	5
History Teacher (091.227-010)	5
Home-Service Director (096.161-010)	5
Manager, Education & Training (166.167-026)	5
Training Instructor (166.227-010)	5

CODE: SEA	ED
Superintendent, Recreation (187.117-054)	6
Employment Supervisor (166.167-030)	5
Foreign-Service Officer (188.117-106)	5
Recreation Supervisor (187.137-010)	5
Supervisor, Volunteer Services (187.137-014)	5

CODE: SCE	ED
Executive Housekeeper (187.167-046)	5
Production Coordinator (221.167-018)	5
Public Health Service Officer (187.117-050)	5
Theatre Manager (187.167-154)	5
Caterer (187.167-106)	4
Credit-Reference Clerk (209.362-010)	4
Liquor Store Manager (187.167-126)	4
Restaurant Proprietor (187.167-106)	4
Ticket Agent (238.367-026)	4
Bellhop (324.677-010)	2

CODE: SRI	ED
Extension Worker (096.127-010)	5

CODE: SRE	ED
Athletic Coach (099.224-010)	5
Building Superintendent (187.167-190)	5
Physical Instructor (153.227-018)	5
Children's Tutor (Governess) (099.227-010)	4
Driving Instructor (099.223-010)	4
Housekeeper (321.137-010)	4
Occupational Therapist (076.121-010)	4
Detective (376.367-014)	3
Houseparent (359.677-010)	3
Professional Athlete (153.341-010)	3
Police Officer (375.263-014)	3

CODE: SRC	ED
Barber (330.371-010)	3
Hospital Attendant (355.674-014)	3

CODE: SIA	ED
Clinical/Counseling Psychologist (045.107-022)	6
College Professor (090.227-010)	6
Political Scientist (051.067-010)	6
Sociologist (054.067-014)	6
Social Scientist*	6
Adult Education Teacher (099.227-030)	5
Group Worker (195.164-010)	5
Nurse, General Duty (075.374-010)	5
Rehabilitation Therapist*	5
School Counselor (045.107-010)	5
Social Worker (195.107-034)	5

CODE: SIE	ED
Principal (099.117-018)	6
Customs Inspector (168.267-022)	4
Dietitian, Chief (077.127-010)	4
Inspector, Quality Assurance (168.287-014)	4

CODE: SIC	ED
School Superintendent (099.117-022)	6
Food and Drug Inspector (168.267-042)	5
Parole Officer (195.167-030)	5
Social Science Teacher (091.227-010)	5

CODE: SIR	ED
Podiatrist (Foot Doctor) (079.101-022)	5
Inhalation Therapist (079.361-010)	4
Physical Therapist (076.121-014)	4
Surgical Technician (079.374-022)	4
Therapist*	4

*May carry other D.O.T. numbers when a more detailed job title is given.

SOCIAL OCCUPATIONS (CONTINUED)

CODE: SAE	ED
Counselor (045.107-010)	5
Elementary School Teacher (092.227-010)	5
Foreign Language Teacher (091.227-010)	5
High School Teacher (091.227-010)	5
Home Economics Teacher (091.227-010)	5
Home Economist (096.121-014)	5
Homemaker (309.354-010)	
Pre-School Teacher (092.227-018)	5
Speech Teacher (091.227-010)	5
Teacher*	5
Vocational-Rehabilitation Counselor (045.107-042)	5
Teacher Aide (099.327-010)	3
Social Service Aide (195.367-010)	3

CODE: SAC	ED
Cosmetologist (332.271-010)	4
Electrologist (339.371-010)	4
Embalmer (338.371-014)	4
Hair Stylist (332.271-018)	4
Physical Therapy Aide (355.354-010)	3
Manicurist (331.674-010)	2

CODE: SAI	ED
Minister/Priest/Rabbi (120.007-010)	6
Librarian (100.127-014)	5
Special Education Teacher (094.227-010)	5
Speech Therapist (076.107-010)	5
Dental Assistant (079.371-010)	4
Licensed Practical Nurse (079.374-014)	4
Medical Record Librarian (079.367-014)	4
Dental Hygienist (078.361-010)	4

ENTERPRISING OCCUPATIONS

CODE: ECI	ED
Bank President (186.117-054)	5

CODE: ECS	ED
Credit Analyst (241.267-022)	5
Insurance Underwriter (169.167-058)	5
Grain Buyer (162.167-010)	5
Real Estate Appraiser (191.267-010)	5
Buyer (Purchasing Agent) (162.157-018)	4
Customer Services Manager (187.167-082)	4
Florist (Retailer) (185.167-046)	4
Furniture Buyer (162.157-018)	4
Manager, Procurement Services (162.167-022)	4
Real Estate Sales Agent (250.357-018)	4
Sales Representative, Farm Equipment (272-357-014)	4
Supervisor, Ticket Sales (238.137-022)	4
Bill Collector (241.367-010)	3

CODE: ERI	ED
Contractor (182.167-010)	4
Farm Manager (180.167-018)	4
Industrial Engineer (012.167-030)	6

CODE: ERS	ED
Warehouse Supervisor (929.137-022)	5

CODE: ERC	ED
Postmaster (188.167-066)	4

CODE: EIS	ED
Sales Engineer*	5

CODE: EAR	ED
Radio/TV Announcer (159.147-010)	5

CODE: ESC	ED
Administrative Assistant (169.167-010)	5
Branch Manager (183.117-010)	5
Business Manager (191.117-018)	5
City Manager (188.117-114)	5
Director, Industrial Relations (166.117-010)	5
Director of Placement (166.167-014)	5
Government Official*	5
Labor Arbitrator (169.107-010)	5
Manager/Administrator*	5
Manager, Insurance Agency (186.167-034)	5
Manager, Restaurant/Bar (187.167-106)	5
Office Manager (169.167-034)	5
Operations Manager (184.117-050)	5
Personnel Manager (166.1/7-018)	5
Personnel Recruiter (166.267-010)	5
Production Manager (183.117-014)	5
Salary & Wage Administrator (166.167-022)	5
Sales Manager (163.167-018)	5
Traffic Manager (184.167-094)	5
Apartment House Manager (186.167-018)	4
Insurance Investigator (241.217-101)	4
Demonstrator (297.354-010)	3
Dispatcher (913.367-010)	3
Hotel Clerk (238.362-010)	3
Peddler (Huckster) (291.457-018)	3
Sales Clerk (290.477-014)	3
Salesperson*	3

CODE: ESR	ED
Automobile Salesperson (273.353-010)	4
Sales Representative, Sporting Goods (277.357-026)	4
Route Driver (292.353-010)	3

*May carry other D.O.T. numbers when a more detailed job title is given.

ENTERPRISING OCCUPATIONS (CONTINUED)

CODE: ESI	ED
Administrator, Social Welfare (195.117-010)	6
Systems Analyst EDP (012.167-066)	5
Wholesaler (185.167-070)	5
Equal-Opportunity Representative (168.167-014)	4
Gift Shop Manager (185.167-046)	4
Grocer (185.167-046)	4
Life Insurance Sales Agent (250.257-010)	4
Manager, Automobile Service Station (185.167-014)	4
Manufacturers Representative (279.157-010)	4

CODE: ESI (cont.)	ED
Retail Merchant (185.167-046)	4
Shoe Store Manager (185.167-046)	4

CODE: ESA	ED
Lawyer, Judge, Attorney (110.107-010)	6
Politician*	5
Stockbroker (251.157-010)	5
Fashion Coordinator (185.157-010)	4
Salesperson, Photographic Equipment & Supplies (277.357-050)	4
Travel Guide (353.167-010)	4
Flight Attendant (352.367-014)	3
Salesperson, Musical Instruments & Accessories (277.357-038)	3

CONVENTIONAL OCCUPATIONS

CODE: CRI	ED
Timekeeper (215.367-022)	4
Linotype Operator (650.582-010)	4
Biller (214.482-010)	3
Key Punch Operator (203.582-030)	3
Tabulating-Machine Operator (213.682-010)	3
Duplicating-Machine Operator (207.682-010)	1

CODE: CRS	ED
File Clerk (206.367-014)	3

CODE: CRE	ED
Electric-Motor Assembler (721.684-022)	3
Sewing Machine Operator (787.682-046)	3

CODE: CIS	ED
Certified Public Accountant (160.167-010)	5
Time Study Analyst (012.267-010)	5
Credit-Card Clerk (210.382-038)	4
Estimator (160.267-010)	4
Posting Clerk (216.587-014)	4
Bookkeeping-Machine Operator (210.382-022)	4
Foreign Trade Clerk (209.262-010)	4
Check-Processing Clerk (216.387-010)	3
Accounting Clerk (216.482-010)	3
High-Speed-Printer Operator (213.382-010)	3
Calculating Machine Operator (216.482-022)	3

CODE: CIE	ED
Office Worker*	4
Payroll Clerk (215.482-010)	4
Proofreader (209.387-030)	3

CODE: CIR	ED
Adding Machine Operator (216.482-014)	3
Telegraphic-Typewriter Operator (203.582-050)	3

CODE: CSE	ED
Business (Commercial) Teacher (091.227-010)	5
Personnel Clerk (209.362-026)	4
Sales Correspondent (221.367-062)	4
Travel Clerk (237.367-018)	4
Receptionist (237.367-038)	3
Typist (203.582-066)	3
Telephone Operator (235.662-022)	3
Teller (211.362-018)	3

CODE: CSR	ED
Reservations Agent (238.367-018)	4
Traffic Checker (205.367-058)	3
Messenger, Office (239.567-010)	2

CODE: CSI	ED
Bookkeeper (210.382-014)	4
Cashier (211.362-010)	4

CODE: CSA	ED
Library Assistant (249.367-046)	4
Medical Secretary (201.362-014)	4
Order Clerk (249.367-054)	4
Secretary* (201.362-030)	4
Social Secretary (201.162-010)	4
Supervisor, Correspondence Section (249.137-018)	4

CODE: CER	ED
Data Processing Worker (213.-)	4
Mail Clerk (209.587-026)	4

CODE: CEI	ED
Financial Analyst (020.167-014)	5

CODE: CES	ED
Accountant (160.167-010)	5
Credit Manager (168.167-054)	5
Clerk, General (209.562-010)	3
Court Reporter (202.362-010)	3
Stenographer (202.362-014)	3

*May carry other D.O.T. numbers when a more detailed job title is given.

APPENDIX B
THE SELF-DIRECTED
SEARCH

The Occupations Finder and the Self-Directed Search are now published by Psychological Assessment Resources, P.O. Drawer 98, Odessa, Florida 33556

OCCUPATIONAL DAYDREAMS

1. List below the occupations you have considered in thinking about your future. List the careers you have daydreamed about as well as those you have discussed with others. Try to give a history of your tentative choices and daydreams. Put your most recent job choice on Line 1 and work backwards to the earlier jobs you have considered.

Occupation   Code

1. _____   ☐ ☐ ☐

2. _____   ☐ ☐ ☐

3. _____   ☐ ☐ ☐

4. _____   ☐ ☐ ☐

5. _____   ☐ ☐ ☐

6. _____   ☐ ☐ ☐

7. _____   ☐ ☐ ☐

8. _____   ☐ ☐ ☐

2. Now use *The Occupations Finder.* Locate the three-letter code for each of the occupations you just wrote down. This search for occupational codes will help you learn about the many occupations in the world. This task usually takes from 5 to 15 minutes.

If you can't find the exact occupation in *The Occupations Finder,* use the occupation that seems most like your occupational choice.

ACTIVITIES

Blacken under "L" for those activities you would like to do. Blacken under "D" for those things you would dislike doing or would be indifferent to.

R   L   D

Fix electrical things ☐ ☐
Repair cars ☐ ☐
Fix mechanical things ☐ ☐
Build things with wood ☐ ☐
Drive a truck or tractor ☐ ☐
Use metalworking or machine tools ☐ ☐
Work on a hot rod or motorcycle ☐ ☐
Take Shop course ☐ ☐
Take Mechanical drawing course ☐ ☐
Take Woodworking course ☐ ☐
Take Auto mechanics course ☐ ☐

Total No. of L's ☐

I

Read scientific books or magazines ☐ ☐
Work in a laboratory ☐ ☐
Work on a scientific project ☐ ☐
Build rocket models ☐ ☐
Work with a chemistry set ☐ ☐
Read about special subjects on my own ☐ ☐
Solve math or chess puzzles ☐ ☐
Take Physics course ☐ ☐
Take Chemistry course ☐ ☐
Take Geometry course ☐ ☐
Take Biology course ☐ ☐

Total No. of L's ☐

A

Sketch, draw, or paint ☐ ☐
Attend plays ☐ ☐
Design furniture or buildings ☐ ☐
Play in a band, group, or orchestra ☐ ☐
Practice a musical instrument ☐ ☐
Go to recitals, concerts, or musicals ☐ ☐
Read popular fiction ☐ ☐
Create portraits or photographs ☐ ☐
Read plays ☐ ☐
Read or write poetry ☐ ☐
Take Art course ☐ ☐

Total No. of L's ☐

S

	L	D
Write letters to friends	☐	☐
Attend religious services	☐	☐
Belong to social clubs	☐	☐
Help others with their personal problems	☐	☐
Take care of children	☐	☐
Go to parties	☐	☐
Dance	☐	☐
Read psychology books	☐	☐
Attend meetings and conferences	☐	☐
Go to sports events	☐	☐
Make new friends	☐	☐

Total No. of L's ☐

E

	L	D
Influence others	☐	☐
Sell something	☐	☐
Discuss politics	☐	☐
Operate my own service or business	☐	☐
Attend conferences	☐	☐
Give talks	☐	☐
Serve as an officer of any group	☐	☐
Supervise the work of others	☐	☐
Meet important people	☐	☐
Lead a group in accomplishing some goal	☐	☐
Participate in political campaign	☐	☐

Total No. of L's ☐

C

	L	D
Keep your desk and room neat	☐	☐
Type papers or letters for yourself or for others	☐	☐
Add, subtract, multiply, and divide numbers in business, or bookkeeping	☐	☐
Operate business machines of any kind	☐	☐
Keep detailed records of expenses	☐	☐
Take Typewriting course	☐	☐
Take Business course	☐	☐
Take Bookkeeping course	☐	☐
Take Commercial math course	☐	☐
File letters, reports, records, etc	☐	☐
Write business letters	☐	☐

Total No. of L's ☐

COMPETENCIES

Blacken under Y for "Yes" for those activities you can do well or competently. Blacken under N for "No" for those activities you have never performed or perform poorly.

R   Y   N

I have used wood shop power tools such as power saw
    or lathe or sander   ☐   ☐
I know how to use a voltmeter   ☐   ☐
I can adjust a carburetor   ☐   ☐
I have operated power tools such as a drill press   ☐   ☐
    or grinder or sewing machine
I can refinish varnished or stained furniture or woodwork   ☐   ☐
I can read blueprints   ☐   ☐
I can make simple electrical repairs   ☐   ☐
I can repair furniture   ☐   ☐
I can make mechanical drawings   ☐   ☐
I can make simple repairs on a TV set   ☐   ☐
I can make simple plumbing repairs   ☐   ☐

                        Total No. of Y's   ☐

I

I understand how a vacuum tube works   ☐   ☐
I can name three foods that are high in protein content   ☐   ☐
I understand the "half-life" of a radioactive element   ☐   ☐
I can use logarithmic tables   ☐   ☐
I can use a slide rule to multiply or divide   ☐   ☐
I can use a microscope   ☐   ☐
I can identify three constellations of the stars   ☐   ☐
I can describe the function of the white blood cells   ☐   ☐
I can interpret simple chemical formulae   ☐   ☐
I understand why man-made satellites do not fall to the earth   ☐   ☐
I have participated in a scientific fair or contest   ☐   ☐

                        Total No. of Y's   ☐

A

I can play a musical instrument   ☐   ☐
I can participate in two- or four-part choral singing   ☐   ☐
I can perform as a musical soloist   ☐   ☐
I can act in a play   ☐   ☐
I can do interpretive reading   ☐   ☐
I can do modern interpretive or ballet dancing   ☐   ☐
I can sketch people so that they can be recognized   ☐   ☐
I can do a painting or sculpture   ☐   ☐
I can make pottery   ☐   ☐
I can design clothing, posters, or furniture   ☐   ☐
I write stories or poetry well   ☐   ☐

                        Total No. of Y's   ☐

S

	Y	N
I am good at explaining things to others	☐	☐
I have participated in charity or benefit drives	☐	☐
I cooperate and work well with others	☐	☐
I am competent at entertaining people older than I	☐	☐
I can be a good host (hostess)	☐	☐
I can teach children easily	☐	☐
I can plan entertainment for a party	☐	☐
I am good at helping people who are upset or troubled	☐	☐
I have worked as a volunteer aide in a hospital, clinic, or home	☐	☐
I can plan school or church social affairs	☐	☐
I am a good judge of personality	☐	☐

Total No. of Y's ☐

E

	Y	N
I have been elected to an office in high school or college	☐	☐
I can supervise the work of others	☐	☐
I have unusual energy and enthusiasm	☐	☐
I am good at getting people to do things my way	☐	☐
I am a good salesperson	☐	☐
I have acted as leader for some group in presenting suggestions or complaints to a person in authority	☐	☐
I won an award for work as a salesperson or leader	☐	☐
I have organized a club, group, or gang	☐	☐
I have started my own business or service	☐	☐
I know how to be a successful leader	☐	☐
I am a good debater	☐	☐

Total No. of Y's ☐

C

	Y	N
I can type 40 words a minute	☐	☐
I can operate a duplicating or adding machine	☐	☐
I can take shorthand	☐	☐
I can file correspondence and other papers	☐	☐
I have held an office job	☐	☐
I can use a bookkeeping machine	☐	☐
I can do a lot of paper work in a short time	☐	☐
I can use a calculating machine	☐	☐
I can use simple data processing equipment such as a keypunch	☐	☐
I can post credits and debits	☐	☐
I can keep accurate records of payments or sales	☐	☐

Total No. of Y's ☐

OCCUPATIONS

This is an inventory of your feelings and attitudes about many kinds of work. Show the occupations that *interest* or *appeal* to you by blackening under Y for "Yes." Show the occupations that you *dislike* or find *uninteresting* by blackening under N for "No."

	Y	N		Y	N
Airplane Mechanic	☐	☐	Sociologist	☐	☐
Fish and Wildlife Specialist	☐	☐	High School Teacher	☐	☐
Auto Mechanic	☐	☐	Juvenile Delinquency Expert	☐	☐
Carpenter	☐	☐	Speech Therapist	☐	☐
Power Shovel Operator	☐	☐	Marriage Counselor	☐	☐
Surveyor	☐	☐	School Principal	☐	☐
Construction Inspector	☐	☐	Playground Director	☐	☐
Radio Operator	☐	☐	Clinical Psychologist	☐	☐
Filling Station Worker	☐	☐	Social Science Teacher	☐	☐
Tree Surgeon	☐	☐	Director of Welfare Agency	☐	☐
Long Distance Bus Driver	☐	☐	Youth Camp Director	☐	☐
Locomotive Engineer	☐	☐	Personal Counselor	☐	☐
Machinist	☐	☐	Psychiatric Case Worker	☐	☐
Electrician	☐	☐	Vocational Counselor	☐	☐

Total **R** Y's ☐   Total **S** Y's ☐

	Y	N		Y	N
Meteorologist	☐	☐	Speculator	☐	☐
Biologist	☐	☐	Buyer	☐	☐
Astronomer	☐	☐	Advertising Executive	☐	☐
Medical Laboratory Technician	☐	☐	Manufacturer's Representative	☐	☐
Anthropologist	☐	☐	Television Producer	☐	☐
Zoologist	☐	☐	Hotel Manager	☐	☐
Chemist	☐	☐	Business Executive	☐	☐
Independent Research Scientist	☐	☐	Restaurant Manager	☐	☐
Writer of Scientific Articles	☐	☐	Master of Ceremonies	☐	☐
Editor of a Scientific Journal	☐	☐	Salesperson	☐	☐
Geologist	☐	☐	Real Estate Salesperson	☐	☐
Botanist	☐	☐	Publicity Director	☐	☐
Scientific Research Worker	☐	☐	Sports Promoter	☐	☐
Physicist	☐	☐	Sales Manager	☐	☐

Total **I** Y's ☐   Total **E** Y's ☐

	Y	N		Y	N
Poet	☐	☐	Bookkeeper	☐	☐
Symphony Conductor	☐	☐	Business Teacher	☐	☐
Musician	☐	☐	Budget Reviewer	☐	☐
Author	☐	☐	Certified Public Accountant	☐	☐
Commercial Artist	☐	☐	Credit Investigator	☐	☐
Free-Lance Writer	☐	☐	Court Stenographer	☐	☐
Musical Arranger	☐	☐	Bank Teller	☐	☐
Journalist	☐	☐	Tax Expert	☐	☐
Portrait Artist	☐	☐	Inventory Controller	☐	☐
Concert Singer	☐	☐	IBM Equipment Operator	☐	☐
Composer	☐	☐	Financial Analyst	☐	☐
Sculptor/Sculptress	☐	☐	Cost Estimator	☐	☐
Playwright	☐	☐	Payroll Clerk	☐	☐
Cartoonist	☐	☐	Bank Examiner	☐	☐

Total **A** Y's ☐   Total **C** Y's ☐

SELF-ESTIMATES

1. Rate yourself on each of the following traits as *you really think you are when compared with other persons your own age.* Give the most accurate estimate of *how you see yourself.* Circle the appropriate number and *avoid rating yourself the same in each ability.*

	Mechanical Ability	Scientific Ability	Artistic Ability	Teaching Ability	Sales Ability	Clerical Ability
High	7	7	7	7	7	7
	6	6	6	6	6	6
	5	5	5	5	5	5
Average	4	4	4	4	4	4
	3	3	3	3	3	3
	2	2	2	2	2	2
Low	1	1	1	1	1	1
	R	I	A	S	E	C

	Manual Skills	Math Ability	Musical Ability	Friend-liness	Managerial Skills	Office Skills
High	7	7	7	7	7	7
	6	6	6	6	6	6
	5	5	5	5	5	5
Average	4	4	4	4	4	4
	3	3	3	3	3	3
	2	2	2	2	2	2
Low	1	1	1	1	1	1
	R	I	A	S	E	C

HOW TO ORGANIZE YOUR ANSWERS

Start on page 4. Count how many times you said L for "Like." Record the number of L's or Y's for each group of Activities, Competencies, or Occupations on the lines below.

Activities

R   I   A   S   E   C

Competencies

R   I   A   S   E   C

Occupations

R   I   A   S   E   C

Self Estimates
(What number did
you circle?)

R   I   A   S   E   C

R   I   A   S   E   C

Total Scores
(Add the five R scores,
the five I scores, the
five A scores, etc.)

R   I   A   S   E   C

The letters with the three highest numbers indicate your summary code. Write your summary code below. (If two scores are the same or tied, put both letters in the same box.)

SUMMARY CODE

☐   ☐   ☐

Highest   2nd   3rd

WHAT YOUR SUMMARY CODE MEANS

The summary code is a simple way of organizing information about people and jobs. Although it is only an estimate, your summary code can be used to discover how your special pattern of interests, self-estimates, and competencies resemble the patterns of interests and competencies that many common occupations demand. In this way, your summary code locates suitable *groups* of occupations for you to consider.

1. Use *The Occupations Finder* and locate the occupations whose codes are *identical* with yours. For instance, if your summary code is I R E, occupations with codes of I R E are *identical* with yours. List some of these occupations below. If you do not find an occupation with an identical code, go the the next paragraph.

Occupation	Education	Occupation	Education

2. Make a list of some occupations whose summary codes *resemble* yours. For instance, if your code is I R E, search *The Occupations Finder* for occupations with all possible arrangements of I R E. Look for occupations with codes of R I E, R E I, I E R, E R I. (If your summary code includes a tie such as R IE A, you must look up more combinations such as R I E, R I A, R E A, etc.) Start by writing down the six possible letter arrangements of your summary code.

Summary Code   **Similar Codes**

Occupation	Education	Occupation	Education

APPENDIX C
RESEARCH SUGGESTIONS
FOR STUDENTS

The following ideas for new research are provided for several reasons: to help students perform better research, to direct them to the more pressing research needs, and to help them avoid the sins of others—especially those of the faculty. The ideas outlined here have a single pragmatic orientation. Students will find it helpful to consult other points of view.

SOME HELPFUL PRINCIPLES AND HOMILIES

If you would like to use the theory in your research, you may find it helpful to use the following principles:

1. Read and reread this book until you understand the main ideas. (This will prevent your testing the usefulness of some other theory and will also make you more knowledgeable than your advisor.) If you don't believe the theory makes sense, try testing another.
2. Don't make up your own definitions of the theoretical concepts. This practice is occasionally useful, but it more often leads to the testing of some other theory. If you cannot resist the urge to create new definitions, at least compare and report the results for the old and new definitions.
3. Plan your experiment by following the theory as closely as possible. When in doubt, follow the theory whatever its ambiguities. The theory is not

intended to be a projective device, although it occasionally serves this function.

4. Avoid unusual populations. It is unlikely that the theory will be useful for understanding people who are mentally retarded, grossly psychotic, and so on. Theories don't have to do everything to be useful.

5. Be selective about your research models. Replications are important, but if you see an old research study you like, don't simply repeat it using new data. Capitalize on its substantive or design strengths, but try to improve the quality of the design, the instrumentation, and so on.

6. Pretend you have your data in hand and everything has come out just as expected. What does it mean? Conduct a thorough run-through of the results with some friends. This kind of review should lead to a more explicit research plan or to abandoning a bad idea.

7. Write your research report so your parents could understand the main ideas. Resist the temptation to impress your advisor or a potential editor with your ability to include every bit of jargon that you've learned in your training.

8. Try to perform the most important study you can within the limits of your resources. Ask yourself whether positive results would make any practical or theoretical difference to anybody. Compare two or more proposals by putting this same question to each.

9. Beware of small N's. Typological studies usually require large N's. Small N's usually restrict the number of analyses you can perform and the number of hypotheses you can cope with. If you must use a small N, try to make sure that all types, environments, or interactions are represented.

10. Read the literature. Because only a few people read research reports, you will be at a considerable advantage if you read them.

11. Be clear about "what's the question?". Unless you have a definite idea to test, everything that follows is likely to be unclear: Analyses of data will be unrelated to the question; discussions and conclusions will be ambiguous. If you are clear about the question, then the design, the analysis, and the writing become easier for you and more useful to others.

12. Avoid programmers, methodologists, and statisticians until you are clear about the problem you want to study. They are prone to forget your problem and substitute an elegant analysis of a problem you may not be interested in. They can be helpful, but they must be used as production managers and engineers, not as architects or artists. You may find it helpful to read Rothkopf's (1973) discussion of some common deficiencies in educational research that apply to the social sciences generally.

13. Spend at least as much time thinking about a potential project as you do fixing your hair or shaving. The quality of research depends more upon daydreaming, thinking, and persistence than upon computers, recording devices, and statistical methods.

NEW RESEARCH

The following sections indicate some research needs and problems that I think are important. These problems are not equally important, nor do they exhaust the major possibilities. You will be able to think of many more. Only the questions have been indicated; these require clarification as well as appropriate research plans. Some questions may turn out to be trivial.

Types. The formulations of the personality types suggest numerous questions: Do people assessed as particular types exhibit characteristic interests, competencies, perceptions, and traits? Similarly, do people assessed as particular subtypes exhibit the expected characteristics? What are the most differentiating characteristics of the types? The subtypes?

Do types produce types? Study both parents and their children. Examine the consistency, differentiation and identity of parents and the apparent effects upon children. Do parents of different types treat their children differently? Consistent, well-differentiated parents with a clear sense of identity should have more predictable influences and child-rearing practices (friendships and social groupings may follow similar principles). Explore the social inheritance of types in three or four generations.

Do types search not only for characteristic occupational clusters, but also for characteristic recreational activities, friendships, problems, and roles? Consider repeating the Staats et al. (1973) experiments by using the six types rather than people with two kinds of interests. What happens when searching behavior is blocked or frustrated? Do people then search for closely related (hexagonal model) activities, friends, and problems? Does searching behavior become more focused with increasing age? For example, partial reinforcement may lead to more and more precise searching behavior as a person narrows the range of activities and environments he or she finds rewarding.

Do types perceive occupations in terms of the typological formulations—activities, competencies, perceptions, values, and traits? Do types perceive similar types more accurately than dissimilar types? More differentially? What is the effect of training and other experience on a type's ability to perceive other types?

Compare the predictive validity of the SCII, SDS, or VPI with a person's vocational aspirations, categorized or organized according to current aspirations and first three aspirations (coded for their coherence: three aspirations belong to the same category, two belong to the same category, and three belong to three categories). Go beyond earlier studies to explore the relation of identity, differentiation, and consistency to the coherence of aspirations and predictive validity of aspirations. Perform these analyses for both students and workers.

Determine the relations among the concepts of identity (Holland et al., 1980), neuroticism (Costa and McCrae, 1976), and personality integration (Seeman, 1983). My speculation is that identity and integration are similar concepts and that neuroticism may be the opposite pole of both concepts.

Repeat Csikszentmihalyi's (1975) experiment on the effect of having people refrain from engaging in their favorite activities and hobbies. This experiment could be performed and analyzed according to type. Likewise, Ridgeway's (1976) study of musical involvement is congenial with a typological analysis.

Test the hypotheses about level of occupational achievement using adult work histories. Compare the work histories of people in *Who's Who* or other biographical references with the histories of typical adults.

Compare the work histories of people in special fields of science, education, business, and so on. Code, interpret, and summarize the work histories of the members of your state legislature or the U.S. Congress. Some federal agencies such as the Office of Education publish organizational charts. Code, interpret, and summarize the work histories of people at each level of this vast bureaucracy to describe it in typological terms. Try the same procedure on other organizations. Perform a longitudinal study of an organization by studying the organizational charts at different times to see if changes in organizational behavior show patterns that are consistent with the environmental formulations.

ENVIRONMENTS

Using the Environmental Assessment Technique (EAT), assess educational or occupational environments and compare the EAT with other environmental assessment techniques such as CUES. Explore ways to map relatively independent subenvironmental units. Identify the major environmental influences—size, power, educational level, and so on—that the EAT does not account for; then develop and test research designs to cope with this problem. See if the formulations of environmental identity and manning have validity. Are they related to organizational structure and size?

Plan a study and test your ideas. Select a particular population and code all the environments that population lives in. Try to segregate the environments that form each person's psychological field at different times. Examine these environmental data for their consistency. Analyze life histories in terms of environments only: relatives as environments, teachers as environments, and so on. Assess neighborhoods as environments and map a city or county according to the types of the heads of households and other adults. U.S. Census data can be used for this purpose.

INTERACTIONS

Study the following kinds of interactions: student-teacher, parent-child, counselor-client, employee-supervisor, husband-wife, child-child, and so on. Observe the following cautions in the study of interactions:

1. Examine the character of the interaction—amount of time, intensity, involvement, nature of task, degree of risk.
2. Define the degree of congruence carefully. Use the Cole planar method, the hexagonal model, the Zener-Schnuelle Index, or the Iachon Index.
3. Assess the subject's perception of the interaction (is he or she involved?).
4. Use your judgment. Rule out some interactions as tangential and rule others in as central.
5. Incorporate the degrees of consistency, differentiation, and identity of both persons and environments in your design.
6. Look for statistical interactions.

In general, test hypotheses as analytically as possible: Study individual permutations (combining of permutations—such as RIs plus REs plus RSs—hides information). Control for environmental opportunity and type of person—for example, RIs vs RSs, or ESs vs EAs, and so on. And determine the feasibility of outcome or dependent variables. Of special importance, review the interactive studies in Chapter 5 for promising ideas.

CLASSIFICATION

Use the classification to organize and interpret work histories, census data, and occupational aspirations. Test the limits of the classification: for instance, are RIEs different from RISs, and are the differences according to the formulations for Es and Ss? Why do some subcategories such as CA, AC, and so on never occur among the occupational codes and rarely occur in SDS or VPI profiles? Try some cross-cultural comparisons of work forces. Do the differences appear consistent with sociological and anthropological interpretations of national character?

Develop codes for occupations previously unclassified, or check the validity of the categorization of selected occupations by testing employed samples to see if they possess the characteristics that the classification attributes to them.

SPECIAL PROBLEMS

There are a host of other problems that need better solutions. Compare the validity and usefulness of the Cole planar method, the Zener-Schnuelle Index, the Iachon Index, and the hexagonal model as techniques for determining congruency. Use the theory to plan interventions for helping women and minorities. Hollinger's study (1983) illustrates one application of the theory, and Turner's (1983) annotated bibliography provides a useful beginning. Use the typology to study how people cope with careers and aging. Stage theory treats people as if everyone were a single type.

The present typology assumes that people of the same age act according to the types they resemble.

Finally, we need many more evaluative studies of the effects of career counseling and career courses. The theory has been useful in planning these treatments, but there has been no comprehensive application to a single career course or to individual career counseling. See Rayman et al. (1983) as another beginning.

The typology provides a tool for studying the validity generalizations in industrial work. Closely related occupations in the classification should have similar predictors: aptitudes, interests, values, and so on. Divergent occupations should have different predictors.

NAME INDEX

SUBJECT INDEX